FOLGER SHAKESPEARE
LIBRARY PUBLICATIONS
General Editor: Joseph Quincy Adams

HENGIST, KING OF KENT
OR
THE MAYOR OF QUEENBOROUGH

HENGIST, KING OF KENT; OR THE MAYOR OF QUEENBOROUGH

BY

THOMAS MIDDLETON

Edited from the Manuscript in the Folger Shakespeare Library

BY

R. C. BALD

Professor of English in Cornell University

FOR THE TRUSTEES OF AMHERST COLLEGE

Charles Scribner's Sons

NEW YORK AND LONDON

1938

Printed in the United States of America by
E. L. Hildreth & Company, Inc., Brattleboro, Vermont

AS A MEMORIAL
TO HER ENDURING AFFECTION FOR
MRS. HENRY CLAY FOLGER
THE COST OF PRODUCING THIS VOLUME
WAS BORNE BY
MRS. JAMES PARMELEE

FOREWORD

IT is strange that of the major English dramatists contemporary with Shakespeare Thomas Middleton, who at several points touched the master, has been the most neglected by modern scholarship. The only real attempt at a careful edition of his works was made by Alexander Dyce in 1840, for Bullen's text of 1885–6 is little more than a reprint of Dyce's; and both editions are by present-day standards unsatisfactory. It will, I am sure, be generally agreed that a definitive edition of the works of this highly important dramatist is a crying need.

And yet before such an edition can successfully be attempted much detailed research by individual scholars must be undertaken, and carried to completion. A glance at the meagre bibliographies cited by Sir Edmund Chambers (*The Elizabethan Stage,* iii, 437–44) under the name of the playwright and the titles of his separate works will reveal how little has been accomplished. Indeed, almost every aspect of Middleton's life and literary career calls for further and assiduous investigation. The bibliographical problems associated with his original editions have been scarcely touched. The details of his biography remain for the most part unexplored; not until 1931 were such elementary facts as the date of his birth (1580) and the university at which he matriculated (Oxford) disclosed. The history of his long connection with the stage and of his labors for various theatrical companies is, in spite of the efforts of Dyce and Bullen, distressingly obscure. The canon of his works, dramatic and non-dramatic, is far from determined: for example, it is a question whether he had a hand in *Blurt Master Constable* generally accepted as his on the authority of Kirkman; *The Revenger's Tragedy,* the important pseudo-Shakespearian *The Puritan,* and other dramas have been with plausibility attributed to him; his share in certain of the Beaumont and Fletcher plays is still speculative; in the case of his non-dramatic works, frank skepticism has been expressed as to his responsibility for *The Wisdom of Solomon Paraphrased,* 1597, *Micro-Cynicon,* 1599, *The Ante and the Nightingale,* 1604, and *The Blacke Booke,* 1604, and the suggestion has lately been made that he was concerned in the plague pamphlet *The Meeting of Gallants at an Ordinarie,* 1604. Finally, the chronology of those plays known to have been written by him is very doubtful; the only serious attempt to deal with the subject was made as recently as the present year, with results that are confessedly tentative. Yet it is likely that such problems as I have mentioned are no more insoluble than those that have been successfully attacked by scholars in the case of other great Elizabethan dramatists, and we have every reason to believe that research, well-directed and painstakingly executed, will yield equally gratifying results.

The present edition of *Hengist, King of Kent; or The Mayor of Queenborough* by Professor Bald (who has already in his edition of *A Game at Chess* made a notable contribution to Middleton scholarship) will, I am confident, materially advance the cause for which I am pleading. Reproducing as it does a seventeenth-century manuscript in the Folger Shakespeare Library that gives a much fuller, and a much better, text than that supplied by the quarto of 1661, it considerably enhances the literary value of the play. Moreover, in its editorial equipment it furnishes a careful record of all the significant textual variants to be found in another and slightly later manuscript in the possession of the Duke of Portland and in the first quarto of 1661, traces in detail the sources and analogues of the story dramatized, deals with the early stage history of the play, and establishes a new date of composition.

Concurrently with this edition of *Hengist,* the Folger Shakespeare Library is issuing in facsimile, with a modernized and fully annotated text, Middleton's recently discovered and hitherto unreproduced poem *The Ghost of Lucrece,* 1600, important as a continuation and imitation of Shakespeare's famous poem. The Introduction deals not only with *The Ghost* itself but also with all the early non-dramatic works of the author, which are in certain ways interrelated. Incidentally, in a footnote, it prints a freshly discovered document relating to the poet and his family—an indication that much more can probably be found if due effort is made.

In setting forth these two volumes the Library hopes to ring the bell that will call the scholars together to labor in this much-neglected and important field of Elizabethan research.

Joseph Quincy Adams

EDITOR'S ACKNOWLEDGEMENTS

THE completion of this edition of Middleton's play was made possible by the grant of a Research Fellowship at the Folger Shakespeare Library, and the editor's debt of gratitude to the Director, the Trustees, and the staff of the Library is consequently a very heavy one. He trusts that the book may not prove unworthy of their kindness and hospitality.

The Duke of Portland generously granted facilities for the examination of the manuscript of the play in his possession, and allowed full use to be made of it for the purposes of this edition. His Librarian, Mr. Francis Needham, has given useful help, and Dr. W. W. Greg generously lent his photostats of the manuscript until a second set could be made.

Others who have been kind enough to help with advice or suggestions are Professor Kemp Malone, Professor A. C. Bouman, and Dr. J. C. Adams. To all the editor tenders his sincere thanks.

R. C. B.

CONTENTS

INTRODUCTION

I

Date and Authorship

THE earliest reference to the play which is reprinted in this volume occurs on one of the Revels Office slips, containing cancelled play-lists, which were used by Sir George Buc, James I's Master of the Revels, for making insertions in the manuscript of his *History of the Life and Reigne of Richard III* (now Cotton MS. Tib. E. x in the British Museum).[1] The second of these lists occurs at f. 197^{v}; it is written in a clerkly hand, and the first item is "[The] Maior of Quinborough," to which Buc has added the alternative title "or Hengist K. of Kent."[2] These lists, Sir Edmund Chambers conjectures, "represent plays which the Revels Office had at some time or other under consideration for performance at court."[3] At first sight the lists might belong to any period between 1608, when Buc took over the duties of Master of the Revels, and the end of 1620, when he went mad. However, the dedication of the *History,* which is dated 1619, was doubtless written on the completion of the work, and the corrections on the inserted scraps were probably still later in date. Furthermore, other scraps indicate a date about 1619, and Chambers points out that one of the play-lists certainly belongs to the winter of 1619–20. In any case, the list in which *Hengist* is mentioned also includes "The Cambridge Playe of Albumazar and Trinculo," which was written for James I's visit to the University in March 1615. Accordingly, Buc's reference to the play must have been made between 1615 and the end of 1620, and there is a strong presumption that it belongs to the later part of this period, say 1619 or 1620.

That the play, in its present form at least, was written about this date may perhaps be conjectured from the reference at I, ii, 103 to "a great enormitie in

[1] These slips were first described and reproduced in facsimile by F. Marcham, *The King's Office of the Revels, 1610–1622* (1925).

[2] The two handwritings were first distinguished by M. Eccles in his study of Buc in *Thomas Lodge and other Elizabethans* (1933), 478–479.

[3] See his review of Marcham's book, *R.E.S.*, i (1925), 479–484, at 484.

wool." If it is correct to interpret this as a reference to a glut of wool on the market and a general disorganisation of the wool trade, it can be explained by certain attempts to extend and develop the wool industry in James I's reign. During the reign of Elizabeth, England had owed much of her commercial prosperity to the export of woollen cloths, a great deal of which was sent abroad undyed. However, during James's reign a serious attempt was made by a company organised by Sir William Cockayne (whose mayoral pageant Middleton designed in 1619) to do all the dyeing in England, and in February 1615 the Merchant Adventurers surrendered their ancient charter permitting them to export undyed cloths. The new company prospered for a year or so until foreign countries, resenting this blow at their dyeing industries, prohibited the importation of English dyed stuffs. Holland, in particular, also made vigorous efforts, aided in part by Puritan refugees from the eastern counties of England, to improve the quality of its weaving. The situation rapidly became so bad, and so many English weavers were thrown out of work, that the ban on the export of undyed cloth was gradually lifted, and in January 1617 the charter of Cockayne's company was revoked. There was a brief improvement, but foreign competition was now well organised and many markets were permanently lost. Eventually the situation became so alarming that at the beginning of 1622 the Privy Council was compelled to institute an enquiry into the state of the cloth trade which revealed enormous stocks of unsold material all over the country.[1] Thus a reference to the unsatisfactory state of the woollen trade would be appropriate in 1616 and 1617 and again, say, from 1619 onwards. It is therefore likely that when the play was included in one of the lists submitted to Buc it was still fairly new.

The next reference to the play occurs in a list of plays supplied by the King's Men in 1641 to the Lord Chamberlain when they secured from him a warrant to prevent the printing of their plays.[2] There it is referred to as "The Maior of Quinborow &c.," and its inclusion in this list shows that it still had a place in the company's repertoire. During the Civil War the play passed with a large batch of others from the remaining members of the King's Men into the hands of the booksellers Humphrey Moseley and Humphrey Robinson, who entered it in the Stationers' Register with forty-seven other plays on 4 September 1646. That it had held its place on the boards right up to the closing of the theatres

[1] These facts are summarised from M. C. Linthicum, *Costume in the Drama of Shakespeare and his Contemporaries* (1936), 11–12, 65–68.

[2] Printed with comments by Sir Edmund Chambers, "Plays of the King's Men in 1641" in the Malone Society's *Collections*, i, 364–369.

is clear, I think, not only from the publisher's allusion in the 1661 quarto to "this *Mayor of Quinborough* whom you have all heard of, and some of you beheld upon the Stage," but also from a reference to Don Quixote's wardrobe as "not much exceeding the Mayor of Queenborough's" on page 2 of Edmund Gayton's *Pleasant Notes upon Don Quixote* (1654).[1] In *Wit Restored* (1658) the brief scene IV, i was printed under the title of *A Prologue to the Mayor of Quinborough,* and in 1661 the play itself was published, not by Moseley or his widow, but by Henry Herringman who, apparently unaware of the previous entry, had entered it himself in the Stationers' Register on 13 February 1660/61.[2] It was on sale very soon afterwards, for the Thomason copy in the British Museum (644. f. 10) has the date "March 28" in Thomason's hand on the title-page.

It would hardly be necessary to insist on the fact that the play seems to have held the boards from 1620 to 1640 and lingered on in men's memories until the Restoration if there had not been until recently an almost universal tendency to regard it as one of Middleton's early and immature works. It may be said emphatically, however, that it is a play of his full maturity, and that if it contains traces of earlier work they are to be found only in a few isolated scenes. The verse has an ease and mastery of which Middleton was incapable in the early part of his career. The change from the earlier to the later style is first observable in *A Chaste Maid in Cheapside,* which comes at the very end of his early comic period, and may be dated 1613.[3] Rather than attempt to convince the reader with statistics of run-on and end-stopped lines, rhymes, and feminine endings, it will be better to ask him to trust his ears, and to put side by side two passages of verse, one from a typical early comedy such as *A Mad World My Masters* (c. 1604) and the other from *A Chaste Maid.* Both extracts are formal set speeches. The first is a soliloquy in which Penitent Brothel, reading in a book, finds cause for repentance (IV, i, 1–18):

[1] My knowledge of this allusion is due to Dyce, who has noted it in one of his copies of the quarto, now in the South Kensington Museum. He also mentions another allusion in J. Philips's translation of *Don Quixote* (1687), 442, but by this time the play had been in print for twenty-six years. Nevertheless, the allusion shows that Simon had become a proverbial figure.

[2] It is interesting to observe that on the title-page of the 1661 quarto of *Beggars Bush* Humphrey Robinson and Anne Moseley, the publishers, assert that "you may speedily expect those other Playes, which Kirkman, and his Hawkers have deceived the buyers withall, selling them at treble the value, that this and the rest will be Sold for, which were first purchased by us at no mean rate, and since printed by us." Dr. Greg, commenting on this statement (*List of Masques and Pageants,* Essay Introductory, v), says that Kirkman's "competition appears to have been perfectly legitimate, since I have failed to discover any case in which he pirated Moseley's editions, or in which their editions clashed." It is odd that Kirkman should have been singled out for attack without any apparent justification when they had a genuine cause for complaint against Herringman over his edition of *The Mayor of Quinborough.*

[3] See "The Chronology of Middleton's Plays," *M.L.R.,* xxxii (1937), at 39–40.

Ha? read that place again—*Adultery*
Draws the divorce 'twixt heaven and the soul.
Accursed man, that stand'st divorc'd from heaven!
Thou wretched unthrift, that hast play'd away
Thy eternal portion at a minute's game;
To please the flesh hast blotted out thy name!
Where were thy nobler meditations busied,
That they durst trust this body with itself;
This natural drunkard, that undoes us all,
And makes our shame apparent in our fall?
Then let my blood pay for't, and vex and boil!
My soul, I know, would never grieve to th' death
Th' eternal spirit, that feeds her with his breath:
Nay, I that knew the price of life and sin,
What crown is kept for continence, what for lust,
The end of man, and glory of that end,
As endless as the giver,
To doat on weakness, slime, corruption, woman!

The other passage is Touchwood senior's speech at the mock funeral of Moll and his brother (*A Chaste Maid,* V, iv, 1–20), and is one of those which sometimes occur in the Elizabethan drama, and, as Miss Bradbrook has pointed out, "permit a kind of double emotional response by which the spectator or reader is allowed to indulge a feeling which does not lead anywhere, and is contradicted later on":[1]

Never could death boast of a richer prize
From the first parent; let the world bring forth
A pair of truer hearts. To speak but truth
Of this departed gentleman, in a brother
Might, by hard censure, be call'd flattery,
Which makes me rather silent in his right
Than so to be deliver'd to the thoughts
Of any envious hearer, starv'd in virtue,
And therefore pining to hear others thrive;
But for this maid, whom envy cannot hurt
With all her poisons, having left to ages

[1] *Themes and Conventions of Elizabethan Tragedy* (1935), 60. This passage, however, is not included among those cited as examples.

The true, chaste monument of her living name,
Which no time can deface, I say of her
The full truth freely, without fear of censure;
What nature could there shrine, that might redeem
Perfection home to woman, but in her
Was fully glorious? beauty set in goodness
Speaks what she was; that jewel so infix'd,
There was no want of anything of life
To make these virtuous precedents man and wife.

It should be immediately clear that the verse of *Hengist* is at least as mature as, if not more mature than, the verse of *A Chaste Maid,* and for this reason alone it is impossible to assign it to an early date.

Other features of the play which have been singled out as evidence of an early date are the choruses, spoken by Raynulph as presenter, and the dumb-shows,[1] but neither has any weight. It is true that there is a fairly close parallel between the functions of Raynulph in this play and those of Lydgate in the "plot" of *The second parte of the Seuen Deadlie sinns,* which dates from 1590, but Middleton might just as easily have been indebted to Shakespeare, as K. Christ suggested,[2] for his example of the use of Gower as chorus and presenter in *Pericles,* or to Heywood, who had used Homer similarly in the *Golden, Silver* and *Brazen Ages.* It is far more important to realise that the presenter, though he may have been a relic of an earlier and cruder time, was not entirely outmoded in 1608, when *Pericles* was written, nor even a decade later. Indeed, even in Fletcher and Massinger's *Prophetess* (licensed by Sir Henry Herbert on 14 May 1622) one finds the Chorus acting as the presenter of a dumb-show and bridging with a speech a gap in the action somewhat later in the play. Furthermore, it has recently been demonstrated that the dumb-show which carried forward the main action of the plot is not a sign of early date at all, but retained its popularity throughout the whole period.[3]

One can say, then, that *Hengist* was almost certainly written between 1616 and 1620, and that substantially the whole of the play belongs to this period. However, one must not disregard the fact that an earlier play on the same sub-

[1] E. H. C. Oliphant on various occasions (e.g., *The Plays of Beaumont and Fletcher* [1927], 119) adduced as further evidence of an early date the fact that the play "is vouched for as the 'first flight' of the author." He has, however, misunderstood the import of Herringman's words in the prefatory epistle to the quarto. Herringman merely means that the play had not been previously printed.

[2] *Quellenstudien zu den Dramen Thomas Middletons* (Borna-Leipzig, 1905), 15.

[3] B. R. Pearn, "The Dumb Show in Elizabethan Drama," *R.E.S.,* xi (1935), 385 ff.

ject is mentioned in Henslowe's *Diary*. This, which Henslowe generally refers to as "valteger," was performed as a new play on 4 December 1596, and was given twelve times in all during the ensuing four months; it may also beyond any question of doubt be identified with "henges," of which a single performance (not as a new play) is recorded on 22 June 1597.[1] "Valteger" was fairly successful, and was followed up by sequels: the first, "vterpendragon," was new on 29 April 1597, and the other, *King Arthur,* by Richard Hathaway, was paid for nearly a year later on 11 and 12 April 1598.[2] The Admiral's Men evidently put on a closely related series of plays on early British pseudo-history. Henslowe's papers supply one or two other details about *Vortiger*. During the last few days of November 1596 Henslowe lent the company £8–5–0 in all towards the costumes and properties of the new play which was then within a week of its first production,[3] and in the inventory of the wardrobe of the Admiral's Men made in March 1598 he recorded the following costumes:

> j payer of hosse, & a gercken for Valteger.
> Vartemar sewtte.
> Valteger robe of rich tafitie.[4]

The last items are not much, but the second of them does at least suggest that Vortimer played a far more important part in the old play than in Middleton's; and, considering how he appears in the chronicles as a patriot and a successful general, he may well have been its hero, occupying a position in it somewhat analogous to that of Falconbridge in Shakespeare's *King John*. One more fact emerges from the *Diary:* namely, that the play belonged to Alleyn and that Henslowe bought it from him on behalf of the company for £2 on 20 November 1601.[5] Though its value had somewhat depreciated, it was not yet worthless.

There had existed, then, an old play on which Middleton might have based his work, and one can, in fact, find certain passages in his text that can reasonably be held to support the view that he did so. The fourth chorus is more deliberately archaic in style than the others, and is written so clumsily that one may entertain serious doubts as to whether it is Middleton's. The brief opening scene of Act IV is likewise suspect; its rhyming doggerel and its fourteeners seem to hark back to a much earlier period. In the comic part of III, iii and the first half of V,i there are also suggestions of a more primitive style, which

1 *Diary,* ed. W. W. Greg, ff. 25^{v}, 26, 27.
2 *Op. cit.,* ff. 26^{v}, 45^{v}, 46.
3 F. 22^{v}.
4 *Henslowe Papers,* 116, 119.
5 F. 95.

seem to betray an earlier stratum that has been overlaid by later revision. Not only is the line-division of these scenes often very difficult to determine, as reference to the textual notes will show, but prose and verse are sometimes mixed indiscriminately together in Simon's speeches. One cannot be sure, for instance, to what extent III, iii, 179–184 or V, i, 22–27 and 40–48 are prose or verse, except where rhymes clearly indicate couplets. From other speeches, clearly in prose, one is able to rescue what seem to be scraps of verse. For instance, "But being worne thread bare, the shame will be as greate" at V, i, 13–14 has the ring of verse; "to yo^u^ good neighbours now I bend my speech" at III, iii, 194–195 makes a blank verse line, and the words immediately following can with little difficulty be fitted into the rhythm of a fourteener: "first to say more than a Man Can say, I hold it not soe fitt." There seems to be another fourteener at V, i, 195, and there is certainly one in Simon's speech at line 131:

A man
vndon in Law the day before; ye saddest Case that Can be.

Occasionally, too, there are snatches of braggart blank verse such as one would have expected from Pistol rather than from Simon, as at V, i, 154–155:

What ioyfull throat is that Aminadab
What is ye meaneing of this Crye.

Furthermore, rhyme is far more frequent in these two scenes than in the other normal parts of the play, and not only are many of the couplets forced and clumsy, but so are the speeches in which they occur. Reference may be made to III, iii, 21–22, 76–78, 93–97 and V, i, 22–48, 134–139, 154–190; in the last passage in particular two separate styles seem to be intermingled.

If it be held that the evidence provided by these passages is sufficient to prove that Middleton was rewriting an old play, and that that play is most likely to have been Henslowe's *Vortiger,* a problem still remains. How did a play performed by the Admiral's Men in 1596 come eventually in revised form into the possession of the King's Men? In spite of the fact that Mr. Eccles believes that such a thing could not have happened,[1] one answer to the problem may perhaps be found in the somewhat involved and obscure careers of men like Joseph Taylor and William Rowley, who first acted in the Duke of York's company (afterwards Prince Charles's Men), were next connected with the Lady Elizabeth's Men, and eventually joined the King's Men.[2] The Lady

[1] "Middleton's Birth and Education," *R.E.S.,* vii (1931), 431–441, at 433.

[2] The authorities for the biographical details in this paragraph are E. K. Chambers, *The Elizabethan Stage,* ii, 345–346 and iii, 473, and C. J. Sisson, *Lost Plays of the Age of Shakespeare,* 102.

Elizabeth's Men were for some years under the thumb of Henslowe, as were the Prince's Men for a somewhat briefer period, and Henslowe may well have provided the link between an old and abandoned play of the Admiral's Men and its revision for performance by one of the companies under his management at a later date. Taylor left the Duke of York's Men for the Lady Elizabeth's in 1611, and joined the King's Men after Burbage's death in 1619. As for Rowley, it was apparently through writing for the Lady Elizabeth's Men when Henslowe was interested in the two companies that Middleton began his partnership with him. Though Rowley continued nominally to maintain his status as one of the Prince's servants, and in that capacity received a suit of mourning on the death of James I in 1625, he was collaborating with Middleton during 1621 and 1622 in plays for the Lady Elizabeth's Men at the Cockpit, and in 1623 was both writing and acting for the King's Men. Finally, when Prince Charles became King, Rowley and several other members of the Prince's company were officially incorporated with the King's Men in the patent issued on 24 June 1625, some six months before Rowley's death. That one play at least passed from the Lady Elizabeth's Men to the King's Men we know; the former had acted *The Honest Man's Fortune* in 1613, but on 8 February 1624/5 it was relicensed as an old play to the King's Men by Sir Henry Herbert "at the entreaty of Mr. Taylor."

Even if Middleton's *Hengist* was not based on an old play, it is still extremely probable that it was not originally written for the King's Men. The two manuscripts of the play have preserved the names of some minor actors who took part in it.[1] We know so much more about the King's Men than about the other companies at this time—as such a study as T. W. Baldwin's *Organization and Personnel of the Shakespearean Company* amply witnesses—that if these actors had been supers for the King's Men we should doubtless have heard of them. Of the three men mentioned, viz. Robert Briggs, Blackstone, and Robert "Str", Briggs is untraceable,[2] and a sole reference to an actor called "Blaxton" furnishes no information beyond the fact that at one period of his obscure career he was apparently a member of a company of strollers.[3] The only actor of whom any record has survived who can possibly be identified with the third

[1] See below, p. xxviii.

[2] A manuscript *Dictionary of the Old Actors*, compiled by Halliwell-Phillipps, which is now in the Folger Shakespeare Library, contains the following entry: "*Brigges.* One of the Qu. of Bohemia's players, mentd in MS. Coll: Phys: 1630," but it is practically certain that the reference is to John Bugges. See the Malone Society's *Collections*, ii, 403.

[3] The name appears in a manuscript list of actors in a copy of the 1601 quarto of *Every Man in his Humour* formerly owned by F. G. Waldron, which was printed by him on p. 26 of the section on *The English Stage* in his *Shakespearean Miscellany*, 1802.

man is Robert Stratford, who appears in the list of the cast prefixed to Shakerley Marmion's *Holland's Leaguer*. This play was acted by the later Prince Charles's Men at Salisbury Court in 1631, and was printed in the following year. Nothing is known of Stratford beyond the fact that he played the part of Triphœna, wife to Philautus, in this play. It is quite possible that he was still a boy in 1631; on the other hand, he may have been a mature actor capable of filling female rôles, and it is worth noticing both that his part is a very small one and that there are in all eight female parts in the play, so that there may not have been enough boys in the company to take them all. Thus, even assuming that Stratford is the actor referred to in the *Hengist* manuscript, and that he was a hired man capable of playing an occasional female part, we still have no information about the length either of his career as an actor or of his service with Prince Charles's Men. It would therefore be rash to conjecture that *Hengist* belonged to Prince Charles's Men as late as 1631, and passed to the King's Men after this date. Mr. Eccles, indeed, refers to the Revels Office scrap as "Buc's list of what can be shown to have been King's plays,"[1] and, if he is right, it would mean that *Hengist* belonged to the King's Men as early as about 1620. However, though the list may well be one of plays belonging to the King's Men, this is by no means certain. Out of the eight legible titles, there are only four which can be definitely assigned to them; of the other four we have no information. It is thus still possible to conjecture that the play was originally written by Middleton for a company other than the King's Men, and what is known of his career during the years before 1620 suggests that this company is likely to have been either the Prince's or the Lady Elizabeth's Men—more probably the Lady Elizabeth's Men, for whom *The Changeling* and *The Spanish Gipsy* were also written.

A number of critics, who have been sufficiently conscious of the discrepancy between parts of the comic scenes and the style of the rest of the play to feel that some explanation was needed, have avoided the difficulties involved in finding the origin of *Hengist* in the old play of *Vortiger* by providing Middleton with a collaborator. For this post Rowley is the obvious candidate, and his claims have been supported by writers as different as Swinburne[2] and C. W. Stork.[3] This theory, however, is definitely less satisfactory than the one which

[1] "Middleton's Birth and Education," *R.E.S.*, vii (1931), at 433. The three other scraps, it is true, are lists of plays belonging to the King's Men; those at ff. 70^v and 211^v contain only plays which are known to have been theirs, and Dr. Greg has been kind enough to confirm my opinion that the longest list (that on f. 247) is in the hand of the scribe and book-keeper of the King's Men, who wrote out the surviving manuscripts of *Bonduca* and *The Honest Man's Fortune* and added the prompter's notes to the manuscript of *Believe as You List*.

[2] Essay on Middleton in *The Age of Shakespeare* and the Mermaid edition of Middleton, i, xxii.

[3] *William Rowley* (University of Pennsylvania, 1910), 46.

credits Middleton with revising an older play. In both III, iii and V, i there is, interspersed with what may be older work, much that is undoubtedly Middleton's; in particular, the speeches of Hengist in the first half of III, iii could have been written by no one else. Even if it is admitted that the comic parts of the play are kindlier and less ironical than is Middleton's wont, this provides no justification for crediting them to Rowley. The spirit of Rowley's comedy is cruder, clumsier, and grosser than the spirit of these scenes, and one has only to compare them with the comic scenes in *The Birth of Merlin* to detect the difference. I am confident that Rowley's hand is not to be found in this play.

There is no doubt, however, that there is some relationship between *The Birth of Merlin* and *Hengist, King of Kent;* exactly what it is, is less easy to define.[1] Rowley's play covers a part of the reign of Vortiger, the whole of that of Aurelius Ambrosius, and the beginning of Uther's, and it takes for granted a knowledge of some of the events dramatised by Middleton, such as Vortiger's responsibility for the presence of the Saxons in Britain. It is clearly later than Middleton's play, for it not only concentrates on a number of incidents in the chronicles which Middleton might have used but deliberately rejected—using, in fact, what he had left over—but it also repeats a number of his themes. Artesia, the sister of the Saxon general, who attracts Aurelius and marries him, and then is guilty not only of base treachery but of infidelity to her husband, has a part analogous to that of Roxena, while the piety of Constantius and Castiza finds a parallel in the conversion of the two sisters Modestia and Constantia, who refuse husbands and enter a nunnery. The Saxons maintain their reputation for treachery, established in IV, iii of Middleton's play, and a comic underplot is provided which in this case is furnished by Merlin and the Clown.[2] Though C. W. Stork dated *The Birth of Merlin c.* 1608,[3] the consensus of opinion seems to place it, in its present form, about 1620–22[4]—on very slender grounds, it must be confessed. The later date, fortunately, does not conflict with that already decided on for Middleton's play. Fleay believed that *The Birth of Merlin* was a revision of an old play, and suggested that it had its origin in Henslowe's *Uther Pendragon,* but E. H. C. Oliphant's suggestion that it is, or was based upon, a rival play to Middleton's, or to Middleton's original,[5] seems

[1] The suggestions made by P. A. Daniel, Fleay (later withdrawn), and Stork that Middleton was part-author of *The Birth of Merlin* may be disregarded.

[2] See F. A. Howe, "The Authorship of *The Birth of Merlin,*" *M.P.*, iv (1906), 193 ff. for a discussion of these and other parallels.

[3] *Op. cit.*, 58.

[4] See Fleay, *Life of Shakespeare,* 289; A. F. Hopkinson, *Doubtful Plays of Shakespeare,* vol. ii, introduction to *The Birth of Merlin,* 1; and F. A. Howe, *op. cit.*

[5] *The Plays of Beaumont and Fletcher,* 404.

to be nearer to the truth. It is difficult, however, to say more, for we do not, in actual fact, know the exact date of either play; we cannot assert with complete confidence that either is based on an earlier play; we cannot be sure whether *Hengist* was originally written for the King's Men; and we can only guess for whom *The Birth of Merlin* was written.[1] Indeed, the most that seems at all certain is that Rowley attempted to follow up the success of his friend's play with another in the same vein. Evidence, to be adduced later,[2] suggests that *Hengist* and *The Birth of Merlin* were at one time played in conjunction with one another by the same company, and the condition of both plays is most satisfactorily explained on the hypothesis that about 1620 they were rival plays, but that *Hengist* changed hands and came into the possession of the King's Men, already the owners of Rowley's play, who then made certain revisions in *Hengist,* and possibly also in *The Birth of Merlin,* to bring the two plays more closely into line with one another.

Another play about Vortiger and Hengist was written about the same time as Middleton's. It has never been published—doubtless because it was written in Latin—but it has survived as MS. Lansd. 723 in the British Museum. Its title is *Fatum Vortigerni,* and it covers very much the same ground as Middleton's play.[3] It does not follow or suggest any of the more important of Middleton's unhistorical elaborations, but keeps closely to the story of the chronicles. In spite of one or two similarities which cannot be explained by common sources (for instance, the appearance of Vortimer's ghost to Roxena just before her death, and Hengist's grief for her in both plays) it is unlikely that *Fatum Vortigerni* influenced, or was influenced by, *Hengist,* in view of the authorship and provenance of the former. W. H. McCabe has shown[4] that it was written by Thomas Carleton (*alias* Medcalf) student and later Professor of Rhetoric at the English College at Douay, where it was performed on 22 August 1619. It is probably, he adds, an allegorical attack on the English Reformation, with Vortiger representing Henry VIII and Ronowen, Ann Boleyn. For our present purposes the play is interesting only because it shows that the legend of Hengist and Vortiger furnished dramatic materials for other writers besides Middleton.

[1] It may be noted that Fleay (*Biog. Chron.*, ii, 105) asserts that "the ascription to Shakespeare justifies my assigning it to the King's company."

[2] See below, pp. xxxiv–xxxv.

[3] The play is summarised by G. R. Churchill and W. Keller in "Die lateinischen Universitäts-Dramen in der Zeit der Königin Elisabeth," *Shakespeare Jahrbuch,* xxxiv (1898), 258–264.

[4] *T.L.S.,* 15 August 1935.

II

The Texts

The texts of the play are as follows:

1. Manuscript, in the Lambarde volume of seventeenth century plays, in the Folger Shakespeare Library, Washington.

This is now the last play in the Lambarde volume, although it was formerly followed by George Wilde's *Lovers' Hospital*. The play occupies 46 leaves, which measure 11¾ × 7¾ inches, and have been badly cropped by a binder. The first and last leaves are half-sheets; the rest of the play consists of successive sheets in folio which were originally numbered, but, owing to the trimming, portions of the numbers or of the lines enclosing them are now visible only on folios 12, 20, 30, 32, 36, and 40. The first half-sheet was not included in the numbering.

There is no watermark on the first half-sheet. On the first 21 sheets there is a watermark of three circles, one above the other, surmounted by a cross crosslet; in the uppermost circle is a crescent, in the second 6D above 6, and the lowest is empty. On the twenty-second sheet and the final half-sheet the watermark consists of three circles surmounted by a three-pointed crown, with a cross at each point and the central one surmounted by a ball; the upper circle contains a cross crosslet, the second the letters AO, and the third is empty. Watermarks of this type originated in Genoa, but were widely imitated in France, and persisted throughout the seventeenth century.[1]

There is no title-page. Fol. 1^a: [a list of dramatis personæ]; fol. 1^b: [blank]. Fol. 2^a: begins *"Actus Primus Scena Prima."*

Fol. 46^a, at the foot of the page: *"Finis / Hengist King off Kent"*; fol. 46^b: begins *"Enter Raynulph"*; ends *"Musique."*

[1] Briquet (*Les Filigranes*, i, no. 3246) illustrates a watermark closely resembling the first of these two (viz. three circles surmounted by a cross crosslet, a crescent in the upper circle, 6D in the second, and A in the lowest) which he found at Brussels. He assigns to this mark the conjectural date of 1598, but, he adds (p. 218), "une variation du groupe 3245 et 3246, mais où le cercle inférieur est vide, se trouve à Perpignan postérieure de 1639." In "Papiers et filigranes des Archives de Gênes," *Atti della Società Ligure di Storia Patria*, xix, fasc. ii (1888), at 347, the same authority states that watermarks of this type ("croissaint au dessus de deux lunes") were common between 1626 and 1643. However, as Mr. E. Heawood has shown ("Papers used in England after 1600, II. *c.* 1680–1750," *The Library*, ser. 4, xi [1931], 473–474 and fig. 123) watermarks of this type survived right up to the end of the century.

The manuscript is written in a not very elegant hand, belonging probably to the second quarter of the seventeenth century. The body of the text is in the secretary hand, but an Italian hand is used for act and scene headings, speakers' names, nearly all the stage-directions, and occasionally for proper names in the text. A few corrections, recorded in the textual notes, have been made by another, contemporary, hand.

The sheet, after being folded into two leaves, was folded twice lengthways, and a margin of a quarter of the width of the page was observed on the left side, speech prefixes being written in the margin. Speeches are separated by strokes.

The play is divided into acts, and in acts III and V the scenes are numbered as well. Scenes are always separated by double rules, and the one entrance which is centred during the course of a scene also has them. Stage-directions at the beginning of a scene, and one at I, i, 28, are centred; directions for music and noises are usually in the left margin, but normal entrances and exits during a scene are at the right of the text, and are usually enclosed by penstrokes.

The text of the play given in this volume is based on this manuscript, which is referred to as *L* in the ensuing discussion and in the textual notes.

2. Manuscript in the library of his Grace the Duke of Portland at Welbeck Abbey.

The manuscript is bound in a modern binding, and contains the bookplate of the present Duke of Portland. The pages measure $11\frac{5}{8} \times 7\frac{5}{8}$ inches. The text of the play is written on 21 successive sheets (42 leaves) numbered from 1 to 21, preceded by a half-sheet containing a list of dramatis personæ. The watermark of the first six sheets consists of three circles (the upper contains a cross crosslet, the second TC, the lowest A) surmounted by a three-pointed crown with a cross at each point. In the remaining sheets the watermark is of similar design, but has SR in the middle circle, and the lowest one is empty. Blank leaves at the beginning and end of the play are apparently a sheet of eighteenth century French paper. In addition, the play is preceded by a title-page, in the same hand as the rest of the manuscript, written on a half-sheet of grey paper that is possibly part of an original wrapper.[1]

Fol. 1^a: [title-page, reproduced in plate vi]. The figures "52" at the top are in the same hand as the rest of the page; another hand has written "<?>36" in the left upper corner, and the number "457" is written on a diamond-shaped label pasted near the left lower corner. Fol. 1^b: [blank]. Fol. 2: [blank].

[1] The manuscript of *Sir John van Olden Barnavelt* also has a grey title-page, which is thought to be all that remains of a wrapper. See W. W. Greg, *Dramatic Documents from the Elizabethan Playhouses,* 193.

Fol. 3^a: [list of dramatis personæ, and, in pencil, near the upper right corner, "0–10–6"]; fol. 3^b: [blank].

Fol. 4^a: begins *"Actus Primus Sce^a: Pri^a:"*.

Fol. 45^a: ends *"Finis / Hengist King of Kent"* / [flourish]; fol. 45^b: begins *"Enter Raynulph,"* ends *"Musique."* Fol. 46: [blank].

This manuscript is a transcript by the same scribe as that of *L*, and has many features in common with it. A quarter of the page is reserved for the margin, and the rather unusual division into acts and scenes is exactly the same. Stage-directions are similarly treated. There are only two differences to be noted: in this manuscript the scribe frequently ignores the line-division, running verse speeches together as if they were prose, and he does not observe a margin for the directions for the dumb-shows, but writes them right across the page.

This manuscript is cited as *P* in the following pages and in the textual notes.

3. Quarto:

THE / MAYOR / OF / Quinborough: / A / COMEDY. / As it hath been often Acted with much / Applause at *Black-Fryars,* By His / Majesties Servants. / [rule] / *Written by* THO. MIDDLETON. / [double rule] / LONDON, / Printed for *Henry Herringman,* and are to be sold at his / Shop at the Sign of the *Blew-Anchor* in the Lower- / Walk of the *New-Exchange.* 1661

Collation. A–I^4 K^2.

[A]1: recto, [title-page]; verso, [blank].

A2: recto, [publisher's epistle]:

GENTLEMEN,

Y*ou have the first flight of him I assure you; this* Mayor *of* Quinborough *whom you have all heard of, and some of you beheld upon the Stage, now begins to walk abroad in Print; he has been known sufficiently by the reputation of his Wit, which is enough (by the way) to distinguish him from ordinary Mayors; but Wit you know, has skulk'd in Corners for many years past and he was thought to have most of it that could best hide himself: Now whether this Magistrate fear'd the decimating times, or kept up the state of other Mayors, that are bound not to go out of their Liberties during the time of their Mayoralty, I know not; 'tis enough for me to put him into your hands, under the title of an honest man, which will appear plainly to you, because you shall find him all along to have a great picque to the Rebel* Oliver; *I am told his drollery yields to none the* English Drama *did ever produce; and though I would not put his modesty to the blush, by speaking too much in his Commendation, yet I know you will agree with* *me, upon your better acquaintance with him, that there is some difference in point of Wit, betwixt the* Mayor *of* Quinborough, *and the* Mayor *of* Huntingdon.

A2, verso: begins "Drammatis Personæ."

A3–K2[v]: [text].

Pagination. A3[r] is page 5, and from there onwards pagination is continuous until K2[v] (page 76).

Copies consulted: British Museum (shelf-mark, 644. f. 10); Dyce Collection, Victoria and Albert Museum, South Kensington (2 copies); Folger Shakespeare Library; Copy sold at the Anderson Galleries, New York, 27 February 1937.

Several slight differences between the various copies of the quartos are recorded in the textual notes. Since most of these variants, however, concern turned letters or letters low in the line, they are of little importance.

This edition is referred to as *Q* in the following pages and in the textual notes.

Before proceeding to discuss the relations of the three texts it will be well to revert to the statement made above that the two manuscripts are in the handwriting of the same scribe. The plates will immediately reveal the general similarity between the handwritings of the two manuscripts, but a more detailed examination will show apparently consistent differences in the formation of certain letters, of which some typical examples may be mentioned. In *L* one notices a tendency to terminate *d* with a curly flourish above the line, and, not quite so frequently, to terminate *g* and *y* with similar flourishes below; in *P* these final curls are absent. Again, in *L* the downstroke of a final *h* is interrupted by an abbreviated shoulder, but in *P* it is an uninterrupted curve; in the text of *L* secretary *C*'s, *J*'s, *K*'s, and *k*'s are generally used, in *P* Italian ones. Nevertheless, these differences are not entirely consistent, since a more extensive examination shows that these forms are not peculiar to the manuscript in which they occur frequently, although in some cases they are of very rare occurrence in the other. The many other similarities are sufficient to outweigh these differences, and some of them are very striking. The final *u* in *you* (made like a Greek ω), and the *w* are, for instance, characteristic of both manuscripts. Further, a detailed examination of significant general characteristics, such as slope or pen-pressure, will convince any student who undertakes it that the two manuscripts are by the same hand. One may also mention a number of common scribal characteristics which seem to be distinctive. There is a marked tendency to link words together without any separating pen-lift; it is a habit from which the scribe rarely departs to use a majuscule instead of a minuscule for words beginning with *c*; and he frequently ends words with a long *s*. At the end of words *-neſſ* appears instead of *-neſſe* or *-nes,* and present participles often end in *-eing*. Finally, the lines separating the speeches project into the left margins further than is usual in dramatic manuscripts of the period. *P,* it would seem, reveals that there has been a gradual transition from secretary to the more fluent Italian forms; it is the work of a more practised writer, and for that reason it is likely to have been transcribed later, possibly some years later, than *L.*

Both manuscripts preserve a number of features specially characteristic of theatrical prompt-copies. At II, i, 40–41, on the right side of the page, *P* has, enclosed by a line, "Brigs / Robrt str / Blackson" (see plate v);[1] these are presumably the names of minor actors who had parts in the dumb-show which followed soon afterwards. A similar direction probably occurred in *L,* but it has been trimmed by the binder, and only a portion of the line surrounding it has survived. At the beginning of II, iii (at l. 2) *L* adds the name "Rob: Briggs" and *P* "Robb Briggs" (cf. plate i); he apparently acted the part of the Gentleman in this scene. Finally, at IV, ii, 280–282 *L* alone has, within the usual surrounding line, "Lor<des> / Black<son> / Bri<ggs>"; again the reference seems to be to actors who took part in the succeeding dumb-show. Unfortunately, no reliable information about Briggs or Blackstone has survived, and the identification of the third actor with Robert Stratford raises more difficulties than it solves, so what might have been a valuable clue to the date and provenance of the play merely provides additional matter for speculation.[2]

In both manuscripts also the same two passages are marked for omission in the manner commonly used in prompt-books to indicate theatrical cuts. Beside III, i, 56–63 (see plate ii) and V, ii, 162–176 there is a vertical line in the left margin, and a horizontal line at the end to indicate the exact extent of the cut. In addition there are in *L* alone certain symbols which may possibly have some stage significance (cf. plate i); they resemble an *O* with a cross on top of it, and they occur at the beginnings of II, iii (where there are two of them), III, iii, IV, i, and V, i. What meaning, if any, was attached to these signs is not easy to decide, and, in any case, it is possible that they were added later by another hand.

A dramatic manuscript containing such clearly marked theatrical cuts and

[1] There is some doubt as to the way in which the second line should be read; the last letter of the first word is given as *t* because it can hardly be *e,* and does not make sense as ρ; the last letter of the second word may be either *r* or *o*. It is evident that the scribe's writing is cramped because he is so near to the edge of the page.

[2] See above, p. xx.

various actors' names in stage-directions would, under normal circumstances, be unhesitatingly pronounced a prompt-book, but here, where the same features appear in the two manuscripts of the play, and where the manuscripts are in the hand of the same scribe, both can scarcely be prompt-copies, and it is probable that neither is. It seems to be more reasonable to assume that if the scribe was capable of mechanically transcribing theatrical notes when he made one copy of the play, he was capable of doing it when he made a second one later. That a prompter's notes might find their way into a private transcript is proved by another play in the Lambarde volume. The manuscript of Berkeley's *Lost Lady* there was apparently made for presentation to Queen Henrietta Maria, but it contains a number of obvious prompter's notes which have been included by the scribe, but which were deleted by the author when he corrected the manuscript.[1] The two manuscripts of *Hengist,* therefore, are probably private transcripts; but there is little doubt that the scribe's "copy" was an annotated prompt-book.[2] One may perhaps express, too, a general impression that the text given by *L* and *P* is not quite accurate enough for a prompt-book; both manuscripts contain too many mistakes (many of them common mistakes) which are often of such a nature that they would almost inevitably have been corrected had either of the manuscripts been used in the theatre.

Comparison with *Q* reveals even more clearly the theatrical origin of a number of other features in *L* and *P*. The latter contain in all twenty-four directions for music and noises off stage; *Q* has only four such directions, viz., two for shouts (at I, i, 1 and V, i, 155), one for "Alarms and excursions" (at the beginning of II, iii), and one for a flourish (II, iii, 218). The musical directions in the manuscripts are unusually full and systematic. They provide for music at each act interval, at the conclusion of the epilogue, and before each dumb-show ("Musique" for the first, and "Hoboys" for the other two). Directions for music also introduce the two songs (I, i, 28 and IV, ii, 39), and "hoboys" accompanied the processional entry to the banquet at the beginning of IV, ii. Flourishes generally mark solemn royal entrances and exits (I, i, 175; II, iii, 218; II, iii, 299), though "musique" is used for Vortiger's exits at IV, i, 19 and IV, ii, 269. Flourishes also occur at the coronation of Constantius (I, i, 117), and as the characters march off at the end of the play. It is significant, too, that the manuscripts have two directions for drums in the military scenes (at II, ii, 24–26

[1] See the description of the manuscript in *The Library,* ser. 4, xvii (1936–37), at 407–409.

[2] In view of the very close agreement of *L* and *P,* even over minor errors, it might be argued that *P* was transcribed from *L*. But in a few places (II, iii, 236, III, iii, 129 and 298) the scribe has made a mistake in *L* and then corrected it, whereas in *P* the error is found uncorrected. This would seem to be decisive.

and II, iii, 8) which are lacking in *Q*. One can hardly doubt that these directions are due to theatrical annotation.[1]

There are two other directions in the manuscripts which suggest the influence of a prompter. At the beginning of III, ii one finds *Enter Castiza A Booke: two Ladyes:*, and here the words *A Booke* seem to be the prompter's curt insertion to make provision for a property that was to be brought on to the stage. At I, i, 28, in *Enter Certaine Muncks, Germanicus; Constantius being one . . .* the name "Germanicus" looks like another insertion. It not only interrupts the syntax of the sentence, but, being a mistake for "Germanus," was obviously written by someone not as familiar with the play as the author would have been. Apparently Germanus was felt to be a sufficiently important character to be named specifically, and his name was added to the stage-direction for the sake of clarity. There is no mention, it may be noted, of Germanus in the corresponding direction in *Q*.

The stage-directions of *Q*, on the other hand, have in the main been purged of references to the actual details of stage production. The minor stage-directions of *Q* are also not as careful as those of *L* and *P*, for, though *Q* has three exits not to be found in *L,P* (I, ii, 221; V, i, 38; and V, i, 258), *Q* omits six exits and three entrances which are in the manuscripts.[2] Nevertheless, the directions of *Q* have a distinctive character of their own, especially in the fifth act. This can best be illustrated by putting the most significant of them alongside the corresponding directions from *L,P:*

	MSS.	Q
I, i, 28	*Musick Enter Certaine Muncks, Germanicus; Constantius being one as at Precession*	*Enter Constantius as a Monck, attended by other Moncks) Vortiger stays him.*
I, ii, 193	*Enter Vort: & Gentleman*	*As he kisses her, Enter Vortiger and Gentleman.*
II, ii, 1	*Enter Vortiger a Gentleman*	*Enter Vortiger (Crowned) a Gentleman meeting him.*
III, ii, 20	*Enter Vort: & Hersus*	*Enter Vortiger and Horsus disguised.*
III, ii, 115	*Ex^t vort: Castiza*	*Vort. snatches her away.*

1 For a further discussion of this topic in relation to other plays, see *Bibliographical Studies in the Beaumont and Fletcher Folio of 1647*, Supplement to the Transactions of the Bibliographical Society, no. 13, 78–79 and 106–108.

2 Viz., at I, ii, 75, 196; II, ii, 11; II, iii, 129; III, ii, 34; III, iii, 79, 117; IV, ii, 204; V, i, 351.

IV, i, 1	*. . . Symon And his Brethren . . .*	*. . . Symon and his Brethren, a Mace and Sword before him, . . .*
V, i, 156	*Enter Oliuer*	*Oliver is brought in.*
V, i, 234	(omitted)	*They draw.*
V, i, 250	(omitted)	*They pick his pocket.*
V, i, 286	(omitted)	*He throws off his Gown, discovering his doublet with a satten forepart, and a Canvas back.*
V, i, 319	*Exit*	*Throws meal in his face, takes his purse, & Exit.*
V, ii, 105	(omitted)	*stabs him*
V, ii, 140	(omitted)	*They stab each other, Rox. enters in fear.*
V, ii, 179	(omitted)	*Both stab, Hor. falls.*
V, ii, 190	(omitted)	*She falls.*

These directions make it clear that in *Q* there is much more description of the action than in the manuscripts. They are, in fact, more literary in type, and seem to be there to help a reader who has not actually seen the play on the stage.[1]

Of far greater importance than anything yet mentioned is the fact that the manuscripts present a much fuller text of the play than does the previously known quarto version. In all, the manuscripts contain 175 lines not in *Q*, although *Q* has about 25 lines not in the manuscripts. The omissions of *Q* extend far beyond the two passages marked as cuts in the manuscripts.[2] A large number of the other omissions are also ordinary theatrical cuts,[3] and, although

[1] A somewhat similar difference exists in the stage-directions of the two versions of *The Humorous Lieutenant;* see *Bibliographical Studies in the Beaumont and Fletcher Folio,* 76–77. It must be made clear, however, that some of the stage-directions in *Q* are not necessarily of a type that would not be found in a prompt-copy. Such directions as those in Act V, for example, might very well be found in an author's fair copy, and would have been inserted by the author as a guide to the producer; cf. *Believe as You List,* ll. 1766, 2118, 2122. Nevertheless, the evidence seems to suggest that *Q* traces its descent through the prompt-copy behind *L* and *P* (see below, p. xxxiv), and that at least some of the directions just cited are likely to have received their present form late in the process of transmission.

[2] The following is a list of passages of two lines and over which are omitted in *Q:* I, i, 9–14, 29–40, 190–192; II, ii, 5–7, 14–15; II, iii, 143–145; III, i, 56–63, 105–109; III, iii, 218–230, 277–282; IV, ii, 51–57, 187–188, 273–279; IV, iii, 15–20, 25–31, 137–140; V, i, 292–295; V, ii, 47–56, 163–174, 197–199, 209–211, 257–290, and Epilogue.

[3] E.g., I, i, 9–14; II, ii, 5–7; III, i, 56–63; III, iii, 218–230, 277–282; IV, ii, 273–279; IV, iii, 15–20, 25–31, 137–140; V, i, 292–295; V, ii, 47–56, 163–174.

they sometimes leave a line incomplete, in three instances the stage-adapter of the version from which *Q* is descended has bridged the gap in the sense or metre by inserting a few words of his own.[1]

Whether censorship can be held responsible for any omissions in *Q* is a moot point, but there are three passages where one may perhaps sense official interference. They are sufficiently important to be quoted, with *Q*'s omissions italicised:

they hated him aliue,
Grew weary of ye minute of his raigne
Compared with some kings time, & poysoned him
Often before he died, in there black wishes;
Calld him an evill of there own electing,
[II, ii, 12–17]

Heng: Theirs the fruitee
Of their religious shewes too, to lye rotting
Vnder a Million spent in gold and marble
When thousandes left behind dyes without shelter
Haueing not house nor food;
Hers: *A pretious Charitye*
But wheire shall we make Choice of o^r ground Captaine
[II, iii, 140–146]

such as wee
Know not ye way to suffer, then to doot
How most prepostrous tis: *whats all o^r greateness*
Iff we y^t prescribe bovndes to meaner men
Must not passe these ourselues, oh most ridiculous,
This makes ye vulger merry to endure,
Knowing our state is strict, and less secure;
Ile breake through Custome, . . .
[III, i, 103–110]

The omission in *Q* of these lines suggests the sensitiveness to anything that might be conceived as criticism of the throne that was especially characteristic of the years of Charles I's despotism, and recalls Sir Henry Herbert's memorandum of 18 October 1633 that

[1] Viz. the cuts at I, i, 9–14; III, i, 56–63; V, ii, 163–174.

> All ould plays ought to bee brought to the Master of the Revells, and have his allowance to them, for which he should have his fee, since they may be full of offensive things against church and state; ye rather that in former time the poetts tooke greater liberty than is allowed them by mee.[1]

Of course, one cannot be certain when this censoring took place, if, indeed, it took place at all; nevertheless, the balance of probability seems to suggest censoring at a fairly late date.

The omission in *Q* of the two songs (at I, i, 29–40 and IV, ii, 51–57), which were undoubtedly written by Middleton, is also significant, though here again one is treading on rather uncertain ground. One may perhaps venture to say that when an author intended a song to be introduced, but left it to the discretion of the stage-manager to choose a suitable song, he would not do more than include a direction for its insertion (as in *Believe as You List,* l. 2025), but when he wrote the words of the song himself as part of the play they would be *in situ* in his papers, and thus in the prompt-book, especially if the author's own fair copy was used as the prompt-book. If, however, a fresh prompt-book were made later, the words of the song would not be likely to be included,[2] since the prompter obviously did not need to prompt during a song, and the singer would learn the words from a sheet containing both words and music; indeed, if he sang behind the stage he would have been able to do so with both words and music in front of him.[3]

From the foregoing discussion it will be seen that *Q* is most likely to have been set up from a private transcript which lacked such directions as a prompter would add, but which contained a number of others describing the action, for which the scribe of the private transcript was probably responsible, although it is possible that some of them may go back to the author's original directions. However, there is no doubt that this private transcript was based on a text used in the theatre, since it observes all the cuts made in performance, and shows

[1] J. Q. Adams, *Dramatic Records of Sir Henry Herbert,* 21.

[2] It may be objected that the omission in *Q* of any directions for the songs indicates that they were omitted altogether from performances. It is true that the song in I,i has disappeared without leaving any trace, but in IV,ii *Q* retains lines 41–42 and 58–60, which would be meaningless without the music and the song. One is therefore justified in concluding that, like most of the other directions for music and noises, those affecting the two songs were also omitted when the manuscript on which *Q* is based was being prepared.

[3] Dr. J. Q. Adams points out to me that sometimes one finds the songs printed together at the beginning or end of a play (e.g., *The Shoemakers Holiday,* 1600), and that in other quartos there is a note to the effect that the songs have been lost. This may indicate that songs were often appended at the beginning or end of the "book" of the play, and hence that they were easily lost.

traces of censorship, made possibly as late as the middle of Charles I's reign.[1] It therefore represents a private transcript of a more normal type than the surviving manuscripts, such a one, in fact, as Moseley refers to in his foreword to the Beaumont and Fletcher folio of 1647:

> When these *Comedies* and *Tragedies* were presented on the stage, the *Actours* omitted some *Scenes* and Passages (with the *Authour's* consent) as occasion led them; and when private friends desir'd a Copy, they then (and justly too) transcribed what they Acted.

If, as has been suggested earlier, *Hengist* had a fairly long and successful stage career, it is likely, especially in view of the omission of the songs in *Q*, that the prompt-copy on which the stage version, represented at two removes by *Q*, is based was not the same as that behind *L* and *P*, but a later one, made because the earlier one was old and worn. Confirmation of this may perhaps be found in the obscurity of one or two passages found only in *L* and *P*, and in some of their common errors and omissions. Nevertheless, there are two features of *Q* which show that ultimately it can trace its descent back to the earlier prompt-book. As in the two manuscripts, only the third and fifth acts are divided into scenes,[2] and, like them, it has all the stage-directions except those at the beginning of the scenes in the right margin. To the last statement there is one exception, but it is common to all three texts: the stage-direction at I, i, 28 is centred.

One further difference between *Q* and the two manuscripts still remains. The quarto version has a different ending, and one probably not written by Middleton. *Q* omits from V, ii, 257 to the end of the play, and instead substitutes eleven lines of much stiffer verse than any to be found elsewhere in the serious parts of the play. This alteration was obviously not made for the same reason as impelled a change at the end of *The Honest Man's Fortune,* another play of the period for which alternative endings are known, for there are no obscenities here. Nor could the motive have been materially to shorten the play, for, if one leaves out of consideration the ten-lined epilogue, eleven lines in *Q* replace only twenty-eight in the manuscripts. The effect of the alteration is to cut out

[1] The official prompt-copy of the play belonging to the King's Men before the closing of the theatres doubtless passed to Humphrey Moseley, and was in his possession when the play was entered on the Stationers' Register on 4 September 1646.

[2] In *Q* in Act IV also the first scene is followed by a heading for the second scene, but none of the later scenes in this act have headings. This sporadic indication of scenes seems to have been the work of Middleton himself, since in two of the manuscripts of *A Game at Chess* (one of them autograph) the last scene has a separate heading, although none of the earlier acts have any such divisions.

the final appearance of Castiza, who is brought on to the stage after her innocence has been vindicated, and is then hailed by Aurelius as his future bride. It seems as if the alteration had been made to omit all reference to a marriage between Aurelius and Castiza, and for such a change, with the limited evidence now available, only one explanation seems possible. An important part of the plot of Rowley's *Birth of Merlin* hinges on the marriage of Aurelius with the Saxon maid Artesia and its consequences. This would have caused no worry to anyone if the two plays had been rival plays performed by different companies, but if the plays had passed into the hands of the same company from different sources, and had ever been performed in conjunction with one another, there would be a real inconsistency in providing Aurelius with two different wives on, let us say, two successive afternoons. Only the possibility of such a *contretemps* would, it seems, suffice to explain the need for a new ending to *Hengist*.[1]

The passages in *Q* which are omitted in the manuscripts[2] are brief and of slight importance, and their omission was probably due to accident. This was certainly the case with the longest omission, IV, ii, 171–178. Lines 170 and 178 both end with the words "landes & honor," and the omission is due to a scribe's eye having caught the end of the wrong line, so that he went on without noticing that he had left out eight lines.[3]

For most textual purposes *L* and *P* may almost be considered as a single text, so close is their agreement. Nevertheless, *L* is superior to *P,* which gives the impression of having been more carelessly written, and is rarely able to correct *L.* Fortunately, however, it is able to fill in the gaps in *L* caused by the binder's trimming of the edges of the paper. On the other hand, the manuscripts have a number of mistakes in common, and here *Q,* which is a carefully printed text, is generally able to set them right, so that it is very rarely necessary to resort to emendation. The most troublesome passages are one or two which were cut or altered in *Q,*[4] and which, by reason of their very obscurity,

[1] It is worth noting that Vortiger appears as a character in Act IV of *The Birth of Merlin.* He is there King of Welsh Britain, and the time occupied by the earlier action of the play is presumably after the landing of Aurelius and Uther, but before their complete subjugation of Britain. Vortiger appears primarily as a subject for Merlin's magic exploits (IV, i). There is one short scene in which his forces come into conflict with those of Aurelius (IV, iii) and then, in a later scene, his death is briefly alluded to (IV, v, 12–16). It is possible either that there has been a cut or some revision here, or that Rowley is taking for granted a knowledge of the manner of Vortiger's death. In any case, there is not the same glaring inconsistency with *Hengist* in the references to Vortiger's death as in those concerning the wife of Aurelius.

[2] Viz., I, ii, 87; III, iii, 263; IV, ii, 171–178; IV, iii, 143; V, i, 39, 124, 273–275.

[3] The omission of V, i, 273–275 can also be similarly explained.

[4] E.g., III, i, 56–63; IV, ii, 160–171.

may thus have been simplified in the acting version to which the text of *Q* goes back.

The text of the play given in this volume is an edited text, based on *L*. Gaps due to the trimming of the binder have been supplied from *P*. The pages of *L* have been indicated; verse-lining, when incorrect, has been corrected, and the original arrangement recorded in the textual notes, but the prose passages are printed line for line. The first word of each line of verse has been given a capital letter, if it did not already have one, and the very light punctuation of *L* has been added to only where it seemed necessary to clarify the sense. The stage-directions, which contain occasional words or letters in the secretary hand, have been uniformly italicized, and such as are not in *L* are enclosed in square brackets. The textual notes attempt to record as faithfully as possible the exact state of *L*. Although the strokes separating the speeches have been omitted, the other features of the manuscript have been reproduced as far as it was possible typographically to do so.

The textual notes do not treat the other two texts with the same scrupulous respect as that accorded to *L*. For instance, *P*'s incorrect line-division has been ignored, and no mention has been made of its punctuation unless, in disagreeing with *L*, it alters the sense of a passage. The punctuation of *Q* has been similarly treated.

Corrections from *Q* have been frequently incorporated into the text, but when *Q* is quoted as the source of such a correction it does not necessarily mean that *Q* has been followed *literatim; Q*'s spelling may have been modified to that which one would have expected from the scribe of *L* and *P*. For instance, at III, iii, 124 "watle faide," which is the reading of *L,P,* has been altered, on the authority of *Q,* to "watle facde," although *Q* actually reads "wattle-fac'd." Again, where two texts are reported as agreeing on a reading it has not been thought necessary to record mere differences of spelling or capitalisation. For example, at I, i, 17 *L* and *P* are both reported as reading "kind Lordes," whereas only *L* does so, and *P* has "kinde lordes." *Minutiæ,* such as those just alluded to, would only swell the textual notes without any commensurate gain, although all *Q*'s variant colloquial contractions have been included. The editor, acknowledging the limitations imposed by human fallibility, can only hope that it will be found that everything of any significance has been recorded.

III

Sources

The question of Middleton's use of Henslowe's play of *Vortiger* has been broached earlier in this introduction, and if, as is possible, he drew on the old play it would naturally have constituted his principal source. On the other hand, it must be admitted that the case for his indebtedness to it is not conclusive, and one might reasonably maintain that in the comic scenes he attempted, not without success, to portray rustic uncouthness and pomposity in some of the exaggerated jargon which the London stage had outgrown. In fact, one of the very passages which seems most certainly to bear traces of old-fashioned crudity (IV, i) was sufficiently popular with the more sophisticated audiences of the second quarter of the seventeenth century to be included in *Wit Restored* in 1658. And even if Middleton did rewrite the old play, there can be little doubt that he refashioned it thoroughly, especially if the suggestion already made that Vortimer was originally a prominent character in it is to be given weight. The story of Castiza and the intrigue of Horsus and Roxena—both of them interpolations into the historical legend—so completely express the natural bent of Middleton's mind at this period, and are so characteristic of his individual manner in their treatment, that their introduction must have been due to him. The historical parts, too, attest an independent consultation of Holinshed and other chronicles, so that, in any case, his principal indebtedness to an old play, apart from its suggestion of a subject, may at most have been to its framework of presenter and chorus, and to certain scraps of its comic scenes which he fitted into the new pattern.

The story of Hengist and Horsa and the coming of the Saxons still has a place in English history-books in spite of the destructive criticism that has been levelled against it. In Middleton's day it was firmly entrenched as authentic history, although it had been decorated during the early Middle Ages with many romantic ornaments which were still undiscarded.[1] It was to be found in all the Elizabethan chronicles, from Fabyan to Stow and Speed; it had been retold or referred to by most of the principal poets, in *The Mirrour for Magistrates, Albions England, The Faerie Queene,* and *Polyolbion,* and there had even been

[1] For an account of the early development of the legend see the Appendix, p. 127.

a ballad on the subject.[1] Among so many possible sources it becomes a matter of some difficulty to decide from which of them Middleton may have drawn, but fortunately for our study an exhaustive analysis of the chronicles was made by Dr. K. Christ in 1905.[2] Christ was primarily concerned with refuting the earlier thoughtless statements, current since Langbaine and based on the appearance of Raynulph as chorus in the play, that its source was Higden's *Polychronicon*. He succeeded in showing that Middleton's principal source was Holinshed's *Chronicles,* and that he made use of both versions of the story in Holinshed: the fuller one in the *Historie of England,* compiled from a variety of sources, and the briefer one, based solely on Hector Boethius's *Scotorum Historiæ,* in the *Historie of Scotland*. However, certain details were apparently derived from another chronicle, which might have been either Fabyan or Grafton. Christ finally decided that Fabyan was the more likely of the two, since Fabyan adds in a side-note a piece of information which is not to be found in Grafton, and which actually contradicts his own text, viz. that "Thonge Castell standyth within 4 Miles of Feuersham by Thamys syde, nat ferre from Quynburghe."[3]

Middleton's use of Fabyan is further revealed by several details which are either not to be found in Holinshed or are contradicted by him. In Holinshed Constantius had been sent to a monastery because he was "dull of wit, and not verie toward," "soft and childish in wit" and "not meete to gouerne"; Fabyan, however, offers an alternative explanation: "as some writers meane, the sayde Constante of pure devociõ that he had to God & saynt Amphiabyl made himselfe a monke," and this is the conception of Constantius's character of which Middleton makes use. Again, Hengist and Horsus are brothers in both Holinshed's accounts; this relationship would have been fatal to Middleton's additions to the story, so he follows Fabyan, who in one place only speaks of any kinship between them, and then says that Horsus was "brother to Hengist or cosin"; usually he refers to them merely as the "two leders" of the Saxons. The first dumb-show, too, may perhaps owe one of its features to Fabyan. In making the Saxons explain to Vortiger the circumstances which had brought them to Britain, Fabyan uses a phrase which has no parallel in the other versions:

[1] A "ballade of the lewde life of Vortiger kinge of Bryttaine and of the firste commynge of Hingeste and the Saxons into this Lande" was entered in the Stationers' Register on 10 May 1589.

[2] *Quellenstudien zu den Dramen Thomas Middletons,* 6–15.

[3] This side-note is found only in the first edition of Fabyan (1516) and not in the later editions. It is therefore likely that Middleton used a copy of the 1516 edition.

Fabyan in his text and the other authorities place Thong Castle in Lindsey. The sole exception is William Lambarde in his *Perambulation of Kent;* he also asserts that it was near Feversham. The relevant passage is quoted in the note on II, iii, 26–46.

"sins *fortune*[1] hadde brought them to this land, they besought the king that he wolde take them to his seruice." This sentence contains the only explanation I have been able to find for the appearance of Fortune as the goddess of the Saxons. Again, it is possible that Fabyan's frequent citations of Higden, introduced by the formula "as witnesseth Polycronica" and "as affermeth Polycronica" may have helped to determine the choice of Raynulph as the presenter. Finally, it may be mentioned that the story of the thong, which is so important a feature of the story of the earlier part of the play, is omitted from Holinshed's *Historie of England,* is only very briefly related in the *Historie of Scotland,* but is told in full by Fabyan.

From the *Historie of Scotland* Middleton chose the name Roxena in preference to Rowen or Ronowen, the more usual forms of the name. In this part of Holinshed, too, there are various references to the effects of popular opinion on Vortiger's behaviour after the murder of Constantius and Vortiger's accession to the throne; for a time he "durst not commit himselfe to the sight of a multitude," and after a subsequent defeat of his armies by the Picts and Scots "through want of good wils in his commons, . . . he was minded to have auoided the realme."[2] These statements have left their mark on the play in II, ii, 1–23. A further fact used by Middleton, which is stated in this part of Holinshed but not in the other authorities, is that after Vortimer's death Vortiger, as a condition of his restoration, was "first forced by oth to promise neuer to aid the Saxons, nor to receiue by way of aid anie forreine people into the realme."[3] In the main, however, Middleton relied on the fullest available version of the story—that in Holinshed's *Historie of England.* His obligations to this part of the work are general as well as particular, and are fully illustrated by the extracts quoted in the notes.

The study of the chronicle versions of the story elucidates not only a number of incidents in the play itself but throws light on Middleton's dramatic craftsmanship as well, and this fact furnishes additional justification for the copious quotations from the chronicles included in the commentary. In the play, however, Middleton rarely paraphrased extracts from his sources as he did in *A Game at Chess,* or as Shakespeare did, say, in the discussion of the French succession in the opening scene of *Henry V;* in fact, there is only one single line in the whole play (V, ii, 32) which can be said to have come *verba-*

1 Italics not in the original. Cf. also

we are all my Lord
The sons of fortune, she has sent vs forth
To thriue. (II, ii, 38–40)

2 Ed. 1587, 92.

3 P. 97; cf. dumb-show iii and chor. iv, 6–7.

tim from the chronicles. Middleton seems rather to have thoroughly absorbed his facts and formed his conceptions of character before putting pen to paper. Indeed, when the full significance of an incident is understood only by reference to the sources, as in the passage already referred to at the beginning of II, ii, one feels that he assimilated his materials almost to the extent of taking for granted knowledge that his audiences could not possess. There is, however, much to admire in the skill with which Middleton has made use of his sources, and in the qualities of compression, selection, and emphasis which a close study of the play reveals. Compression is mainly achieved by means of the dumb-shows, but it can also be seen in such a scene as II, iii. Here the Saxon successes, the thong story, the arrival of Roxena, and the King's sudden infatuation are all successfully blended. On the other hand, it will be noticed that Middleton has refrained from making Vortiger meet Roxena at a banquet; the suggestion of a banquet was reserved for a later occasion, and was used as the basis of IV, ii. Middleton's emphasis on his central theme is shown mainly by what he has omitted from the chronicles, and especially in his refusal to be attracted by the dramatic possibilities of Vortimer. Rowley's *Birth of Merlin* also illustrates the depths to which the play might have sunk if Middleton had been seduced by the opportunities for cheap dramatic effect which Rowley did not scruple to use when he made Merlin the centre of his comic underplot. Fortunately, Middleton was not entirely without an artistic conscience, and the play he wrote does not altogether lack strength and coherence.

If the play had been based solely on the chronicles we should probably have had nothing more than a sensational and loosely constructed chronicle play consisting mainly of battle scenes, and depending for variety on the comic scenes or on such an episode as Vortiger's infatuation for Roxena. However, all the episodes of Constantius's futile reign—except its beginning and its end—were added by Middleton. Castiza is not a "historical" figure at all; the chronicles, it is true, mention that in order to marry Roxena Vortiger "forsooke his lawfull wife," but that is all. Middleton has not only elaborated the means by which Vortiger concentrated the power into his hands and made kingship a burden to Constantius, but has made the greater part of two acts revolve round Vortiger's foul attempt to rid himself of his wife. It is quite likely that this part of the play is based on some other story, possibly of Italian origin, which has not been found, for the theme might well have been the subject of one of the later Italian *novelle*. Nevertheless, it need not be thought of as beyond Middleton's powers of invention, for the stratagem propounded by Horsus has more than one analogue in the drama of the time, although the parallel does not extend so far as to include the victimisation of a married woman by her husband. In both *The Laws of Candy* and the somewhat later *Spanish Gipsy* an unmarried girl falls a victim to the unchecked lust of a wilful gallant. But whatever may have been the source for the plot against Castiza, one can hardly doubt that the intrigue of Horsus and Roxena was an ironic complication which had its suggestion in Middleton's own mind. The chronicles knew nothing of it, and they all agree in making Horsus die in battle fighting against Vortimer, but the situation in the play is so much a part of Middleton's whole conception of the plot that it is unlikely that it could have had an independent origin.

Of the comic underplot there is less to be said. The first scene in which Simon appears is one based on the traditional story, and his clowning is in the conventional manner of comic relief. The play scene (V, i) is the only one in this part of the plot which demands fuller consideration. In conception it certainly owes something to Nashe's story of the absurd behaviour of a country justice at a play,[1] while the episode from *The Cheater and the Clown,* presented before Simon by the cheaters, has an interesting analogue in a later drama. *The Knave in Graine, New Vampt* (1640) by J.D.[2] concludes with a scene in which Julio, the knave of the play, cozens a countryman of a gold piece in spite of the fact that its owner has hidden it in his mouth for safety. Not only is the countryman's behaviour on his first appearance strikingly similar to that of the Clown in Middleton's play, but the first sentence he speaks echoes the Clown's very words:

> *Country fel.* They talke of Cheaters, here is a twenty shillings peece that I put into my mouth, let any Cheater in Christendom cousen me of this, and carry it away cleanly, and Ile not only forgive him, but hugge him and imbrace him for it, and say he is a very *Hocus Pocus* indeed.
>
> *Iulio.* What said that fellow?
>
> *Pusse.* He saith he hath a peece in his mouth, that all *Europe* shall not cheate him of.
>
> *Iulio.* I have markt him, 'tis mine owne: and notwithstanding all this melancholy we'le spend it at night in Wine and Musicke.
>
> *Count. fel.* He that can plucke this peece out of my jawes, spight of my teeth, and I keepe my mouth fast shut, Ile say hee is more than a Cheater, and a Doctor *Faustus,* or *Mephostophilus* at least.

[1] *Pierce Penniles,* in Nashe's *Works,* ed. R. B. McKerrow, i, 88. The passage is quoted in the note to V, i, 299–306.

[2] I am grateful to Dr. J. Q. Adams for drawing my attention to this play.

Then, when the countryman has been forced by an officer of the law to disgorge the coin, which Julio asserts that he has lost, the stock phrase used in *Hengist* also appears:

> *Iulio.* Marry twenty shillings good and lawfull currant mony, *Puss,* was not this the piece that I put in my pocket this morning?[1]

The Knave in Graine was clearly, as the title-page states, "new vampt."[2] The condition of its text would repay careful examination, but there seems to be no doubt that it represents an old play that has been livened up by the insertion of a number of cheating episodes, and one can hardly doubt that it echoes Middleton's play rather than that the reverse should have happened. There is some evidence, however, to suggest that the inserted scenes were not written for the revision, but were lifted bodily from another play.[3] If this happened in *The Knave in Graine,* an interesting possibility is suggested for Middleton's play: namely, that *The Cheater and the Clown* is substantially what it purports to be, an episode from an old rogue play which Simon might well have seen when he was an apprentice, even though it was never printed or sold to the cheaters in Canterbury. In that case the climax of the play, including Simon's discomfiture, would have been a genuine new addition, and, though the trick by which the Clown was cheated would have presented little that was new to Middleton's audiences, the interest and humour of this part of the scene would have lain in the dialogue, and especially in the comments of Simon and his fellow townsmen. Nevertheless, this is no more than a possibility, and a great deal more evidence than is at present available must come to light before it can be considered even as a probability.

1 Sigs. M–M_2.

2 Another play of a similar title, *The Whore New Vampt,* acted, apparently, by the same company, got the actors into trouble. See *Cal. State Papers* (*Dom.*), 29 Sept. 1637.

3 In the S.R. entry of 18 June 1639 *The Knave in Graine* is given the alternative title of *Jack Cottington,* although no character of this name appears in the printed version. According to Captain Alexander Smith's *History of the Lives of the most noted Highwaymen* (ed. A. L. Hayward [1926], 326) "Mull-Sack, the Chimney Sweeper, *alias* John Cottington," pickpocket, cheat, and highwayman, was hanged at Smithfield in April 1659 at the age of forty-five, but he had attained sufficient notoriety to be alluded to on the stage in John Kirke's *Seven Champions of Christendom,* 1638 (ed. G. E. Dawson, Cleveland, Western Reserve University Bulletin, 1929), at line 627. It is suggested that Cottington had been made the hero of a cheating play of which portions are preserved in *The Knave in Graine.*

IV

The Play

The Mayor of Queenborough, to use the title by which the play has previously been known, has not fared well at the hands of the critics. "The piece, though containing some fine passages, calls for no special notice";[1] "such merit as there is in the play lies almost wholly in individual lines and passages, which stand out from a confused and rather hideous mingling of tragic bombast and strained farce";[2] "the play is obscure, roughly written, and uninteresting."[3] Even when the play has been rated more highly, praise has been tempered with reserve: "Again and again," writes Bullen,[4] "we are arrested by the bold utterance, the fine dramatic ring of the verse. Yet the play as a whole leaves little impression on the mind, and has the appearance of being an immature production. . . . The plot is repulsive. . . . The comic scenes were doubtless effective on the stage; they are somewhat tiresome by the fireside. . . . It is for detached passages of noble poetry that students will value this tragi-comedy." Swinburne, too, after confessing to the confusion and uncertainty wrought in his mind by the incongruous elements of which he found the play to be composed, writes of the serious parts: "The story is ugly and unnatural, but its repulsive effect is transfigured or neutralised by the charm of tender or passionate poetry; and it must be admitted that the hideous villainy of Vortiger and Horsus affords an opening for subsequent scenic effects of striking and genuine tragic interest."[5] The consensus of opinion is clearly that the play is one of Middleton's less significant works; the few who praise it do so half-heartedly, while the majority condemns. Nevertheless, it is the aim of this section to point out that *Hengist, King of Kent* is a product of the same mature power that created *Women Beware Women, The Changeling,* and *A Game at Chess,* and is not unworthy to be ranked beside them.

It is surprising how often the mind automatically turns to Shakespeare rather than to any of his contemporaries to interpret what Middleton was trying to do

[1] A. W. Ward, *History of English Dramatic Literature to the Death of Queen Anne,* ii, 500.
[2] A. Symons, *Studies in Elizabethan Drama,* 217–218.
[3] Havelock Ellis, Preface to *Plays of Middleton* in the Mermaid series, ii, xi.
[4] Introduction to his edition of Middleton's *Works,* i, xix–xx.
[5] *The Age of Shakespeare,* 164–165.

in his latest, and greatest, works. In the popularity of Beaumont and Fletcher, it is true, one finds a partial explanation of the ill-matched, loosely co-ordinated elements of *The Changeling,* and it was imitation of Webster and Tourneur that produced the rather jarring sensationalism of the last act of *Women Beware Women.* Where such external influences are strongest in Middleton the result is something unnatural to him and inharmonious with his more characteristic work. On the other hand, comparison with Shakespeare seems to throw into relief what is best in his work, and it is perhaps his greatest merit that he can endure such comparison. This does not mean, of course, that there are not profound differences both of temperament and of greatness between the two men, and when Shakespeare's works are mentioned in the following pages it must be realised that the similarity is often of kind rather than of quality. Nevertheless, a certain kinship between the minds of the two men is to be found not only in their attitudes to their material and its presentation on the stage but also in a more fundamental likeness. Miss Bradbrook has justly drawn attention to "Middleton's interest in the way the mind works," and has pointed out that he "relies upon action and characterisation in a way which no one else did except Shakespeare."[1] On this last quality, more than any other, Middleton's place among the Elizabethans depends.

In shaping the old stories of Lear and Macbeth to his purposes Shakespeare had allowed himself considerable latitude. It was as if he instinctively sensed, rather than knew, that they were semi-mythical personages, and in his hands they became creatures of the imagination transcending the soberer pages of the history-book. In *Hengist* too there is something of this imposition of a pattern, which had formed itself in the dramatist's mind, upon the "realities" of a commonly accepted historical narrative. The pattern of life, as envisaged by the creative imagination, has become more real than any sequence of recorded facts. This is the fundamental conception of form in the play, although to explain the more superficial elements in its structure one must look elsewhere than to Shakespeare. Structurally *Hengist* is at once pre-Shakespearian and post-Shakespearian. On the one hand, the play is at first sight amorphous, a mere string of events succeeding one another in the loosely-connected narrative manner of the early chronicle plays; on the other hand, its underplot is a concession to the demand for a double plot which, as has been suggested, was encouraged by the success of the plays of Beaumont and Fletcher, and which only writers like Shakespeare, Jonson, and Webster were strong enough to resist. In fact, the loosely-knit structure of the old chronicle play has been slightly adapted and brought up to

[1] *Themes and Conventions of Elizabethan Tragedy,* 239.

date to suit the taste of late Jacobean times. Nevertheless, while it lacks the deftness of *A Game at Chess, Hengist* has structural merits which enable it to compare favourably with Middleton's other plays of this period. The serious parts of *The Changeling* have one real defect: in order to secure an equitable division of labour with Rowley and an even balance between the two incongruous plots which the two writers were handling separately, Middleton cramped himself unduly, especially as he insisted on introducing a number of episodes not to be found in his principal source. There is thus too much action in the main plot, and the compression which compelled Middleton to hurry from one event to another is only emphasised by the power with which he wrote when his dramatic instincts forced him to find room to elaborate situations and characters. In *Hengist,* although his plan allowed for the double plot which convention demanded, he did not have to come to terms with a collaborator, and the comic scenes occupy a more subordinate position. In *Women Beware Women,* on the other hand, Middleton was also working alone, but here the action moves more slowly—too slowly, perhaps—and tends to be held back by the weight of the moralisings it is called upon to bear, until, in the fifth act, it gets out of hand and rushes to its swift and sensational conclusion. In *Hengist* there is a truer proportion between action and situation than in either of these two plays, and the balance between the two elements is produced by the skill with which Middleton has used the old device of the dumb-show. The dumb-show enables certain parts of the necessary narrative to be compressed, leaving the dramatist free to emphasise and heighten the dramatic and psychological interest of the more important episodes. They thus have a definite functional value in the play, and it would be very difficult to find the device used with the same artistic purpose and such genuine effectiveness in any other drama of the period. It is noteworthy, too, that the dumb-shows are the most purely historical parts of the play, for in them Middleton follows the chronicles more closely than anywhere else. Clearly the new elements which he had introduced into the traditional story made it significant to him, and what he most needed was the scope and freedom necessary to mould it to his own purposes. These the dumb-shows gave him.

It is by comparison with such plays as *Lear* and *Macbeth* that the real structural limitations of *Hengist* are most easily perceived. In *Macbeth* the tragic interest is concentrated in the two chief characters; they, as it were, stand in the glare of the spotlight throughout, and the subsidiary figures move, but dimly discerned, in the half-light beyond. In *Lear,* on the other hand, where there is far more richness and variety of characterisation and a secondary plot as well, the underplot is not merely closely intertwined with the main plot, but echoes it also, and emphasises the total tragic impression of the play. In *Hengist,* however, the tragic interest is insufficiently concentrated; Constantius, for instance, is the most important figure in the early scenes, and Hengist himself, though scarcely the leading character, is yet sufficiently prominent to be the titular hero. The underplot, again, though more effectively subordinated to the main plot and more closely linked to various events in it than that of *The Changeling* to the main plot there,[1] fails to emphasise the tragic theme. It really constitutes an excess of comic relief, such as might have occurred if the Porter in *Macbeth* or the gravediggers in *Hamlet* had been elaborated on a scale comparable to that accorded to Dogberry and Verges. Nevertheless, this part of the play so interested audiences whose standards were declining that it was regarded as the principal attraction of *Hengist,* and supplied the title by which the play is best known. When it was published in 1661 the conflict between Simon the Mayor and Oliver the Puritan had a contemporary allusiveness that ensured its popularity, and the publisher's catchpenny description of the piece as a comedy seems to have deluded nearly all the critics. Even Bullen referred to it as a tragi-comedy; others before and since have called it a comedy; and Swinburne was practically alone in calling attention to the interest and significance of the tragic elements of the play.

Hengist is a tragedy and, like *Macbeth,* a tragedy of ambition. But although Vortiger is the hero, there is little of the heroic in him. From the conventional point of view he has scarcely a redeeming quality, except perhaps a certain regal dignity which is inseparable from the Elizabethan portrayal of kingship. Without the original nobility of a Macbeth, without the aspiration of a Tamburlaine, and without even the zest of a Volpone, he can hardly be compared with the villain-heroes of the contemporary stage. It is at once Middleton's peculiar strength and weakness that he saw life entirely in terms of the life of the City to which he belonged, and Jonson recognised this quality both in the man and in his work when he told Drummond that Middleton, like Markham and Day, "was not of the number of the Faithful, i.e., Poets, and but a base fellow." Vortiger is a product of the same mind that could envisage Leantio, in *Women Beware Women,* as incorrigibly a Cockney vulgarian; there is no glorification of his lust and ambition, which are as sordid as anything that Middleton had observed in Cheapside or Fleet Street. Yet, in spite of this, Vortiger does undoubtedly exact sympathy of a sort. Some of it is due to the flashes

[1] In spite of Miss Bradbrook's able and ingenious analysis of the relations of the two plots of *The Changeling* (*Themes and Conventions of Elizabethan Tragedy,* 221–224), I cannot feel that her case is entirely convincing.

of poetry in his best speeches, although they are not connected with any particular emotional state of mind, as they are in Macbeth. Nevertheless, the unconscious evocation of sympathy is inalienable from poetry, and is one of the factors which contribute to the superiority of poetic over prose drama. Still more important is Vortiger's inherent kinship with the man in the street. He shares the common man's attitude of ignorance and wonder towards place and power, which he apostrophises as "sweet power" and "this dream of glory," and he never outgrows it. He seeks these things for themselves, and there is no suggestion that he ever rates them at any other value than that which others place upon them. On the throne he still reveals the naïveté and ingenuousness of a simple mind in the soliloquy which shows that he is stirred by passions as violent as any he had known before:

> Haue I powre
> Of life and death and Cannot Com̃and ease
> In myne owne Blood: After I was a King
> I thought I neuer shold haue felt paine more,
> That there had beene a ceasing of all passions
> And Common stings which subiects vse to feele,
> That were Created with a patience fitt
> For all extremityes; but such as wee
> Know not ye way to suffer, then to doot
> How most prepostrous tis: whats all o^{r} greateness
> Iff we y^{t} prescribe bovndes to meaner men
> Must not passe these ourselues, oh most ridiculous,
> This makes ye vulger merry to endure,
> Knowing our state is strict, and less secure;
> Ile breake thourgh Custome, why shold not ye mind
> The nobler part that's of vs, be allowed
> Change of affections, as our bodyes are
> Still Change of foode and rayment; Ile haue't soe.

Some of these sentiments are platitudes, certainly; but in the concluding lines there is more than a suggestion of that irresponsibility which is normally characteristic only of day-dreaming and wish-fulfilment. Vortiger's case is different from that of the ordinary man only because he is above the normal restraints, and his desires can express themselves in unchecked action.

Vortiger, then, is altogether of lesser calibre than Macbeth. Macbeth is the dupe of supernatural powers, Vortiger of men with greater cunning and singleness of purpose than his own. Macbeth never loses sight of his ultimate responsibility for his actions, but Vortiger, a wilful egoist, is scarcely even conscious of his iniquity. It is true that, for a moment, when he is left alone after Hengist has stripped him of half his kingdom, he faces it half-heartedly, but if there is any such consciousness in his last moments it only lends vehemence to his dying curses. Normally he can suppress without effort all sense of remorse or guilt. The passage which best illustrates this quality of his mind, and is at once the truest and most terrifying piece of psychology in the play, occurs in the early part of the last scene, when Vortiger, with the wild panic of a cornered animal, turns against Horsus and tries to make him the scapegoat for his own crimes. If, as Mr. T. S. Eliot says of the heroine of *The Changeling,* "Beatrice is not a moral creature; she becomes moral only by becoming damned,"[1] one must say of Vortiger that he never becomes a moral creature at all. Vortiger's tragedy lies in his emotional refusal to make any specific acknowledgement of a moral order, even though his humiliation at Hengist's hands, his final disillusionment, and the very agony of his dying curse, are all there to confirm its reality.

The figure of Vortiger is clearer and more original in conception than any other in the play. Though neither Hengist nor Horsus is a typical example of a stock character, both are closer in conception to such types. The Machiavellian element in both is emphasised by the cunning and treachery with which they pursue their ends, and in Horsus one may also see the influence of the malcontent. As a rule, however, the malcontent is primarily a spectator and commentator, and his part in the action is of secondary interest, but Horsus more than any other individual guides and controls the events which lead Vortiger to his doom. The acrid and sinister comments of Horsus may frequently recall the malcontent, but they are not, as they often are in the other stage malcontents of the time, a substitute for action; they are the complement of his actions in the expression of his personality. Horsus's attitude towards his victims in its complete objectivity resembles the detachment of a torturer concerned only with the display of his technical skill, and more than any other factor gives the play its characteristically bitter tone.

Of the other figures in the main plot little need be said. Constantius is sympathetically drawn, but Middleton realised that without development or alteration there was scarcely enough in his conception of the character to sustain the interest beyond a few scenes, and it is natural dramatically that Constantius should disappear from the action just before the entrance of the Saxons. Cas-

[1] *Selected Essays,* 163.

tiza's sufferings are portrayed adequately rather than greatly, but the interest at this point is centred not so much in her sufferings as in the zest and ingenuity with which they are inflicted. The most brilliant touch in the handling of her character occurs earlier in the play, when she informs Vortiger that Constantius has persuaded her to abandon a worldly life:

Ime bound my Lord to marry none but yo^{u}
Youle grant me that, and you Ile neuer marrye
Vort: It drawes into me violence and hazard
I sawe you kiss ye Kinge
Cast: I grant yo^{u} so s^{r}
Where Could I take my leaue of ye world better
I wrongd not yo^{u}; in that yo^{u} will acknowledge
A King is ye best part ont
Vort: Oh my passion
Cast: I see you somewhat yeilding to infirmitie S^{r}.
I take my leaue
Vort: Why tis not possible
Cast: The fault is in yor faith, time I was gon
To giue it Better strengthening
Vort: Hark yo^{u} Ladye
Cast: Send yor intent to ye next monestary,
There yo^{u} shall finde my answer ever after,
And soe with my Last dutye to yor Lordshipp
For whose perfections I will pray as hartely
As for mine owne.

The hint of tartness and self-righteousness in her replies is characteristic of Middleton's unflinching observation of human nature, to which he was faithful even at the risk of temporarily alienating the sympathies of his audience.

It is evident that Middleton's characterisation was not always achieved without effort, and that, while his general conception was clear, in filling in the details his aim was sometimes unsure. For instance, there is no artificiality in the one real touch of tenderness shown by Horsus in an aside in the last scene,

True, my hart findes it that sitts weepeing blood now
For poore Roxenas safetie,

but his momentary relenting towards Castiza at III, ii, 107–109 hardly rings true. It is as if Middleton had felt the necessity of adding these lines to keep him from becoming altogether inhuman. Again, when Hengist nods over his book near the end of III, iii it is uncertain whether his sleep is genuine or feigned; the incident serves no real dramatic purpose, and seems to be inserted only to humanise and individualise the man. There is, indeed, more uncertainty of aim in Hengist than elsewhere. Normally he is presented as combining seemingly open affability with shrewd and utterly unscrupulous opportunism, but Horsus's speech at IV, ii, 283–285,

> the Earle of Kent
> Is calme & smooth, like a deepe dangerous water,
> He has som secret way, I know his blood,
> The graues not greedier, nor hells Lord more proud,

suggests a character of greater depth and intensity, and there are also one or two passages, such as his words at the end of the play,

> I haue a thirst
> Cold never haue bene full quenchd, vnder all;
> The whole land must, or nothing,

where his opportunism acquires the strength of a ruling passion. Possibly Middleton changed his conception of Hengist as the play proceeded, and did not trouble to remove the resulting inconsistencies. In the main, however, Middleton's characterisation is not merely convincing but penetrating, and the true dramatic quality of the play can best be gauged by the fact that a search for parallel passages in the more important of his later plays produced practically nothing. Not only are the utterances of each character the natural outcome of the situations to which they belong, but they reveal so individual a bent of mind that they can belong to no one else. In this sense Middleton's characters may be said genuinely to live. They may reflect their creator's mind, but they do not reflect the minds of his other creatures.

In considering the comic episodes one cannot regard the coarse buffoonery of the petitioners and tradesmen in the earlier scenes as anything more than a device to emphasise the unworldliness of Constantius. The character of Simon, however, is developed from the outset with a much surer hand, so that he soon achieves an independent existence. One's sense of humour is an intensely personal possession, and *de gustibus non est disputandum,* so the present writer can only assert that, in spite of the fact that others have found Simon tiresome, he regards the scenes of Simon's election and of his discomfiture by the cheaters as a particularly happy mingling of humour and farce. In the early comedies Middleton had often ridiculed the pretensions of the upstarts and self-made men who thronged City and Court, but one never acquires any of that affection for his Quomodos and Lethes which one comes to feel for the more rustic Simon. It is true that, even after being rechristened Simonides, he could never have found his way with his crew to the enchanted wood where Bottom the weaver was translated, and the distance from Queenborough to Athens is no greater than that which separates Middleton's play from Shakespeare's; nevertheless, the touches of kindliness and fantasy which give life to the humour of the scenes in which Simon appears are not essentially un-Shakespearian in spirit, and form a not unwelcome intermission from the grim power of the tragedy in which they are set.

The poetic strength of *Hengist* is the one quality of the play which has been previously recognised. In discussing Middleton's poetry, however, one must emphasise the fact that it is essentially dramatic. Webster's poetry is frequently of the same order, as a single example will show. When the Duchess of Malfi bursts into reproaches against the malignant fate that has pursued her, Bosola's reply, "Look you, the stars shine still," is absolutely overwhelming in its effect, but the power of these words to reduce to insignificance any individual protest can scarcely be appreciated apart from their setting. Similarly, some of Middleton's most powerful lines are almost meaningless away from their context. The imagery of the speech of Horsus at III, ii, 63–65,

> Thus, thus, plainely
> To strip my words as naked as my purpose,
> I must and will enioy yo^{u},

owes its startling and sinister effect entirely to its brutal anticipation of what follows, and the simile used by Vortiger as the basis of his appeal to Horsus at V, ii, 42–44,

> You Could not but in Conscience loue me afterward,
> You were bound to Doot, as men in honestie
> That vitiate virgins to giue doweries to em,

is, in the light of the relations of the two men earlier in the play, ironical in the extreme. For this reason it is impossible fully to illustrate by mere quotation Middleton's poetic range, but there are still numerous lines and sentences which are outstanding for their imaginative power and concentrated strength:

Why looke you sir I Can be as Calme as Silence
All ye whiles musick plays, [III, i, 132–133]

Of powre, to turne a greate man to ye state
Of his insencible monument, with orewatching;
[I, i, 145–146]

Methinks it looks as if it mockd all ruin
Saue that greate M^{r}peece of Consumation,
The end of time, wch must Consume even ruin
And eate that into Cinders. [IV, i, 7–10]

Extremitie breedes ye wildness of a desart
Into yor soule; [V, ii, 53–54]

Why Ile be iudgd by those
That knitt death in their Browes, & think me now
Not worthy ye acception off a flaterye.
[V, ii, 57–59]

A longer passage of similar quality occurs at I, ii, 179–187:

Keepe still that holy and im̃aculate fire
You Chaste Lampe of eternitye, tis a treasure
Too pretious for deaths moment to pertake,
This twinckling of short life; Disdaine as much
To lett mortality knowe you, as starrs
To kiss ye pauem^{ts}, y'haue a substance
As excellent as theirs, holding yor pureness;
They looke vpon Coruption as you doe
But are starrs still; be you a virgin too.

However, to appreciate what Middleton could achieve when his imagination was fully distended it is necessary to read lines 1 to 205 of V, ii. This scene, save for the sole blemish of Vortiger's rather unfortunate interjections between lines 125 and 136, is unsurpassed in Middleton, and in very few of his contemporaries, for its sustained and terrifying power.

Reference has already been made to Middleton's unflinching observation of human nature, but his interpretation of what he saw was powerfully influenced by his gift for irony. Mr. T. S. Eliot has said that "his greatest tragedies and his greatest comedies are as if written by two different men,"[1] but a closer scrutiny

[1] *Selected Essays,* 162.

will reveal his characteristic quality of ironic observation in an early comedy like *Your Five Gallants* just as much as in the later tragedies. Middleton's irony, however, is not the impersonal irony of Sophocles and Shakespeare, inherent in the speeches and situations of the drama themselves; it is something so personal as to become the expression of the author's own outlook on life. Middleton's impersonal observation, it is true, makes him more genuinely a realist than any of his contemporaries, but the moments at which he appears himself to intervene, and give some turn to a speech or some twist to the action, are almost always those at which irony is uppermost. In *Hengist* there is irony in plenty. Sometimes it is obvious enough, as when the piety of Constantius gives check after check to Vortiger's rising ambitions, or when Castiza expresses her trust in her husband at the very moment of his treacherous betrayal of it. But it also underlies many of the speeches. One example has already been noticed, and we may also draw attention to the irony, only revealed by subsequent events, which lurks under the surface of such an outwardly splendid passage as Vortiger's greeting to the Saxons:

> Y'haue giuen me such a first tast of yor worth
> Twill neuer from my loue, sure when lifs gone
> Y^{e} memory will follow my soule still
> Participating im̃ortality with't. [II, iii, 11–14]

Again, Vortiger's astonishment at Hengist's ingratitude and rapacity (IV, iii, 57–80) which, in its unconsciousness of personal iniquity, resembles the shocked surprise of Beatrice-Joanna in *The Changeling* when De Flores claims his reward, is fundamentally ironical. So, too, is the final comment on Hengist's ambitions, which may fitly be called his epitaph:

> A strange drowth
> & what a little ground shall death now teach yo^{u}
> To be Content wthall. [V, ii, 252–254]

The irony, however, goes deeper still; it is at the very basis of the action. It is implicit in the relations of Vortiger with Roxena and Horsus; it is constantly emphasised by Horsus's acrid comments; and it blazes forth in Vortiger's disillusionment in the final scene. Irony is, in fact, a vital element in Middleton's conception of tragedy. In *The Changeling* the ironical essence of the tragedy of Beatrice is, as Mr. T. S. Eliot has pointed out, "not that she has lost Alsemero, for whose possession she has played; it is that she has won De Flores." In *Women Beware Women* the irony lies in the fact that at a crucial point in the action Hippolito should be the one to take it upon himself to defend his sister's honour, and thus precipitate the catastrophe. In *Hengist,* finally, it consists in the audience's foreknowledge of the futility of all Vortiger's designs, and underlies all the situations which develop out of his infatuation with Roxena.

FACSIMILES

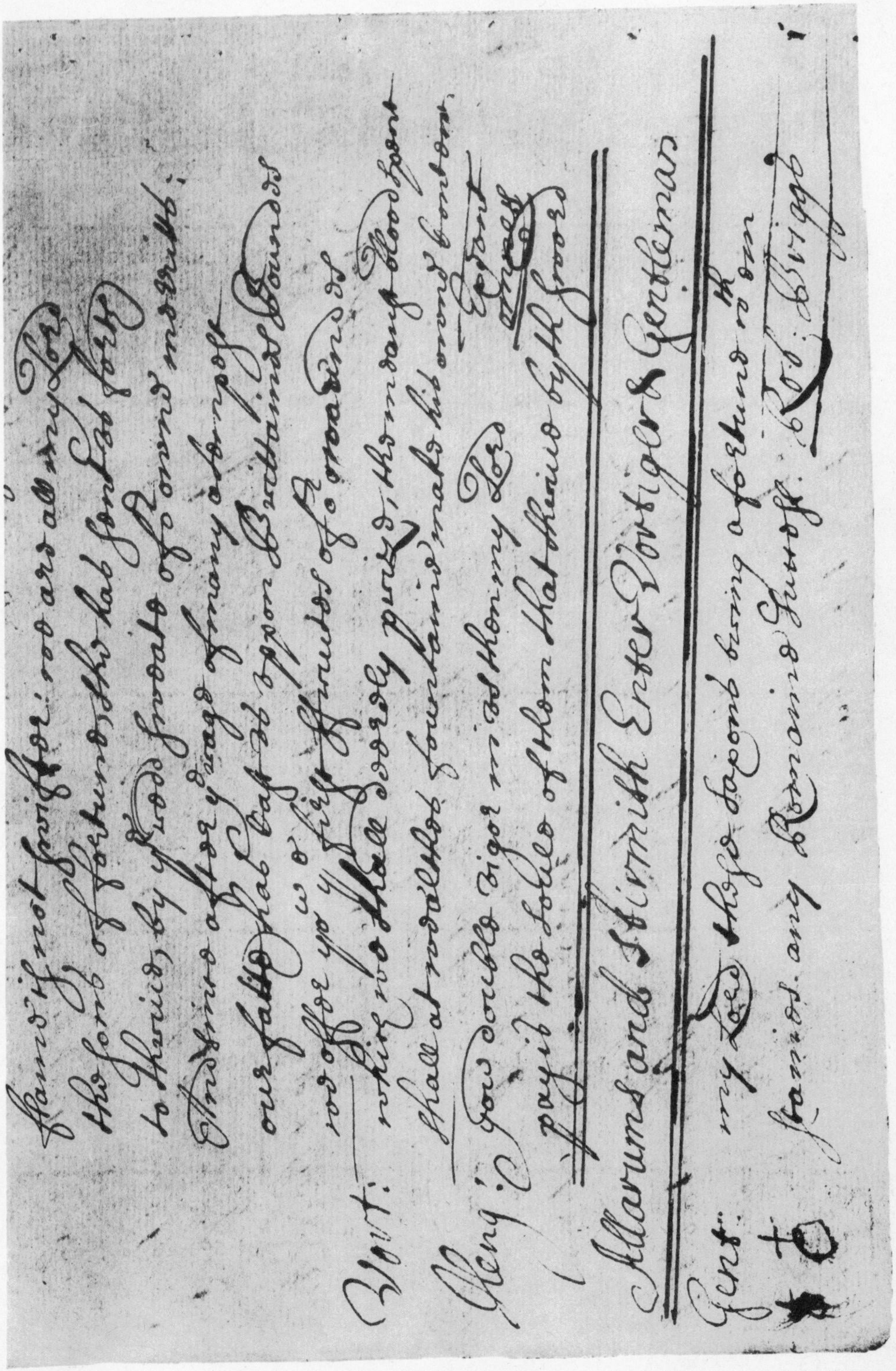

Plate I: Lambarde MS., Folger Shakespeare Library.
Lower portion of fol. 11ᵇ (II, ii, 38—II, iii, 2).

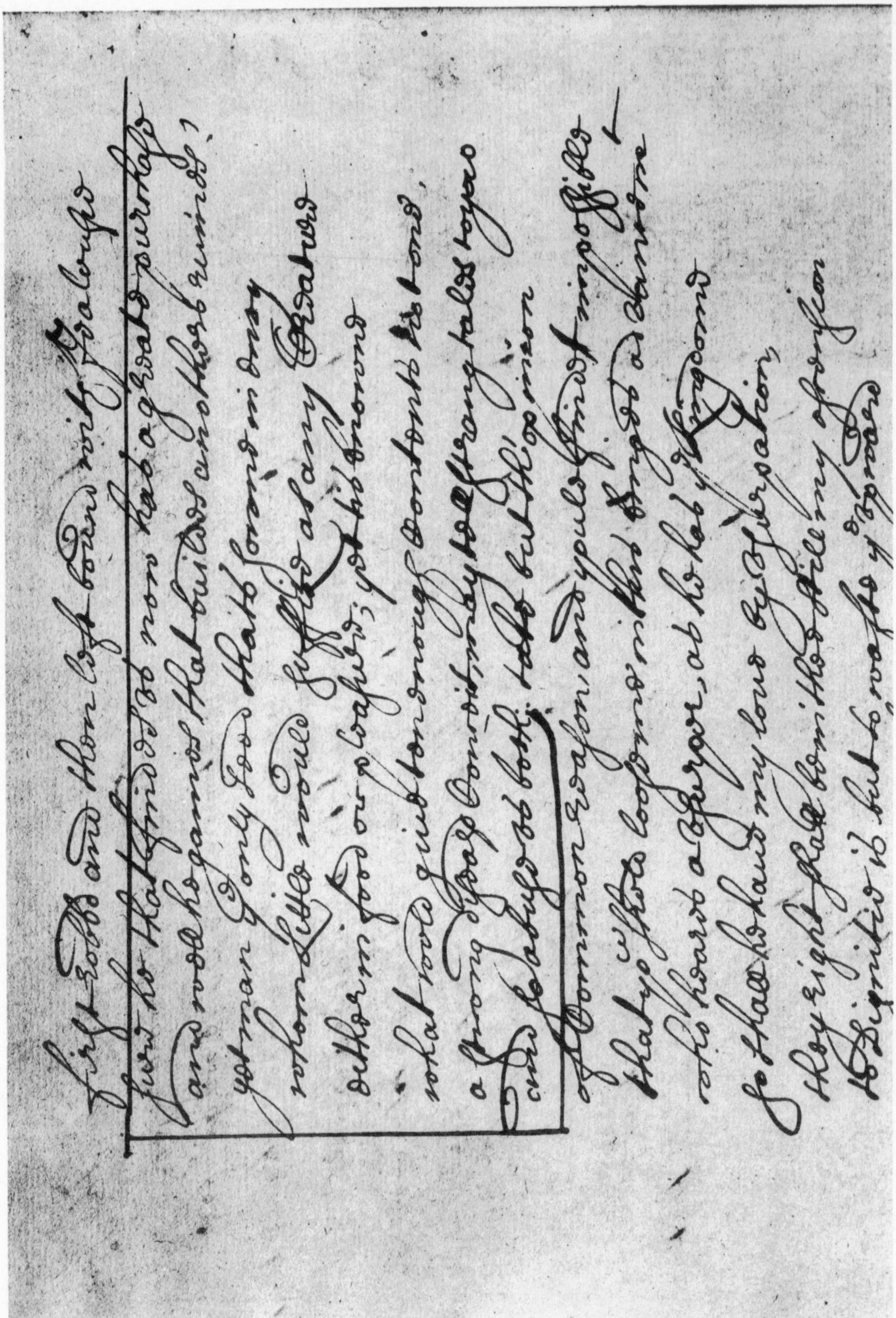

Plate II: Lambarde MS., Folger Shakespeare Library.
Upper portion of fol. 17^{b} (III, i, 55—69).

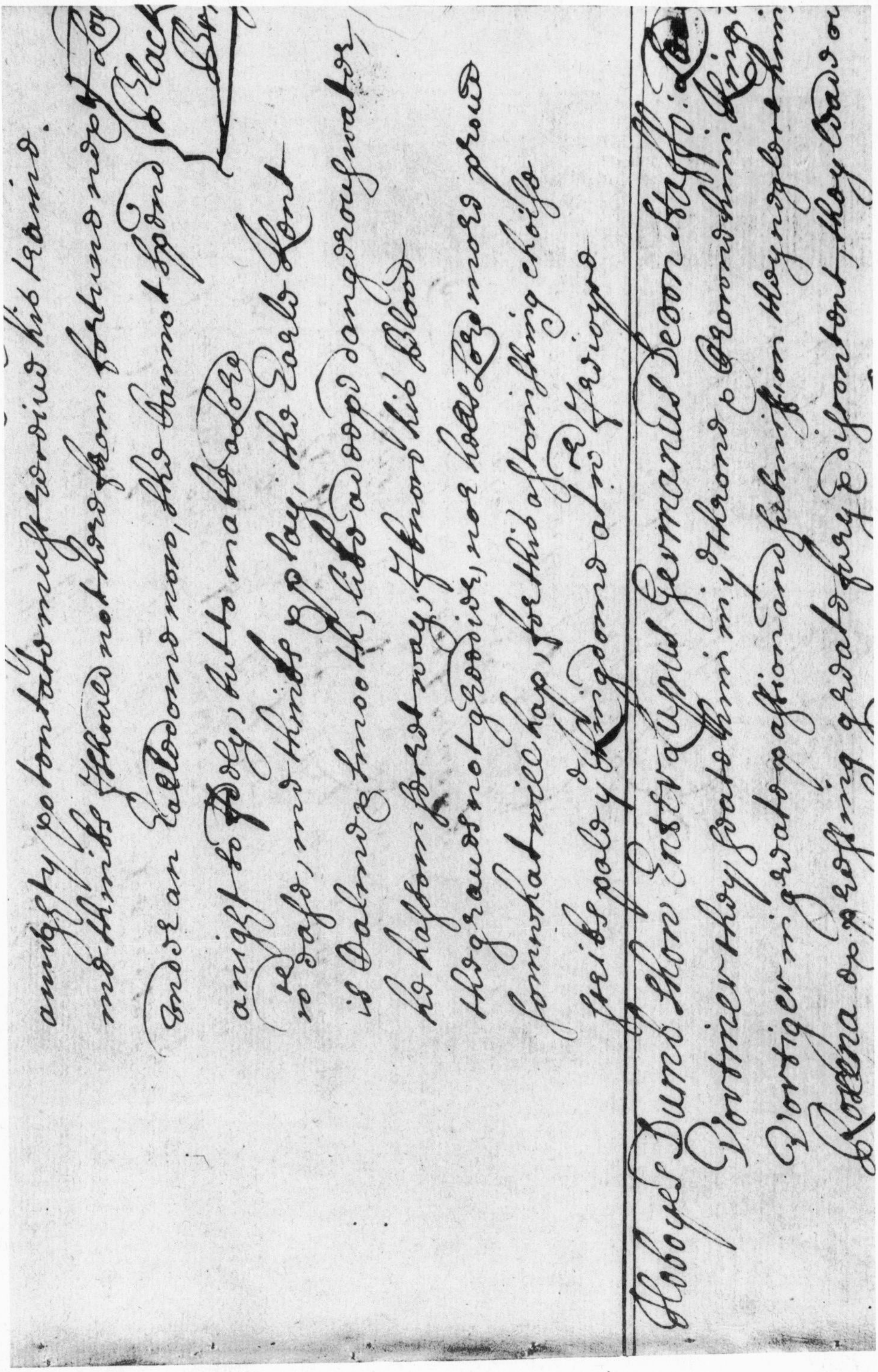

Plate III: Lambarde MS., Folger Shakespeare Library.
Portion of fol. 32ª (IV, ii, 279—D.S. iii, 4).

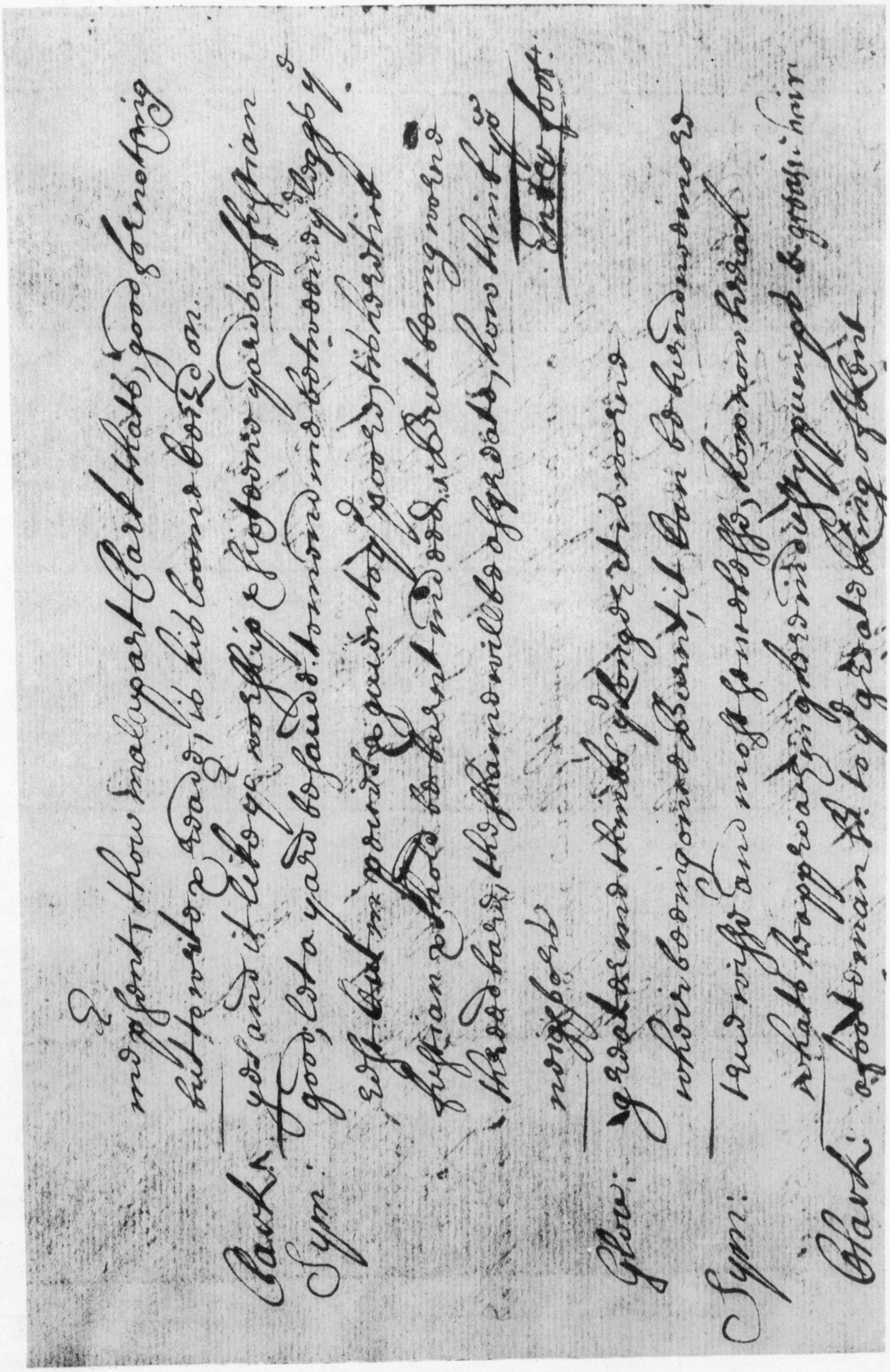

Plate IV: Lambarde MS., Folger Shakespeare Library.
Upper portion of fol. 55[b] (V, i, 5—21).

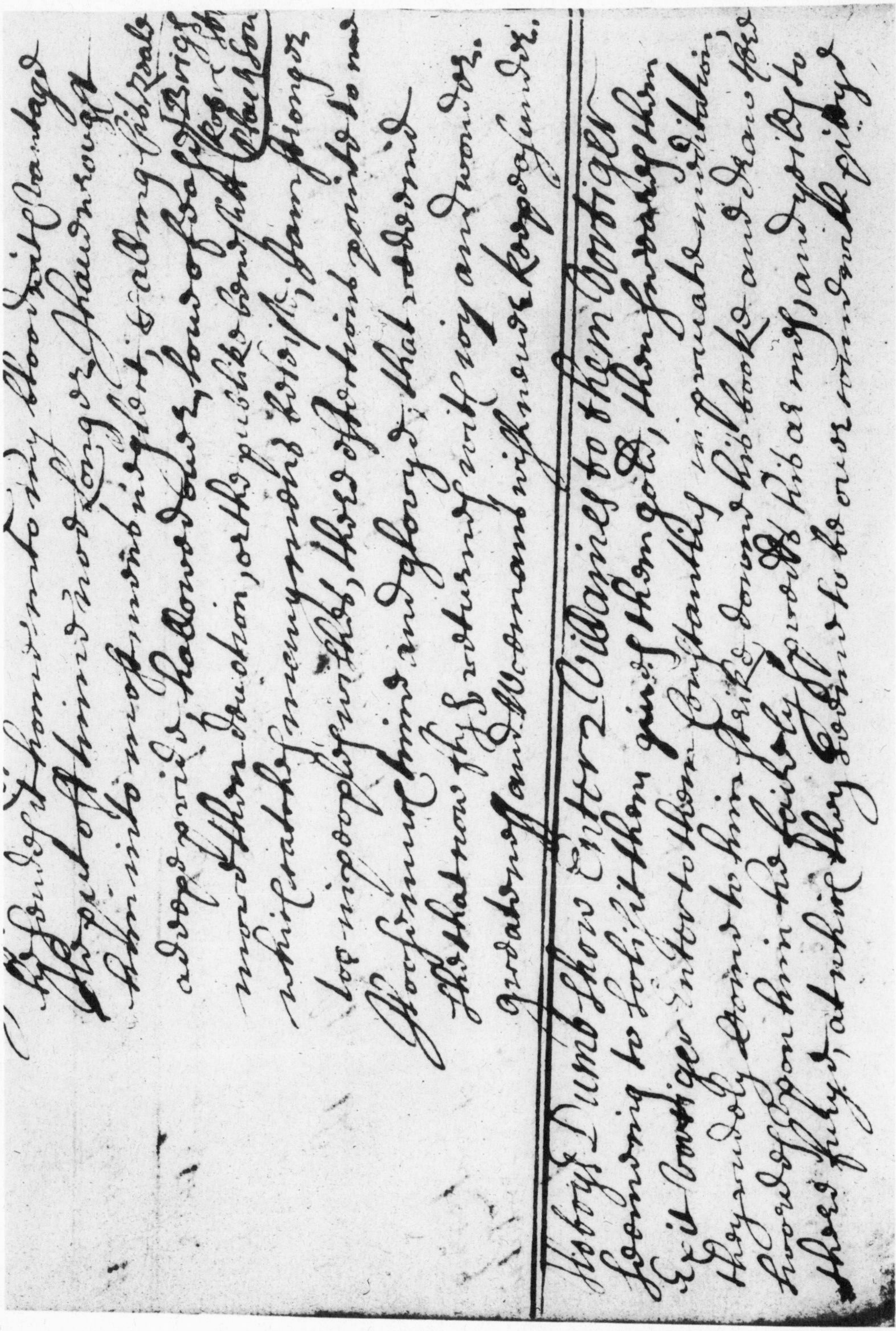

Plate V: MS. in the possession of the Duke of Portland.
Lower portion of fol. 10[b] (II, i, 37—D.S. ii, 7).

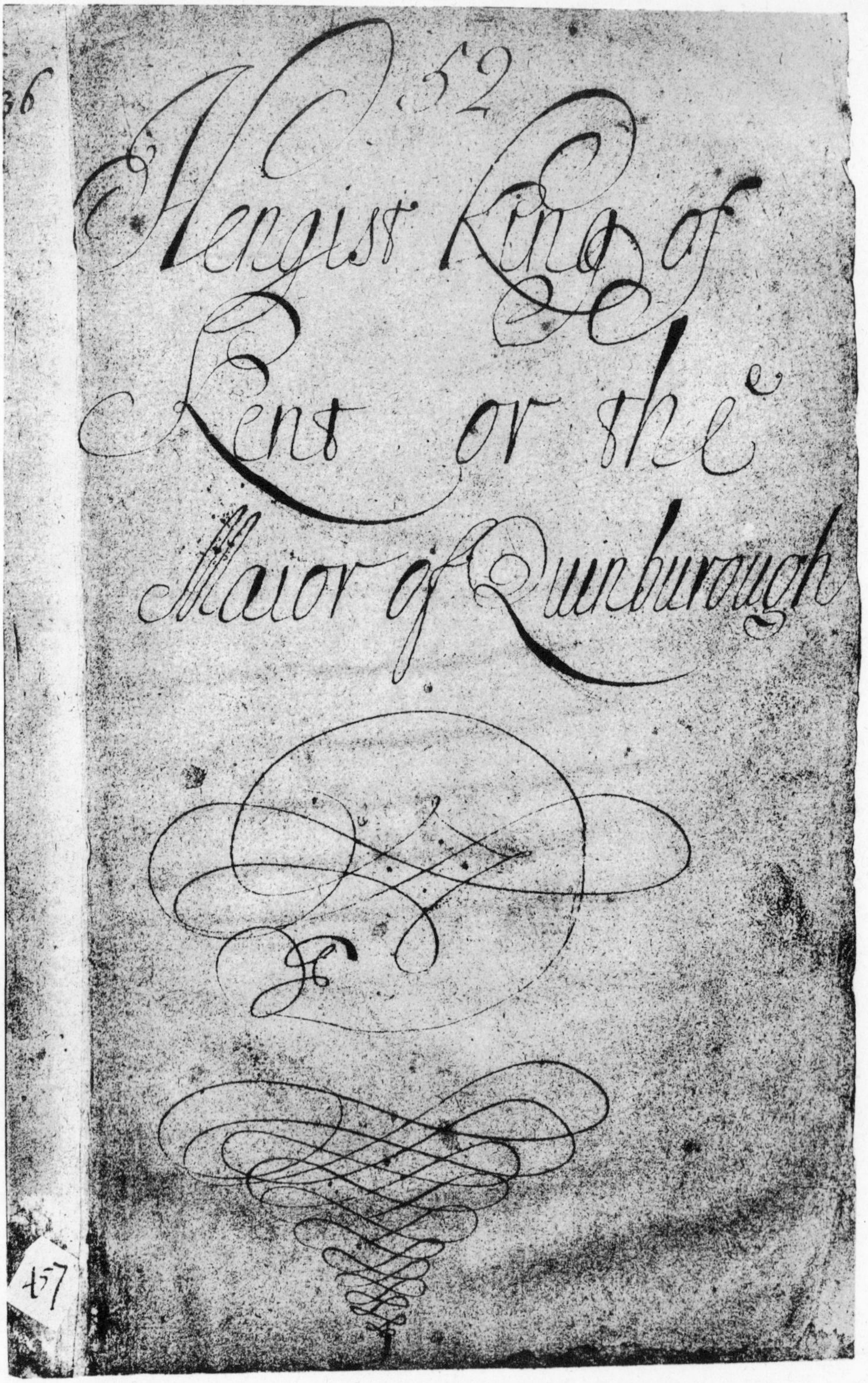

Plate VI: MS. in the possession of the Duke of Portland.
Title-page (reduced).

Hengist King of Kent or the Maior of Quinburough

Adapted from P; no title-page in L. For title-page and prefatory epistle of Q, see Introduction, p. xxvi.

[Fol. 1, *recto*]

DRAMATIS PERSONÆ

Chorus:

Raynulph Munck of Chester

Constantius King of y^{e} Britins

Vortiger

Hengist King of Kent

Aurelius and Vther Brothers to Constantius

Horsus

Deuon: and Stafford two Lordes

Lupus & Germanus two Muncks

Castiza Daughter to Devon:

Roxena Daughter to Hengist

two Ladyes

Symon a tanner Maior of Quinbourough

Oliuer a ffustian Weauer

three Graziers

Glouer

Barbor

Taylor

fellmonger

Buttonmunger

Brazier

Petitioners

Gentlemen

Clarke

Footeman

Saxons, Soldiers,

Captaine, Gaurd

and officers

1 *omitted in L,P;* Drammatis *Q* 2 Chorus *as heading in L,P, and no space between lines 3 and 4* 4 Brittains *P* 6 Hengis *L* 7 Cons: *P* 8 Hersus *P* 9 Staff^{d}: *P* 15 Gentleman *P* 18 Saxons Soldi< *L* 19 Captaine G< *L* 20 officrs *L*

The Dramatis Personæ are in quite a different order in Q, viz. Constantius. / Aurelius Ambrosius. / Uther Pendragon. / Vortiger. / Hengist. / Horsus. / Devonshire, / Stafford. *British Lords.* / Gentlemen. / Symon. / Oliver. / Taylour. / Barber. / Aminadab. / Footmen. / Souldiers. / Cheaters. / Castiza. / Roxena. / Ladies. / Raynulph *Monck of* Chester. / Germanus. / Lupus. *Moncks.* / Grasiers.

[Fol. 2, *recto*]

Actus Primus Scena Prima

Enter Raynulph a Munck ye p^{r}senter

Ray: What Raynulph Munck of Chester Can [Chor. i]
Raise from his policronicon,
(That raises him as works doe Men
To see light so long parted with agen)
That best may please this round faire ring
With sparkleing iudgm^{ts}: Circled in,
I shall produce; if all my powers
Can wyn the grace of too poore howres;
Well apaide I goe to rest.
Ancient storyes haue bene best,
Fashions that are now Calld new
Haue bene worne by more then yo^{u},
Elder times haue vsd ye same
Though these new ones get ye name,
So in story whats now told
That takes not part with days of old?
Then to proue times mutuall glorye
Ioyne new times loue, to old times storye.——*Exit*

Showte *Enter Vortiger* [I, i]

Vort: Will that wide throated Beast the Multitude
Neuer Lyn Bellowing? Courtiers are ill advisd
When they first make such Monsters:
What doe they but make head against themselues by't?
How neere was I to a Scepter and a Crowne,

heading) *full point after* Actus *erased in L;* ACT. 1. SCENA 1. / [rule] / Enter Raynulph: *Q*

Chor. 2 policronicron, *L,P;* Polycranicon *Q* 3 that *L;* raiseth *Q;* does *P* 4 (to *L,P;* To see long parted light agen, *Q* 6 sparkling Diamonds *Q;* Circled *altered from* Circles *in L* 7 I *added from Q; omitted in L,P;* produce, if, all my power *L;* powre *P* 9 rest *L* 13 haue worne *P* 15 what *Q* 16 old *L* 17 approve *Q* 18 follye *altered to* storye *in P*

I. i. *heading*) Shouts within: Then Enter Vortiger. *Q* 1 *prefix omitted in P;* wided *L* 2 neuer luy *P;* leave *Q;* ill / advisd *P,Q* 4 *omitted in Q;* by'< *L*

Faire power was een vpon me, my desires
Were tasting glory, till this forked rable
With their infectious acclamations
Poysoned my fortune; they will here haue none

[Fol. 2, *verso*]

As long as Constantins three sons Suruiue,
As if y[e] vassailles knew not how to obey
But in that line, like theire professions
That all there life time hamer out one way
Beaten into their pates with seauen yeares Bondage;
Well! though I rise not King Ile seeke the meanes
To grow as Close to one as policye Can
And Choake there expectations: now good Lordes
In whose kind loues and wishes I am Built
As high as humane dignitye Can aspire,
Are yet those Truncks that haue no other soules
But noyse and Ignorance, something more quiett?

Enter Devon St afford

Devon: Nor are they like to be for ought we gather;
Their wills are vpp still, nothing will appease 'em,
Good speeches are but Cast away vpon 'em.
Vort: Then since nessesity and fate withstand me
Ile striue to enter at a straighter passage;
Yo[r] suddaine aides and Councells good my Lordes.
Staff: Their ours noe longer then they doe yo[u] seruice.

Musick *Enter Certaine Muncks, Germanus; Constantius being one singing as at Precession*

6 ever *deleted and* een *written above it in another hand in L;* euer *P;* even *Q* 7 casting *Q* 8 ccl *of* acclamations *blotted in L* 9 fortune < *L; the foot of the page is badly cropped in L; P reads* fortune; they will haue none, / they as long *but in L the top of the word* here *is clearly visible* 9–14 they . . . Bondage *omitted in Q and 9 filled in with* Fortunes for Constantines sons. 11 vassailles *altered from* vassalls *in L* 14–16 yeares / Bondage, . . . the / meanes to *L* 16 as neer to *Q;* Enter De- / von. and / Stafford: *Q, after line 17* 17 r *of* there *over* e *in L;* good Lordes) *so Q;* kind Lordes *L,P* 18 whose kind loues) *so Q;* whose loues *L,P* 21 quiett *L* 22 *prefix omitted in P;* t *of* ought *a later addition in L;* gather *L* 23 still *L;* can appease them *Q;* 'em *L* 24 them. *Q* 25 *prefixes omitted in P for the rest of the page, but speeches are separated by strokes;* with stand *L* 26 straighter) *so P,Q;* stranger *L;* passage *L* 27 aid *Q* 28 *prefix omitted in some copies of Q;* They are *Q;* Exit *after this line in L,P; stage-direction*) Germanicus *L,P;* as Precession *L;* as at Precession *P;* Enter Constantius (as a Monck, attended by other Moncks) / Vortiger stays him. *Q*

Song Boast not off high Birth or Blood,
To be greate is to be good;
Holy and religious thinges
Those are vestures ffitt for Kinges;
By how much Man in fame shines Cleerer
He to heauen shold draw the neerer,
He deseruing best of praises
Whom vertue raises;

[Fol. 3, *recto*]

It is not state, it is not Birth;
The way to heauen is grace on earth.
Sing to the Temple him so holy
Sinn may Blush to thinke on ffollye.

Vort: Vessels of sanctity, be pleasd awhile
To giue attention to ye publique peace
Wherein heauen is serud too; though not soe purely;
Constantius eldest son of Constantine
We here seaze on thee for the generall good
And in thy right of Birth,
Const: On me! for what Lordes!
Vort: The Kingdomes gouerm^{t}.
Const: Oh powres of Blessednesse
Keepe me from groweing downwards into earth againe,
I hope I am further on my way then soe;
Sett forward
Vort: You must not
Const: How?
Vort: I know yor wisdome
Will light vpon a way to pardon vs
When you shall read in euery Brittaines brow
The vrgd necessity of ye times.
Const: What necessity
Can be i'th world, but praier and repentance, {*showte*
And that Buisnes I am about.

29–40 *the song is omitted in Q; it is entirely without punctuation in L,P* 29 of *P* 33 shins *P* 41 sanctity *L;* a while *Q* 42 the general peace, *Q* 43 soe holy, *P;* purely < *L* 45 on the for thee for the generall *L, with* r *of* generall *over* e 50 groweing) *from Q;* groaneing *L,P;* ag< *L* 51–2 *all one line in L* 52 forwar< *L;* forward *P;* forwards. *Q* 59–61 What . . . can there be . . . world / But . . . business / I am about now. *Q; no stage-direction in Q* 60 show< *L;* showte / within *P* 61 n *of* Buisnes *over* e *in L*

Vort: Hark, afarr off still,
We loose and hazard much: holy Germanus
And reuerend Lupus, wth all expedition
Sett the Crowne on him.
Const: Noe such mark of fortune
Comes nere my head
Vort: My Lord we are forc'd to rule you
Const: Dare yo^{u} receiue heauens light in at yor eye Lidds
And ofer violence to religion; take heede,

[Fol. 3, *verso*]

The very Beame lett in to Comforth yo^{u}
May be the fire to burne yo^{u}, on these knees
Hardened wth zealous praiers I entreate you,
Bring not my Cares into ye world agen,
Think with how much vnwillingnes and anguish,
A gloryfied soule departed from the Bodye,
Wold to that loathsom gaole returne againe,
With such greate paine, a well subdude efection
Re-enters worldly Buisnes.
Vort Good my Lord
I know yo^{u} Cannot Lodge so many vertues
But patience must be one; as low as earth
Wee Begg the freeness of yor owne Consent
W^{ch} ells must be Constraind, and time it were
Either agreede, or forcd, speake good my Lord
For yo^{u} binde vp more syn in this delaye,
Then thousand praiers Can absolue againe.
Const: Wert but my death you shold not kneele so long for't.
Vort: Twill be the death of millions if yo^{u} rise not,
And that betimes two: lend yor helpes my Lordes
For feare all Come too late,
Const: This is a Crueltye
That peaceful Man did neuer suffer yet,
To make me dye agen, that was once dead
And begin all that ended long before:
Hold Lupus and Germanus yo^{u} are lights

62 hark *L* 63 loose and hazard) *so Q;* loose hazard *L,P;* Germanicus *L,P* 66–7 *all one line in L,P; line-division that of Q* 70–1 religion; / take . . . yo^{u} *L,P,Q* 75 v *over* a *in* vnwillingnes *L* 76 departed) part *P* parted *Q* 77 gaole) goale *L,P* Gaol again return, *Q* 83 dee *erased after* owne *L* 86 binde more *P* sins *Q* 88 not beg *P* 90 help *Q* 94 once was *Q* 95 that was ended *P*

Of holyness and religion, Can yo^{u} ofer
The thing that is not lawfull, stand not I
Cleere from all temporall Charg by my profession?
Germ: Not when a time so violent Calls vpon you;
Who's borne a Prince is borne for generall peace
Not his owne onely, heauen will looke for him
In others buisnes, and require him their;

[Fol. 4, *recto*]

What is in you religious must be showne
In saueing many more soules then yor owne
Const: Did not greate Constantine o^{r} noble ffather
Deeme me vnfitt for gouerment and rule
And theirfore pressed me into this profession:
W^{ch} I haue held strict and loue it aboue glorye?
Nor is there want in me yo^{r}selues Can witness
Heauen has prouided largely for yor peace
And blest yo^{u} wth ye liues of my two Brothers:
Fix yor obedience there, leaue me a servant.
Vort: You may euen at this Instant
Const Oh this Crueltye
All: Long liue Constantius son of Constantine King of the Brittaines. ——— {*flourish*
Aure: They haue Changd there tune already
Const: I feele want
And extreme pouerty of Ioy within me,
The peace I had is parted mongst rude men,
To keepe them quiet I haue lost it all:
What Can ye Kingdome gaine by my vndooing?
That riches is not blest though it be mightye
Thats purchasd wth the spoyle of any man,
Nor Can ye peace so filcht, euer thriue wth 'em:
And ift be worthily held sacredlidge,

99 Charg) rule *P* 100 you *L* 101 Who is *Q;* for) *so some copies of Q only; others read* a *with L,P;* good *deleted after* generall *in L* 102 owne) *so P,Q;* one *L;* only Heauen lookes *P* 103 others actions, and will require *Q; the foot of the page is cropped in L and* their *is barely visible* 107 gouerment. *L* 108 pressed) *so Bullen;* praised *L,P,Q* 110 want of *Q* 111 hath *Q* 112 yor t *deleted after* of *in L* 114–5 *omitted in Q* 116 of < *L;* of the *P;* of Great Britain. *Q* 117 *stage-direction omitted in Q;* flouri< *L* 118 *omitted in Q;* tim *P* 119 I do feel a want *Q;* already *deleted after* want *in L* 120 me *omitted in Q* 122 them *altered from* their *in P* 123 vndooing < *L* 124 best, *Q* 125 wth the spoyle) y *of* spoyle *added to an original* spole *in L;* by the ruine of another; *Q* 126 filcht *deleted before* peace *in P;* with them: *Q*

To robb a Temple, tis no lesse offence
To rauish meditations from a soule
The Consecrated alter in a Man,
And all their hopes will be beguild in me;
I know noe more the way to temporall rule
Then he thats borne and has his years Come to him

[Fol. 4, *verso*]

In a rough desart; well may the waight kill me
And thats the fairest good I looke for from't.

Vort: Not so greate King: here stoopes a faithfull seruant
Wold sooner perish vnder it with Cheerefulness
Then yor meeke soule should feele the least oppresion
Of ruder Cares: such Common Course imployments
Cast vppon me yor subiect, vppon vortiger,
I see yo^{u} are not made for noyse and paines
Clamors of suitors, iniuryes and redresses,
Millions of riseing actions with the sun,
Like laws still ending and yet neuer Dun,
Of powre, to turne a greate man to ye state
Of his insencible monument, with orewatching;
To be opprest, is not required of yo^{u} my Lord
But onely to be King, the Broken sleepes
Let me take from yo^{u} s^{r}, the toyles and troubles,
All that is Burthensome in authoritye
Please yo^{u} to lay't on me, and what is glorious
Receiue it to yor owne Brightness

Const: Worthy vortiger
Iff twere not sin to greiue an others patience
Wth what we Cannot tollerate o^{r}selues
How happy were I in the, and thy Charitye;
Theirs nothing makes man ffeele his miseries,
But knowledge only, reason that is placd
For mans directo^{r}, is his Cheife aflicter,
For though I Cannot beare the waight my selfe

128 o *of* no *a later addition in L* 129 the Soul *Q* 133 years) *so Q;* yeare *L,P;* to < *L,* to him *P,Q* 135 that *L;* from it. *Q* 138 feel oppression *Q* 140 me your servant, *Q;* subiect; *L* 141 perish *deleted before* paines *in L* 143 of Actions, rising *Q* 144 neuer dun, *altered from* newe begun *in P* 146 orewatching *L,P;* Of his marble Monument: with over-watching, *Q* 149 take *altered from* looke *in P* 150 burthenous *P,Q* 151 you lay it *Q* 152 r *of* Brightness *over* u *in L* 154 e *of* greiue *over* i *in L* 155 our self, *Q* 156 Charitye, *L;* and thy love? *Q*

I Cannot haue that Barreness of remorse
To see another groane vnder my Burthen.
Vort: Ime quite blowne vpp, a Conscionable way,
Theirs euen a trick of murdering in som pittye.

[Fol. 5, *recto*]

The death of all my hopes I see allreadye,
Their was noe other likelyhood: for religion
Was neuer friend of mine yett,
Const: Holy parteners
In strictest abstnence, ffasteings and vigills,
Cruell necessitye has forcd me from yo^u,
We part I feare for ever, But in mind
I will be alwayes here, here let me staye.
Devon: My Lord you know the times
Const: Farewell Blest soules, I feare I much offend
flourish He that drawes teares from yo^u, takes yor best friend *Exevnt*
Vort: Can this greate motion of Ambition stand
Like wheeles false wrought by an vnskilfull hand,
Then time stand thou too, let no hopes ariue
At their sweete wishfulness till mine sett forward,
Wold I Could stay this existance; as I Can
Thy glassy Counterfeit in hours of sand;
Ide keepe the turnd downe till my wishes rose,
Then weede both rise together;
What seurall inclinations are in nature:
How much is he disquietted, and weares royaltie
Disdainfullie vpon him like a Curse,
Calls a faire Crowne the waight of his afflictions
When heres a soule wold sing vnder that Burthen.
Yet well recouered: I will seeke all wayes
To vex authoritye from him, I will weary him
As lowe as the Condition of a hound
Before I giue him ouer, and in all

161 *second* e *of* Barreness *over* o *in L* 163 I am *Q;* way *L* 164 pittye *L* 165 allreadye *L* 168–9 *Q omits* ffasteings and vigills *and prints the two lines as one* 170 C *of* Cruell *over some other letter in L;* hath *Q* 174 much) *corrected from* must *in another hand in L;* must *P;* shall *Q* 175 flourish) *omitted in Q;* friend < *L;* Exevnt *P,* Ex. all / but Vor: *Q* 176 Can the *Q* 179 h *of* wishfulness *altered from* l *in L;* forwards: *Q* 180 xistance; *L,* the existence, *Q* 182 I'ld *Q* 183 wee'ld *Q;* rise *altered from* thrice *in P;* together. *P,Q* 184 seudall *written by scribe of L, and* r *added over the* u *in another hand;* nature *L* 187 afflictions! *Q* 188 Burthen *L* sink under the *Q* 189 seeke all wayes) speak always *P;* use all means *Q* 190–2 I will . . . ouer, *omitted in Q*

Studdy what most may discontent his Blood *Enter 3 Graziers*
Makeing my maske my zeale, to'th publique good.
Not possible a richer policye
Can haue Conception in the thought of Man
1 Graiz: An honnorable life inclose yor Lordship

[Fol. 5, *verso*]

Vort: Now what are yo^{u}
2 Graz: Graziers ant like yor Lo^{pp}:
Vort: Soe it shold seeme by yor inclosures
Whats yor affaires with me
1 Graz: We are yor Petitioners my Lord
Vort: What: depart,
Petitioners to me, y'haue well deserud
My grace and friendshipp: haue yo^{u} not a Ruler
After yor owne election, high to Court
Get neere and Close, be lowd and bold enough
You Cannot Chuse but speede
2 Graz: And that will doot,
We haue throates wide enough, weele put em toot——*Ex^{t}*

Musique *Dumb show:* ffortune is discouered vppon an alter, in [D.S. i]
her hand a golden round full of Lotts: Enter *Hengist*
and *Hersus* with others, they Draw Lotts and hang them vp
with Ioy, soe all depart saueing
Hengist and *Hersus* who kneele and imbrace
each other as parteners in one fortune, to them
Enter *Roxena* seemeing to take her leaue of
Hengist her father, But especeally priuately &
warily of *Hersus* her louer; she departs weepeing:

193–4 *stage-direction from P;* Ent< / Gra< *L; in Q the direction* Enter two / Grasiers *comes after line 196* 194 maske, *P;* to the *Q;* good *L* 196 M *of* Man *over* f *in L* 199 ant) and it *P,* if't *Q* 201 affair *Q* 202 Petitioners, / My Lord. *Q* 203–4 *all one line in L;* For what? . . . to me! / You have . . . Ruler / After *Q* 205 grace and favour, *Q* 206 hye you to *Q* 208 Exit. *Q* 209 If that *Q* 210 enough *L;* them to't. Exeunt. *Q;* Exit *P*

Dumb show. *In P the dumb show is written right across the page so that there is no margin as in L.* 2 n *of* hand *over* u *in L* 3 others *L;* hang *inserted above a caret mark between* and *and* them *in L; it is perhaps in another hand* 4 imbrace each o *deleted after* soe *in L;* departs *L,P;* saueing Hengist: and *P* 5 kneeles *L,P* 7 Roxena: *P;* leaue of of *P* 9 louer *L For the dumb show Q omits the direction for* Musique *and reads:* Dumb show. Fortune discovered, in her hand a round Ball full of Lots; then enters Hengist and Horsus, with others; they draw Lots, and having opened them, all depart, save Hengist and Horsus,

[D.S. i]

and *Hengist* and *Hersus* goe to the doore and Bring
in their souldiers with Drum and Collors and so
march forth

Rayn: When Germany was ouer growne [Chor. ii]
With sons of peace two thickly sowen
Seuerall guides wer Chosen then
By destind lots to lead out Men
And they whom fortune here with-standes
Must proue theire fates in other Land^{s}:
On these two Captaines fell that Lott
But that which must not be forgott

[Fol. 6, *recto*]

Was Roxenas Cuning greife
Who from ye father like a theife
Hid her best and truest teares
Which her Lustfull Louer weares
In many a stolne and wary kisse
Vnseene of father: that maydes will doe this
Yet highly scorne to be Cald strumpetts to—
But what they lac'k ont Ile be iudgd by yo^{u}——*Exit*

Enter Vortiger felmonger, Buttonmonger [I, ii]
[Brazier] Graziers Petitioners.

Vort: This way his Matie Comes
all: Thank your good Lordship
Vort: When yo^{u} heare yond doore open
felmon: Very good my Lord
Vort: Be ready wth yor seurall suites, put forward

who kneel and embrace; then enter Roxena, seeming to take leave of Hengist in great passion, but more especially and warily of Horsus, her Lover; she departs one way, Hengist and Horsus another.

Chor. ii. *preceded by* Enter Raynulph *in Q* 6 fate in othere *P* 7 the Lot; *Q;* se *of* these *a later addition in L* 10 her Father *Q* 12 Louer weares *corrected from* Lovers Veares *in P* 14 that *omitted Q;* Maids do *Q* 15 Called *corrected from* Look'd *in P;* strumpett *P;* to) *should possibly be read as* so *in L* 16 ont) of't *Q;* iudgd) *so Q;* iudg *L,* iudge *P*

I. ii. *stage-direction*) Feltmonger, Button-maker, Grasier, *Q;* Brazier *omitted in L,P,Q;* Grazier *L,P;* Petit< *L* 4 *prefix*) All. *Q* 5 seurall) *so Q;* scedall *L,* sceduall *P*

1 Graz: Thats a thing euery Man does naturally s^{r}
Thats a suitor if he meane to speed
Vort: Tis well y'are so deepe Learnd, take no denyalls,
felmon: No my good Lord
Vort: Not any if you loue
The ꝓsperitie of yor suites; you marr all vterly,
And ouer throwe yor fruitfull hopes for euer,
If either fifth or sixth nay tenth repulse
Fasten vpon yor Bashfullnes
Button: Say yo^{u} soe my Lord,
We Can be troublesom and we list
Vort: I knowt,
I felt it but to late in the genrall some
Of yor ranck Brotherhood, wch now Ile thank yo^{u} for;
While this vexation is in play, Ile studdy
To raise a second, then a third to that
One still to back another: Ile make quietness
As deere and pretious too him as nights rest
To a man in suites in lawe, he shall be glad

[Fol. 6, *verso*]

To yield vp powre; if not, it shalbe had ——— *Exit*
Butto: Hark, I professe my heart was Com̄ing vpward,
I thought the doore had opend
Graz: Marry wold it had s^{r}
Butto: I haue such a trecherous heart of myne own, twill throbb at the very falle of a farthingale
Braz: Not if it fall on the rushes
Butto: Yes truely if their bee noe light in ye roome, I shall throbb p^{r}sently; the first time it took me my wife was ith Company, I remember the roome was not halfe so light as this, but Ile be sworne I was a whole houre afinding on her

6 *prefix*) Gras. *Q* 7 That is a Suitor, and doth mean to speed. *Q* 8 well, *L;* you are *Q* 9 *prefix*) All. *Q* 10 loue, *L;* not any if you meane to speede *P* 10–13 *line-division that of Q;* not . . . suites / you . . . throwe / yor . . . either / fifth . . . *L* 11 suites *corrected from* sciters (?) *in L* 13 tenth denyall *P* 15 *prefix*) All. *Q* 15–6 *line-division as in Q; all one line in L* 16 if we *Q;* we < *L* 17–8 *line-division as in Q; all one line in L* 17 knowt *L;* know it *P,Q* 18 gendall *L* 19 I thank *Q;* fo< *L* 22–4 *Q omits* Ile make . . . lawe *and reads* For a second . . . still / To vex another, that he shall 23 as a nights *P* 25 powre *L;* not *L* 26 hark *L;* I protest *Q;* vpward *L;* upwards, *Q* 26–7 *line-division that of Q; as prose in L* 29 *This and all the other tradesmen's speeches for the rest of the scene are printed as verse in Q;* my *Q* 31 *prefix*) Gras: *Q* 33 p^{r}sently *L* 34 in the *Q* 36 in finding her. *Q*

Braz: Byr Ladye y'had a long time of throbbing ont then
Butto: Still I felt men, But I Could finde noe woemen, I
thought they had bene all sunck, I haue made a vowe
fort Ile neuer haue a meeteing by Candlelight agen
Graz: Yes s^{r} in Lanthornes
Butto: Yes sir in Lanthornes, But Ile neuer trust a naked
Candell agen, takt on my word
Enter Constant 2 Gent
Graz: Hark there, stand Close, it opens now indeede
Butto: Oh Maiesty what art thou, Ide giue any man halfe
my suite to deliuer my petition now, tis in the behalfe
of Buttonmakers and so it seemes by my flesh.
Const: Pray doe not follow me, vnles yo^{u} doot
To wonder at my garm^{ts}: theirs noe Cause
I giue yo^{u} why yo^{u} shold: tis shame enough
Me thinks for me to looke vpon my selfe;
It greiues me that more shold: the other weeds
Became me better; but ye Lordes are pleasd
To force mee to weare these, I would not els:
I pray be satisfied, I Calld you not.
Wonder of madness! can you stand soe Idle
And know that you must dye

[Fol. 7, *recto*]

1 Gent: Wee are all Commanded sir,
Besides it is our duty to your grace
To giue attendance
Const: What a wild thing's this:
We maruell though you tremble at Deaths name
When youle not see the Cause why you are Cowardes?
All our attendances are farr to little
On our owne selues, yet youle giue me attendance;
Who lookes to you ye whilst, and soe you vanish
Strangely and fearefully; for Charitys sake

37 *prefix*) Gras. *Q;* you had *P;* of it *Q* 38 felt) could feel *Q;* o *of* woemen *probably a later insertion in L* 39 all sunk't, *P* 40 have meeting while I live by Candle-light again. *Q* 41 *in L a blot extends from the second half of* Lanthornes *to the top of* Ile *in the next line* 42 trust candle naked again. *Q* 43 agen *L;* takt on my word *omitted in Q* 44 Close *L* Hark, hark, stand *Q;* 45 I'ld *Q* 46 petition for me, / tis *P;* petition; It is *Q* 48 do it *Q* 51 me thinks; *L;* Methinks to look *Q;* selfe *L* 57 that) *so Q; omitted in L,P* 59 sir *L* 60 dutyes *P,Q* 62 thing is *P,Q;* this *L* 63 trembeld *altered from* wonder *in P* 64 Cowardes) Carrerdes *L,* Carrerders *P,* fools *Q* 65 little *retouched in L* 65–68 *Q omits* All our . . . fearefully 68 For Charities sake desist here I pray you, / Make *Q*

Make not my p^{r}sence guilty of yo^{ur} sloth;
Withdraw young men and finde you honest buisness

2 Gent: What hopes haue wee to rise by following him?
Ile giue him ouer shortly.

1 Gent: Hees to nice
Too holy for young gentlemen to follow
That haue good faces and sweete runing fortunes *Exevnt Gent^{s}*

Const: Eight houres a day in serious Contemplation
Is But a bare alowance, no higher food
Toth soule, then Bread and water to the Bodye,
And thats but needefull then; more wold doe better

1 Graz: Letts all kneele together, 'twill moue pittye
I haue bene at begging a hundreth suites

Cons: How happy am I in ye sight of yo^{u}:
Here are religious soules that loose noe tyme;
With what Deuotion doe they kneele to heauen
And seeme to Check me that am soe remise.
I Bring my Zeale amongst you, holy men,
If I see any kneel, and I sit out,
That howre is not well serud me thinks: strict soules
You haue bene of som order in yor times

Graz: Graziers and Braziers som and this a felmonger

Braz: Heres my Petition

Butto: Myne ant like yor grace

[Fol. 7, *verso*]

Graz: Looke vpon mine I am ye longest suito^{r}
I was vndone seauen yeares agoe my Lord

Const: I haue mockt my good hopes: call yo^{u} these petitions
Why thers no forme of praier amongst em all

Button: Yes ith Bottom thers some halfe a Line
Prayes for yor Maiestye if yo^{u} looke on mine

69 sloth *L* 70 buisne< *L* 71 him *L* 75 faces) *written above* fortunes *deleted in P; stage-direction) so P; omitted in Q;* Ex< / Ge< *L* 77 alowance *L;* higher *altered from* lither *L* 78 To the Soul *Q;* water for *P;* Bodye *L* 79 needefull then more *L;* needful, then more *Q* 80 *But.* Let us all *Q;* 'twill) *so Q:* together will *L,P;* ben< / begging *L* 80–1 *line-division that of Q; as prose in L* 81 at the begging of a hundred *Q* 82 yo^{u} *L* 83 not time, *Q;* tyme *L* 84 they point at Heaven, *Q* 85 remise *L;* too remiss! *Q* 86 among *Q;* men *L* 87 *this line is found in Q only* 88 well spent; methinks, *Q;* soul< *L* 90 felmonge< *L;* Felt-maker. *Q* 91–2 But. Here's his Petition and mine, if it like your Grace. *Q* 92 ant please *P* 93–4 *as prose in L* 94 my Lord *omitted in Q* 95 You have *Q* 96 s *of* amongst *over* h *in L;* among them *Q* 97 in the *Q;* Botton (*altered from* Button) *L;* some *omitted in L,Q* 98 prayers *P*

Const: Make yor request to heauen not to me
Butto: Las mines a supplicac̄on for brass buttons s^r.
fellmo: Theirs a greate enormitie in woolle, I beseech yor grace
Considert
Graz: Pastures rise to twopence an acre my Lord, w^t will this
world Come too.
Braz: I doe beseech yor grace
Graz: Good yor grace
Const: Oh this is one of my afflictions
That with the Crowne inclosd me, I must beare it
Graz: Yo^r graces answere to my supplication
Braz: To myne my Lord
Consta: No violent storme lasts euer,
Thats all ye Comforth ont
ffell: Yo^r highness answere
Graz: We are almost halfe vndone, the Conttry almost Beggerd
Braz: See see he pointes to heauen, as who should say
Theirs enough there, But tis a greate way thither,
Thers noe good to be don here I see that, we may all spend
our mouthes like a Company of hounds in ye Chase
of a royall deere, and goe home and fall to Cold mutton
bones when we haue don
Buton: My wife will hang me thats my destinye, *Exevnt*
Const: Thankes heauen tis ouer, wee shold neuer know rightly
The sweeteness of a Calme but for a tempest;
Heeres a wish'd howre for Contemplation now;
All still and silent, this is a true Kingdome, *Enter Vortiger*
Vort: My lord

[Fol. 8, *recto*]

Const: Againe
Vort: Alas this is but early
And gentle to the troopes of buisnesses

99 requests *Q;* not *added above the line over a caret mark in P* 101 *prefix)* Felt. *Q;* woolle *L* 102 consider it. *P,Q* 103 rise 2^d an acre, what *Q* 105 *prefix)* But. *Q* 107 this one *L;* a *of* afflictions *over* e *in L* 109 ti *of* supplication *over* c *in L* 110 But. Mine *Q* 111 *no prefix in P, but it is marked off as a separate speech* 111–2 *as one line in L,P,Q* 112 that's the comfort of it. *Q* 113 *prefix)* Felt. *Q* 114 almost all vndon *P,Q;* l *of* halfe *over* o, *and second* g *of* Beggerd *over* e *in L;* the Country begger'd. *Q* 115 *prefix)* But. *Q;* points at *Q* 116 thither, thers / noe *L* 117 there is *P;* done, I see that already, *Q* 118 e *of* like *a later insertion and* ny *of* Company *over* mi *in L;* In chase *Q* 119 and then go *Q* 121 *prefix)* Gra. *Q;* my currish destiny. *Q* 122 ouer *L;* over now, we *Q* 123 for a storm. *Q* 124 wish'd) *so Q;* wisd *L;* wis'h *P;* now *L* 125 All's *Q;* here is *Q* 126 V< *L* 129 buisnes *P*

That flock about authoritye, my Lord
You must forthwith settle yor mind to marrye
Const: To marrye
Vort: Sodainly, thers noe pawse giuen;
The peoples wills are violent
And Couetuous of succession from yor Loynes
Const: From me their Can Come none; a profest abstinence
Hath sett a virgin sele vppon my Blood
And alterd all ye Course; the heate I haue
Is all inclosd within a zeale to vertue,
And thats not fitt for earthly ꝓpogation:
Alas I shall but forfeit all their hopes,
Ime a man made wthout desires tell em
Vort: This giues noe satisfaction to there wills my Lord;
I proude them with such wordes But all were fruitless,
There sturdye voyces Blew em into Cloudes;
A Virgin of the highest Subiects Blood
They haue pickt out for yor imbrace, and send her
Blest with there generall wishes into fruitfullness;
See where she Comes my Lord

Enter Castiza

Const: I neuer felt
Vnhappy hand of miserye till this touch:
A patience I could finde for all but this
Cast: My Lord yor vowd Loue ventures me but dangerously
Vort: Tis but to strengthen a vexation politickly
Cast: Thats an vncharitable practise, trust me s^{r}
Vort: Noe more of that
Cast: But say he shold effect me s^{r}
How shold I scape him then, I haue but one faith my Lord

[Fol. 8, *verso*]

And that yo^{u} haue already, our late Contracts

130–1 *Q omits* my Lord *and divides the lines:* That . . . forthwith / Settle 132 How, to *Q* 133 sodainly *L;* giuen *L;* And suddenly . . . pause to be given, *Q* 134–5 The peoples . . . covetous / Of *Q* 135 for succession *P;* Of a succession *Q* 136 abstinen< *L* 137 hat *P;* sele) scle *L,* Seal *Q,* a Virgins seate *P* 138 the heate *added above the line over a caret mark in P* 139 vortue *L* 142 desire *P;* them. *Q* 143 *line omitted in Q;* giues not *P;* Lord *L* 144 fruitles< *L* 145 *line omitted in Q;* Cloudes *L* 146 s *deleted at the end of* Virgin *in L* 147 send) *so Q;* sends *L,P;* he< *L* 148 fruitfullness *L* 149 Lo, where *Q; the stage-direction has been cropped in L, and only a fragment of one letter of it is visible* 151 Th' unhappy *Q* 153 r *of* your *added later in P;* danger< *written above* strange< *deleted in L* 154 politique. *Q* 157 affect *Q* 158 my < *L* 159 already S^{r} *P;* contract is *Q* 159–60 *as one line in Q*

A Diuine witness toot
Vort: Leaue it to me still
I am not without shifting roomes & helpes ——— *Exit Vort:*
For all my proiects I Com̃itt with you!
Cast: Tis an vngodly way to Come to honnour,
I doe not lik't, I loue Lord *Vortiger*
But not these practises, th'are to vncharitable
Const: Are you a virgin
Cast: Never yet my Lord,
Knowne to the will of Man
Const: Oh blessed Creature
And does to much felicity make yo^{u} surfeyt,
Are you in soule assured their is a state
Prepared for you, for you, a glorious one
In midst of heauen now in the state yo^{u} stand in
And had yo^{u} rather after much knowne miserye
Cares and hard labours mingled with a Curse,
Throng but toth doore and hardly gett a place there?
Think, has ye world a folly like this madnesse;
Keepe still that holy and imãculate fire
You Chaste Lampe of eternitye, tis a treasure
Too pretious for deaths moment to pertake,
This twinckling of short life; Disdaine as much
To lett mortality knowe you, as starrs
To kiss ye pauem^{ts}, y'haue a substance
As excellent as theirs, holding yor pureness;
They looke vpon Coruption as you doe
But are starrs still; be you a virgin too
Cast: Ile neuer marry, what though my troth be ingagd
To vortiger; forsakeing all ye world
I saue it well, and doe my faith noe wrong:
Y'haue mightily prevaild, greate vertuous Lord
Ime bound eternally to praise yor goodness

161 *line omitted in Q* 162 not void of shifting *Q;* Exit. *at end of next line in Q* 163 I)ne *L,P; in L* hee *is written in the right margin in another hand;* all projects that I *Q* 164 this an *L,P;* This is an *Q;* vngodly *altered from* vngolly *in P* 165 lik't *L;* loue, Lord, *L* 166 they are too *P* 168–9 *all one line in L* 174 stand in) *so Q;* in *omitted in L,P* 177 o *added to original* dore *in L;* to the door *Q* 178 think *L;* hath *Q;* your madness; *P* 180 chast lump *Q* 183–6 *Q prints 183–4 as one line, otherwise this is Q's line-division;* to lett . . . pauem^{ts}, / y'haue . . . pure / ness . . . doe *L* 185 pureness *L* 186 Corruptions *P* 187 still *L* 188 truth *Q* 191 vertuous Sir, *Q* 192 I am *Q*

[Fol. 9, *recto*]

I Carry thoughts away as pure from man — *Enter Vort: & Gentleman*
As euer made a virgins name immortall
Const: I will doe that for ioy I neuer did
Nor euer will againe — *Exit Castiza*
Gent: My Lord hees taken
Vort: Ime sorry fort, I like not that soe well,
Their somewhat to familliar for their time methinks;
This way of kissing is no Course to vexe him:
Why I that haue a weaker faith and patience
Cold endure more then that Com̃ing from woman;
Dispatch and Bring his answer speedily — *Exit Vortiger*
Gent: My Lord, my gracious Lord
Const: Beshrew thy heart
Gent: They all atend yor grace
Const: I wold not haue em,
'Twould please me better and they'ld all depart,
And leaue ye Court to me, or put me out
And take it to there selues
Gent: The noone is past my Lord,
Meat's vppon ye Table
Const: Meate, away, gett from me,
Thy memory's diseasd; what saints Eues this
Gent: Saint Agatha I take it
Const: Oh is it soe
I am not worthy to be serude before her,
And so returne I pray
Gent: Heele starue the gaurd, & this be sufferd; if we sett Court
Bellyes by a Monastery Clock, he that breakes a fellowes pate
now, will scarse be able to Crack a lowse within this tweluemonth [*Exit*]

193 My thoughts henceforth shall be as pure *Q;* Vo< *L* 194 immortall *written above* eternall *deleted in P;* Gentl< *L* 193–4 *Q has no exit for Castiza, but at this point has:* As he kisses her, / Enter Vortiger and / Gentlemen. 196 nor neuer *P* 198 I am *Q;* fort *L;* well *L* 199 they are *P;* Th'are something *Q;* methi< *L* 200 is no way *Q* 202 woman *L;* from a woman. *Q* 203 p *of* dispatch *altered from* h *in L;* Vortig< *L;* Exit. *Q* 204 my Lord *L* 207 em *L;* them, *Q* 208 if they'ld *Q;* me and they would *P* 209 leave me to my self, *Q* 210 there *altered from* them *in L;* it there *P;* themselves. *Q* 211–218 *line-division as in Q; L has 211–2 as one line, and then:* meate . . . diseasd / what . . . this / . . . oh is it . . . to be / serude . . . I pray 211 my Lord *omitted in Q* 212 on the table: *Q* 214 memory is *Q;* i *of* diseasd *altered from* e *in L* 215 it *omitted in L;* Agatha's I take it. *Q;* as I take it *P* 216 Oh *omitted in Q* 219–21 *as verse in Q* 219 If this *Q;* sufferd *L;* sett< *L* 220 clock: *L;* fellowes < *L* 221 Will not be *Q;* months. *Q;* twel< *L; stage-direction from Q; omitted in L,P*

Enter Vort Deuon & Staff

Cons: Sure tis forgetfulness and not mans will,
That leades him forth into Licentious wayes,
He Cannot Certainly Com̃itt such errors,
And think vppon 'em truely, as they are acting:
Why's abstinence ordeynd but for such seasons
Vort: My Lord y'haue pleasd to put vs to much paines
But we Confess tis portion of o^{r} Dutyes;
Will yor grace please to walke, dinner stayes for yo^{u}.

[Fol. 9, *verso*]

Const: I haue answerd that alreadye
Vort: But my Lord
We must not soe yeild to you, pardon me,
Tis for ye generall good, yo^{u} must be ruld s^{r}:
Your health and life is dearer to vs now,
Think where yo^{u} are, at Court, this is noe monastery
Const: But sir my Conscience keeps still where it was
I may not eate this day
Vort: We haue sworne yo^{u} shall
And plentifully too, we must p^{r}serue yo^{u} S^{r}:
Though youle be willfull; tis noe slight Condition
To be a King
Const: Wold I were lesse then Man
Vort: What, will you make the people rise my Lord,
In greate dispaire off yor Continuance
If you neglect ye meanes that must sustaine yo^{u}
Cons: I neuer eate on Eues
Vort: But now you must
It Concernes others healths that yo^{u} take food
Y'haue Changd yor life, yo^{u} may well Chang yor mood
Const: This is beyond all Cruelltye
Vort: Tis o^{r} Care my Lord *Exevnt Omnes*

222 'Tis sure *Q* 223–4 *stage-direction as in P;* Ente< / Deuon< *L; Q merely has* Enter Vortiger. *after line 226* 225 them *Q* 228 Dutyes *L;* duty: *Q* 229 grace [Co] plesse *P;* to *erased before* dinner *in P* 231–2 *line-division as in Q; all one line in L* 232 me *L* 235 are,) *so Q;* are *L,P* 238–241 *line-division as in Q:* we haue . . . too / we must . . . willfull / tis . . . King *L* 239 too *L* 240 you be *Q;* willfull. *L* 243 What *L; the word is omitted in Q; this speech lacks a prefix in P, but it is marked off by a stroke as a separate speech* 246 Eues) knes *L;* knees *P;* Eeves. *Q* 249 I have chang'd *Q;* you well may *Q* 251 Exeunt: *Q*

Musique *Actvs: Secundus Sce: Prima* *Enter Vortiger & Castiza*

Casti: My Lord I am resolude, tempt me no further
'Tis all to fruitless purpose
Vort: Are you well
Cast: Neuer soe perfect in ye truth of health
As at this Instant
Vort: Then I doubt mine owne
Or that I am not wakeing,
Casti Would you were then,
You'd praise my resolution.
Vort: This is wondrous
Are yo^{u} not mine by Contract.
Cast: Tis most true my Lord
And Ime better blest int, then I look'd for,
In that I am Confind in faith soe strictly

[Fol. 10, *recto*]

Ime bound my Lord to marry none but yo^{u}
Youle grant me that, and you Ile neuer marrye
Vort: It drawes into me violence and hazard
I sawe you kiss ye Kinge
Cast: I grant yo^{u} so s^{r}
Where Could I take my leaue of ye world better
I wrongd not yo^{u}; in that yo^{u} will acknowledge
A King is ye best part ont
Vort: Oh my passion
Castiz: I see you somewhat yeilding to infirmitie S^{r}
I take my leaue
Vort: Why tis not possible
Cast: The fault is in yor faith, time I was gon

II. i. *heading*) Musique *omitted in Q;* ACT. 2. SCENA 1. *Q stage-direction*) *L has* Entiger (*altered from* Enter) *for* Enter Vortiger; Enter Vort: Cast: *P;* Enter Vortiger and Castiza. *Q* 1 farther *Q* 4 y^{e}: way of truth *P* 6–11 *line-division that of Q; in L 6–7, 8–9 and 10–11 are each written as one line only* 6 my own, *Q* 8 *prefix*) i *of* Casti *altered from* e *in L* 9 you would *L;* Youl'd *Q* 13 And I am *Q* 14 Confind, *L,P* 15 I am *Q* 16 you) *so Q;* youle *L,P* 17 draws me into *Q* 20 take leaue *P;* y^{e} *deleted between* take *and* my *in L* 21 you in that, you *Q* 22 of it. *Q* 24 Infirmity; Sir, / I *Q* 27 wer gon *P,Q*

To giue it Better strengthening
Vort: Hark yo^{u} Ladye
Cast: Send yor intent to ye next monestary,
There yo^{u} shall finde my answer ever after,
And soe with my Last dutye to yor Lordshipp
For whose perfections I will pray as hartely
As for mine owne ———— *Exit*
Vort: How am I serud in this:
I offer a vexation to the King,
He sendes it home into my blood with vantage;
Ile putt off time noe Longer; I haue wrought him
Into most mens neglect; Calling his zeale
A deepe pride, hallowed ouer, loue of ease
More then devotion, or the publique benefitt
W^{ch} Catches many mens beleifes; I am stronger too
In peoples wishes, there effections pointe to me;
I loose much time and glorye; that redeemd,
She that now flyes, returnes with Ioy and wonder

[Fol. 10, *verso*]

Greatenes and Womans wish neuer keepe asunder *Ex^{t}*

Hoboys *Dumb show. Enter 2 Villaines, to them Vortiger* seemeing to solissitt them, giues them gold, then sweares them—Exit *Vortiger Enter* to them *Constantius* in priuate meditation, they rudely Come to him, strike downe his Booke and Draw their swordes vppon him, he fairely spredds his armes, and yeilds to thire furys at wch they seeme to be ouer Come wth pittye, But lookeing on ye gold kill him as hee turns his Back, and hurry away his bodye Enter *Vortiger Deuon: Stafford* in [D.S. ii]

30 re *deleted after* yor *in L;* monestary *L* 31 after *L* 33 whose prosperity *Q* 34 my own. *Q* 35 how I am *P* 35–6 *printed as one line in Q* 36 King *L* 37 vantage *L* 38 Longer *L;* brought him *Q;* hi< *L, with the* i *altered from* e 39 neglects, *Q* 40 *after this line in L there are visible fragments of two letters on different lines and part of a pen stroke which apparently enclosed a stage-direction that has been cropped; at this point P has, enclosed by lines,* Brigs / Robrt str / Blackson 42 catcheth *Q;* beleife; *P;* stron< *L (only one minim and the tail of the* g *are visible at the end of the line)* 43 point at me. *Q;* to m< *L (only two minims of the* m *are visible at the end of the line)* 44 redeemd *L* 46 ne're *Q; no* Exit *in P*

Dumb-show. No margin in P. 1 Villaines *L* 2 them *L* 4 him *L* 6 furye, *P* 8 vpon *P;* kills *L,P* 9 & Stafford *P*

[D.S. ii]

priuate Conference: to them Enter ye murderers p^{r}senting ye head to *Vortiger,* he seems to express much sorrow, and before ye astonished Lordes, makes officers lay hold on em; who offering to Com towardes *Vortiger* are Commanded to be hurryed away as to execution: then ye Lordes, all seemeing respect, Crowne *Vortiger,* then bring in *Castiza,* who seems to be brought in vnwillingly by *Deuon:* & *Stafford* who Crowne her and then giue her to *Vortiger,* she going forth with him, wth a kind of Constraind Consent; then enter *Aurelius* & *Vther* ye two *Brothers* who much astonished seeme to fly for there safety:

[Chor. iii]

Ray: When nothing Could prevaile to tyre
The good Kings patience, Death had hyre
In wicked strengths to take his life,
In whom a while there fell a strife
Of Pittye and furye, but ye gold
Made pittye faint, and furye bold;
Then to Vortiger they Bring
The head of that religious King
Who faineing greife to Cleere his guilt

[Fol. 11, *recto*]

Makes ye slaughterers Blood be spilt:
Then Crowne they him, and force ye mayd
That vowd a virgin life to wedd,
Such a strength greate power extendes

11 pres/ting the head *P* 15 Lordes *L;* Lordes seemeing *P* 16 respect *L;* brings *L,P* 17 vnwillingly Deuon: *L,P* 18 *second* her *written over* it *in P* 20 a Constraind *P* 22 there *omitted in P. Q omits* Hoboys *and reads* who seems . . . them with gold, *in line 2, and in line 3 has* them, and Exit. Enter Constantius meditating, they rudely strike *From line 5 Q continues:* Book, draw their Swords, he kneels and spreads his arms, they kill him, hurry him off. Enter Vortiger, Devonshire, and Stafford in Conference, to them the Villains presenting the head, he seems sorrowful, and in rage stabbs them both. Then they crown Vortiger, and fetch in Castiza, who comes unwillingly, he hales her, and they crown her. Aurelius and Uther Brothers of Constantius, seeing him crowned, draw and fly.

Chor. iii. prefaced in Q by Enter Raynulph. 2 they did hire *Q* 3 Two wicked Rogues *Q* 5 Of *omitted in L,P;* furye *L* 6 bold *L* 8 thee head *L* 10 slaughterers) *so Q;* slaughterous *L,P* 11 ye King *deleted between* Crowne *and* they *in L;* may< *L* 12 virgins *P*

It Conquers fathers, kinn, and friendes;
And since fate's pleasd to Change her Life
She prooues as holy in a wife:
More to tell were to betraye
What deeds in there owne tounges must saye,
Only this ye good King dead
The Brothers poore in safetye fledd. ——— *Exit*

Enter Vortiger a Gentleman [II, ii]

Gent: My Lord
Vort: I feare thy news will fetch a Curse
It Comes wth such a violence
Gent: The people are vpp in armes against yo^{u}
Vort: Oh this dreame of glorye, I Cold wish
A sting into thee; theirs noe such felt in *Hell,*
The fellow but to mine I feele now:
Sweete power before I Can haue power to tast thee
Must I foreuer Loose thee: whats the impostume
That swells em now,
Gent: Y^{e} murder of Constantius ——— *Exit Gentleman*
Vort: Vlcers of realmes, they hated him aliue,
Grew weary of ye minuite of his raigne
Compared with some kings time, & poysoned him
Often before he died, in there black wishes;
Calld him an evill of there owne electing,
And is there ignorant zeale so fierye now,
Showte When all their thanks are Cold, the mutable hearts
That moue in their falce breasts: prouide me safety;
Hark I heare ruin threaten me, wth a voice
That imitates thunder. *Enter Gent*

[Fol. 11, *verso*]

Gent: Wheirs the King

14 him and friends *P;* Kindred, Friends. *Q;* e *inserted later between* d *and* s *of* friendes *in L* 15 to Chang'd *P*

II. ii. *stage-direction*) Enter Vortiger (Crowned) a Gentleman meeting him. *Q* 2 thy *altered from* the *in L* 4 up / In Armes *Q* 5–7 I Cold wish . . . feele now: *omitted in Q* 8 tast< *L;* have time to *Q* 9 impostum< *L* 10 them *Q* 11 *stage-direction omitted in Q; only one minim of final* n *visible in L* 12 realmes *L;* aliue *L* 14–15 *omitted in Q* 14 time *L* 16 electing *L* 18 Showte *omitted in Q;* their) *so Q;* this *L,P;* hea< *L* 19 saf< *L* 21 Gen< *L;* Enter a second / Gentleman. *Q* 22 *prefix*) 2^{d} Gent. *Q*

Vort: Who takes him
Gent Send peace to all yor royall thoughts my Lord *Enter Hengist Hersus Drum and soldiers*
A ffleete of valiant saxons newly Landed
Offer ye truth of all their seruice to you
Vort: Saxons! my wishes; let 'em haue free Entrance
And plenteous welcoms from all harts y^{t} loue vs,
They neuer Could Come happier
Heng: Health powre and victorye to *Vortiger*
Vort: Their Can be noe more wishd to a Kings pleasures
If all the Languadges earth speakes were ransackd;
Yo^{r} names I know not, But so much good fortune
And warrented worth lightens yor faire aspects!
I Cannot But in armes of loue enfold you;
Heng The Mistris of o^{r} Births, hope-fruitfull-Germanie
Calls me *Hengistus* and this Captaine Horsus,
A man low built, But s^{r} in acts of valour
Flame is not swifter: we are all my Lord
The sons of fortune, she has sent vs forth
To thriue, by ye redd sweate of o^{r} owne merritts:
And since after ye rage of many a tempest
Our fate has Cast vs vppon Brittaines Boundes
We offer yo^{u} ye first ffruites of o^{r} woundes
Vort: Which we shall deerely prize, the meanst blood spent
Shall at wealthes fountaine make his owne Content.
Heng: You double vigor in vs then my Lord *Exevnt omnes*
Pay is the soule of them that thriue byth sword

24 *prefix)* 2^{d} Gent. *Q; stage-direction)* Hengist *added later above the line over a caret mark in L; Q has the direction after line 29 and omits* Drum and 27 them *Q* 28 all hats *P;* vs *L* 31 h *of* wishd *a later insertion in L;* wish to a kins pleasure *P;* no more pleasure to a King *Q* 32 spake *Q;* ransackd *L* 36 hope-faithfull-Germanie *L,P;* births hope, fruitfull Germany, *Q* 37 Horsus) *this is normally the spelling of Q only, and is not usually found in the MSS; P has Hersus here* 38 but in acts *P;* but yet in deeds of Arms *Q* 43 fate *altered from original* faith *in L;* Fates have *Q;* Boundes *altered from* Lands *in P* 44 woundes *written over an original* owne *in both L and P* 45 shall euer prize, *P* 46 its own *Q;* t *of* Content *added later by scribe in a very small hand in L* 47 *no prefix in P, although the speech is marked off as a separate one by a stroke;* vs now *P* 48 of such as *Q;* that liue *P;* Exeunt *only after line 48 in Q*

Allarums and skirmish Enter Vortiger & Gentleman [II, iii]

Gent: My Lord these saxons bring a fortune wth em
Staines any Romaine success.

[Fol. 12, *recto*]

Vort: On, speake forward,
I will not take a moment ffrom thy tydings
Gent: The maine supporters of this insurrection
They haue taken prisoners, and the rest soe tame
They stoope to the least grace that flowes from mercye
Vort: Neuer Came powre guided wth better starrs
Then these mens ffortitudes, yet th'are misbeleeuers
Tis to my reason wondrous ————
Y'haue giuen me such a first tast of yor worth
Twill neuer from my loue, sure when lifs gone
Y^{e} memory will follow my soule still
Participateing im̃ortality with't:
And hers ye misery of earthes limited glory
Theirs not a way reveald to giue yo^{u} hono^{r}
Aboue ye sume wch yor owne praises giue you.

Enter Heng: Horsus wth Drums & Colours soldiers leading prisoners

Heng: Indeed my lord we hold when alls somd vpp
That Can be made for worth to be exprest
The fame that a Man wins himselfe is best;
That he may Call his owne, hono^{rs} put to him
Make him noe more a man then his Cloathes doe
And as soone taken off, for as in warmth
The heate Comes from ye bodye, not ye weedes,

II. iii. *stage-direction) In Q* Enter Vortiger and Gentlemen. *is centred and* Alarm and / Skirmishes. *is in the right margin* 1 *prefix)* 1 Gent. *Q;* them *Q* 2 Stay any *Q; in L there are two marks* ŏ ŏ *opposite this line in the left margin, and after it in L and P comes an actor's name:* Rob: Briggs *in L and* Robb Briggs *in P* 3 on *L;* forward *L;* forwards, *Q* 4 one minute *Q* 5 *prefix)* 1 Gent. *Q; first* r *of* insurrection *a later insertion in L* 6 and, *L* 7 from m< *L* 8 by better *Q;* Enter H< / Horsus < / Co< / soldiers l< / prisoner< *L;* Enter Heng: Hers: with / Drum Collours soldiers / leading prisoners *P;* Enter Hengist and Horsus / with Prisoners. *Q* 9 th'are) *so Q;* yet are *L,P* 10 Which to my reason is wonderous. *Q* 12 love, when life is *Q* 13 memory sure will follow, my *Q* 14 my soule still *deleted before* immortallity *in P;* with it *P,Q* 15 But here's *Q* 16 to any honour *Q* 17 the same *Q;* the fame *Bullen;* own merits *Q;* giues *P* 18 all'is *P* 20 a Man wins) *so P,Q;* a Mans wines *L;* best *L* 22 Cloathe< *L* 23 And are as soon ta'ne off; for in the warmth *Q* 24 weedes *L*

So mans true fame, must strike from his owne deedes;
And since by this event wch fortune speakes vs
This Land appeares the faire predistind soyle
Ordaind for o^{r} good hap: we Craue my Lord
A little earth to thriue on: what yo^{u} please
Wheir weele but keepe a Nursery of good spirrits
To fight for yo^{u} and yours.

Enter Symon with a hide

Vort: S^{r} for o^{r} treasure

[Fol. 12, *verso*]

Tis open to yor merits, as our loue,
But for y'are strangers in religion Cheifly,
W^{ch} is ye greatest alienation Can bee,
And breeds most factions in ye bloods of men
I must not grant yo^{u} that.

Heng: Spretious my lord
I see a paterne, Bee it but soe little
As yond poore hide will Compasse

Vort: How, ye hide

Heng: Rather then nothing s^{r}

Vorti: Since y'are so reasonable
Take soe much in the best part of our Kingdome

Heng: We thank yor grace, riuers from bubbling springs [*Exit Vortiger*]
Haue rise at first, and greate from abiect things:
Stay yonder fellow, hee Came Luckilye
And he shall fare well fort, what ere hee bee;
Weele thank our fortune in rewarding him

Hers: Stay fellow

Symo: How, fellow, tis more then yo^{u} know whether I be yor fellow or noe for I am sure you see me not

Hers: Come whats ye price of yor Hide

Symo Oh vnreasonable villaine, he wold buy ye house ore a mans head, Ile be sure now to make my bargaine wisely, they may buy me out of my skine else;

25 true fame true fame *P;* owne d< *L* 26 fortunes speake *P* 30 wehere will *with* we *also inserted over a caret mark between* wehere *and* will *in P* 31 *the stage-direction comes four lines later in Q* 32 S^{r} *omitted in P* 33 to, yor *L* 35 greatess *L* 35–36 *within parentheses in Q* 36 of people *P* 37 not yield to that. *Q* 40 yon *Q* 41 how *L* 45 bubbling) *so Q;* blushing *L,P; no stage-direction in L,P,Q* 47 L *of* luckilye *over* l *in L* 48 bee *L* 51 *This and the rest of Simon's speeches in this scene are printed as verse in Q;* how fellow *L* 52 no, I am *Q* 53 Heng. *Q* 54 villaine *L;* u *above the line over a caret mark in* buy *in L;* buy house *P;* over *Q* 55 head *L*

whose hide wold yo^u haue, mine or the Beasts, theirs
little difference in there Complexions, I thinke mine
be the better o'th twaine, you shall see for yor loue
and buy for yor mony, a pestlence on yo^u all, how
haue yo^u guld me; you buy an oxehide, yo^u buy a
good Calffes gather: they are all hungry soldiers
and I tooke em for shomakers

Heng: Hold fellow; prethee hold: right a foole worldling
That kickes at all good fortune, whose man art thou

[Fol. 13, *recto*]

Symo: I am a seruant, yet I am a Masterless man s^r.

Heng: How; prethee hows that now

Symo: Very nimbly s^r: my Maisters dead and I serue my Mistris.
I am a Masterlesse man s^r, shees now a widdow, and I
am ye foreman of her tannpitt

Heng: Hold you and thank yor fortune not yor witt

Symo: Faith and I thank yor Bounty and not yor wisdome, yo^u are
not troubled greatly with witt neither it seemes; now
by this light a nest of yellow whammers, what will
become of me; if I Can keepe all these without hanging
of my selfe, I am happier then a hundred of my nei
ghbours: you shall haue my skin into the bargaine to,
willingly s^r, then if I Chaunse to die like a dogg, the labour
will be saued of fleaing. Ile vndertake s^r. you shall
haue all ye skins of our ꝑish at this rate, man and
womans;

Heng: Sirrah giue eare to me now; take yor hide
And Cutt it all into ye slenderest thongs
That Can beare strength to hold.

Symo: That were a Iest indeed, goe and spoyle all the Leather;

57 would you buy, *Q;* Beasts *L;* There is *Q* 58 o *of* Complexions *altered from* t *in L* 59 by'th better *L;* be the better of the *P;* Is the blacker of the two; *Q* 61 deceiv'd me? *Q* 62 a Calves *Q* 63 them for honest Shoomakers. *Q* 66 Maister *deleted between* a *and* seruant *in L;* yet a masterless *Q;* Masterless m< *L* 67 how that *L;* how, that *P;* Heng. Prithee how can that be? *Q* 68 Master is *P,Q;* and now I *Q;* I haue *P;* serue *written over original* haue *in L;* my < *L* 69 s^r *omitted in Q;* she is *Q;* Ergo, I am *Q;* and < *L;* 72 and *above the line over a caret mark between* Bounty *and* not *in L;* yo^u < *L* 73 troubled with wit neither greatly, it seems: *Q;* seemes < *L* 74 what < *L* 75 ha< *L;* hanging / My self, *Q* 76 selfe. *L;* my < *L* 77 to < *L;* bargain, / Then if *Q* 78 s^r *L;* the l< *L* 79 fleaing me; *Q;* you s< *L* 80 of *altered from* in *in L;* in our *Q;* man a< *L;* this price, mens and womens. *Q* 82 give good ear *Q;* now *L;* me; now *Q;* the Hide *Q* 85 jest y'faith, / Spoil all *Q;* the L< *L*

sin and pity, why twold shoe halfe yor armye
Heng: Doot I bid you
Symo: What, Cut it all in thongs: hunch: this is like ye vanitie of
yor Romane gallants that Cannot were good suites
but they must haue em Cutt and slasht into Iiggets
that ye very Crimson Tafity sitts blushing at theire
follyes: I would I might perswade you s^{r} from the
humo^{r} of Cutting, tis but a kind of swaggering Condition
and nothing profitable, what ant were but well
pinckt, twold last Longer for a somer suit.
Heng: What a grosse lumpe of ignorance haue I lighted on
I must be forcd to beat my drift into him:

[Fol. 13, *verso*]

Looke you, to make yo^{u} wiser then yor parents,
I haue soe much ground giuen me, as this hide will Compas
W^{ch} as it is, is nothing
Symo: Nothing quotha,
Why twill not keepe a hog
Heng: Now with the vantage
Cutt into seuerall parcells 'twill stretch farr
And make a liberall sircuitt
Symo: A shame on yor Crafty Hide, is this yor Cuning; I haue
learnd more knauery now then ever I shall
shake off while I liue: Ile goe purchase landes by Cowes
tailes, and vndoe the ꝑish: three good Bulls pizels wold sett
vpp a Man for ever, this is like a pin a day dubled to sett vp
a haberdasher of small wares
Heng: Thus men as meane to thriue, as we must learne Captaine
Sett in a foot at first
Symo: A foote doe you Call it,

86 pity *L* 87 Do it *Q* 88 what *L;* hum, *Q;* the is *L;* vani< *L* 89 Romane *altered from* Romans *in L;* sh< *L,* suites *P,Q* 90 them *Q;* slasht in *Q;* Ii< *L* 91 Taffaties sit *Q;* at the< *L* 92 you from this *Q;* from < *L;* from the *P;* 93 Cutting *L;* swaggering < *L;* swagger in *P;* but a swaggering *Q* 94 and it were *P;* if it / Were *Q;* but < *L* 96 a cross lump *Q;* I lig< *L* 98 you *L;* parents *L* 99 r *of* ground *over* u *in L;* will Compas / W^{ch}) *line-division that of Q;* will / Compas *L,P* 101–2 *line-division of Q; all one line in L,P* 103 w *of* with *altered from* is *in L* 103–5 *line-division of Q;* now . . . parcells / 'twill stretch . . . sircuitt *L* 104 parcells *altered from* peices *in L;* pieces *Q;* stretch far) *so Q;* far *omitted in L,P* 105 i *of* sircuitt *over* e *in L* 106 Hide *L;* Cuning *L* 108 claw off *Q;* land *Q;* Cowtailes *P,Q* 110 a day to set *Q* 112 that mean *Q;* Captaine *omitted in Q* 114–6 *as prose in L; lines 115–6 printed as one in Q*

The Deuills in that foote, y^{t} takes vpp all
This Leather.
Heng: Dispatch, away, and Cutt it Carefully
With all ye advantage sirrah
Sym: You Could neuer haue lighted vpon such a fellow Captaine
to serue yor turne; I haue such a trick of stretching too, I
learnt it of a tanners Man that was hangd last sessions,
that Ile warrant yo^{u} Ile get you in a mile and a
halfe more then yo^{u} are aware of
Heng: Pray serue me soe as oft as yo^{u} will sir.
Sym: Ime Casting about for nine Acres to make yo^{u} a gar
den plott, out of one of ye Buttocks
Heng: Twill be a good soyle for nosegayes
Symo: Twill be a good soyle for Cabiges, to stuff out the guts
of yor ffellowes there —————— *Exit Symo:*
Heng: You sirs goe see it Carefully performd
It is ye first foundations of o^{r} fortunes
On Brittaines earth, & ought to be imbracd

[Fol. 14, *recto*]

With a respect, nere linckt to adoration:
Me thinks it soundes to me a faire assurance
Of large hono^{rs} and hopes; dos't not Captaine?
Hers: How many haue begun wth less at first
That haue departed Emperours from theire Bodyes
And left there Carcasses as much in monument
As would erect a Colledge,
Heng: Theirs the fruiteę
Of their religious shewes too, to lye rotting
Vnder a Million spent in gold and marble
When thousandes left behind dyes without shelter
Haueing nor house nor food;

115 Devil is *Q;* e *of* Deuills *over* i *in L* 117 Dispatch away and *L;* Dispatch, and *Q* 117–8 *printed as one line in Q* 119–20 fellow / To serve your turn, Captain; *Q* 121 Last Sessions at Maidstone, / I'le warrant *Q* 122 you Ile get *added later in the left margin in P;* get you a mile *Q;* mile and and *L* 123 y'are *Q* 124 as *above the line over a caret mark between* soe *and* oft *in L* 125 I am *Q;* make a *Q* 129 your Followers *Q; no stage-direction in Q* 130 You sirs *omitted in Q* 131 foundation *Q* 132 a *of* earth *over* r *and* c *of* imbracd *retouched in L* 135 promisses *deleted after* large *in P;* does it *Q* 137 have had Emperours from their bodies sprung, *Q;* Body< *L* 138 ca *of* Carcasses *added above the line over a caret mark in L* 139–40 *so Q;* Colledge, theirs the fruiteę. / Heng: of their *L,P* 141 shews shewes *L;* shew *Q,* 143–5 *omitted in Q* 143 shelt< *L* 144 noe house or food *P*

Hers: A pretious Charitye
But wheire shall we make Choice of o^{r} ground Captaine
Heng: About ye fruitfull Bancks of vbrious Kent
A fatt and Oliue soyle, there we Came in
Oh Captaine h'as giuen I know not what
Hers: Long may he giue soe
Heng: I tell ye sirrah he that begd a feild
Of fourescore Acres for a garden plott
'Twas pretty well butt he Came short of this
Hers: Send ouer for more saxons
Heng: With all speede Captaine
Hers: Espetially for Roxena
Heng: Who my daughter
Hers: That starr of Germany, forgett not her s^{r}.
Shees a faire fortunate maide, I shall betray my selfe,
Faire is shee and most fortunate may she bee
But in maide lost for ever, my desire
Has beene ye Close Confusion of that name
A treasure tis, able to make more theeues

[Fol. 14, *verso*]

Then Cabinetts set open to entice,
W^{ch} learnes one theft, y^{t} neuer knew ye vice
Heng: Som Ile dispatch with speede
Hers: Doe you forgett not *showte & flourish*
Heng: Mary pray help my memory if I should.
Her: Roxena you remember
Heng: What more deere sir
Hers: I see you neede no helpe, yor memorys Cleere s^{r}
Heng: Those soundes lept from our Armye *Enter Gent. saxon*
Hers: They were to Cheerefull
To voice a bad event,
Heng: Now s^{r} yor news

146 of ground *P;* Ca< *L* 147 uberous *Q* 149 he has given he knows *Q* 158 Germany *L* 159 She is *Q;* I shall betray my selfe *omitted in Q;* sel< *L* 160 Fair she is, and fortunate *Q* 161–2 *line-division as in Q;* but in . . . beene y^{e} / Close . . . *L* 163 tis *L* 165 learn them theft *Q* 166 Come, I'le *Q;* t *blotted and deleted at the end of* dispatch *in L* 167 Do, forget none. *Q;* showte flourish *P; no stage-direction in Q* 168 helpe me if *P;* if I should *omitted in Q* 171 helpe *L;* I se *deleted in P;* memory is *P;* I see your memory's clear, Sir. *Q* 172 Those shouts *Q;* Enter Gent *P;* Enter a Gentleman *three lines later in Q* 173–4 *all as one line in L; line-division as in Q* 174 voice bad *P*

Gent: Sax: Roxena ye faire
Heng: True she shall be sent for.
Gent: Sax: Shees heere
Heng: What saist
Gent: Sax: Shes Com s^{r}
Hers: A new youth
Begins me ore againe
Gent: Followed yo^{u} Close s^{r}.
With such a zeale as Daughter neuer equald
Exposd herselfe to all ye mercilesse dangers
Sett in mankind or fortune, not regarding
Ought but yor sight
Heng: Her loue is Infinite to me
Hors: Most Charitably sensurd; tis her Cuning,
The loue of her owne lust, wch makes a woman
Gallop downe hill as feareless as a drunkard,
Theirs noe true Loadstone ith world but that;
It drawes em through all stormes, by sea or shame;
Lifs loss is thought too small to pay that game
Gent: What followes more of her will take yo^{u} strongly
Heng: How
Gent: Nay tis worth yor wonder
Heng: I thrist fort

[Fol. 15, *recto*]

Gent: Her heart Ioy rauishd at yor late successe
Being ye early morneing of yor fortunes
So prosperously now opening at her Com̃ing
She takes a Cup of gold and midst ye armye
Teaching her knee a Current Cheerefulnes
W^{ch} well became her, dranck a liberall health
To ye Kinges ioyes and yours, the King in p^{r}sence
Who with her sight but her behauiour Cheifely
Or Cheife I know not which, but one, or both,

176 (and 178 and 180) prefix) >t: Sax: *L;* Gent: *only in P,Q;* a *of* Roxena *added later in L* 178 here, Sir. *Q* 180 S *of* Sax: *over* G *in L* 181 new age *P* 181–2 *all as one line in L* 183 *a stroke to indicate the conclusion of a speech erased after this line in L* 189 Charitable *P* 191 ll *of* hill *over* s *in L;* s *of first* as *a later insertion in L* 192 in the *Q;* that *L* 193 them *Q;* shame *L* 198 *omitted in Q* 199 *prefix omitted in Q;* with your *Q* 200 ne *of* morneing *added above the line over a caret mark in L* 201 prosperously opening *P;* prosperously new opening *Q* 203 a reverend cheerfulnes, *Q* 206 behuuiour *L* 207 which but one, or both *L;* Or chief but one or both, I know not which, *Q*

But hees soe farr boue my expression Caught,
Twere Art enough for one mans time and portion
To speake him and misse nothinge
Heng: This is astonishing
Hers: Oh this endes bitter now, our Close hidd flame
Will breake out of my hart, I Cannot keepe it
Heng: Gaue yo^{u} attention to this Captaine, how now man
Hers: A kind of greife about these times oth moone still,
I feele a paine like a Convulsion
A Crampe at hart, I know not what name fitts it
Heng Nor neuer seeke one fort, let it goe
Wthout a name, wold all greifes were serud soe
Our vseing of em manerly makes em grow

flourish
Enter Vort.
Roxena
attendants

Hors: A loue knott already, arme in arme
Vort: Whats he lays Clame here
Heng: In right of fatherhood
I Challeng an obedient part my Lord
Vort: Tak't and send back ye rest
Heng: What means yor grace
Vort: Youle keepe noe more then w^{t} belongs to yo^{u}, will yo^{u},
Heng: Thats all my Lord, it all belongs to me yet,
I keepe a husbands Interest till he Come,
Yet out of dutye and respect of maiestie

[Fol. 15, *verso*]

I send her back yor seruant
Vort: my M^{rs} s^{r} or nothing
Heng: Com agen
I neuer thought to haue heard so ill of thee
Vort: How s^{r} soe ill
Heng: So beyond detestabell,

208 farr, *L* 209 ons mans *L* 214 attention, Captain? *Q* 215 time *P;* of the *Q;* stil< *L* 217 know what *P;* fitts < *L* 218 for it, *Q;* flourish / Enter <> / Ro<> / <> *L;* flourish Cornet Enter Vort: / Rox: and attendance *P;* Florish. / Enter Vortiger, / Roxena, &c. *Q* 220 *omitted in Q* 221 already *L* 222 claim to her? *Q* 224 my Lord *omitted in Q* 225 take it *P,Q* 227 you will take noe *P;* what / Belongs *Q;* will yo^{u} *omitted in Q* 228 Lord *L;* me, yet *L;* yet *omitted in Q* 229 yet *deleted at the beginning of the line,* her *altered to* y^{e} *deleted before* husbands *and a small* a *inserted before the deleted word in L;* the husbands *Q;* a Husbands part *P* 230 to Majesty *Q* 233–4 *all one line in Q, viz.:* Come again, I never thought to hear so ill of thee. 234 neue *L;* to haue liude to haue heard so ill of / thee *L,P* 235 s^{r} *added above the line over a caret mark in P* 236 soe ill beyond *P;* ill *deleted before* beyond *in L*

To be an honest vassaile is som Calling,
Poore is ye worst off that, shame Comes not toot,
But M^{rs}, thats ye only Com̃on bayte:
Fortune sitts at all ours Catching whores wth it,
And plucks em vp by Clusters: theirs my sword my Lord
And if yor strong desires ayme at my blood
W^{ch} runs too purely their, a nobler way
Quench it in mine
Vort: I neere tooke sword in vaine,
Hengist wee heere Create the Earle of Kent
Hors: Oh that will doot, twill doot,
Vort: What ayles our friend, looke to him
Rox: Oh tis his Epilepsie, I know it well,
I holp him once in Germany, Comst agen?
A virgins right hand stroakt vpon his heart
Giues him ease streight But tmust be a pure virgin
Or ells it brings no Comforth
Vort: What a taske
She puts vppon herselfe vn-vrgd for puritie;
The proofe of this will bring loues rage vpon me
Roxe: Oh this would mad a Woman, theirs no plauge
In loue to indiscretion
Hers: Pish this Cures not
Rox: Doost thinke Ile euer wrong thee
Hers Oh most feelingly

[Fol. 16, *recto*]

But Ile prevent it now, and breake thy necke
Wth thine owne Cuning, thou hast vndertooke
To giue me help, to bring in royall Creditt
Thy Crackt virginitie, But Ile spoyle all;
I will not stand on purpose though I Could,
But fall still to disgrace thee
Rox: What yo^{u} will not
Hers: I haue no other way to help my selfe

238 shame) *so Q;* that shames *L,P* 239 that the *Q;* Mistris is the *P;* worst *deleted before* only *in P* 239–40 bayte / fortune sitts . . . whore wth / and *L;* sets *Q;* whore *L,P,Q;* with it, *P,Q* 241 them *Q* 243 noble *P* 245 vaine *L* 247 twill doot *omitted in Q* 248 friend *L* 249 Epilepsie *L;* well *L* 250 holp) hope *L,P,* helpt *Q;* Comes it agen? *P,Q* 252 it must *P,Q* 255 puritie *L;* unurged purity! *Q* 256 The truth of this *Q;* brings *P;* into me. *Q* 257 there's no proof *Q* 258 *second* i *of* indiscretion *over* e *and blotted in L* 263 thy *Q;* undertaken *Q* 265 virgintie *L;* all *L* 266 Could *L*

For when thou't knowne to be a whoore impostrous
I shall bee sure to keepe thee;
Rox: Oh s^{r} shame me not
Y'haue had w^{ts} pretious, try my faith yet once more,
Vndoe me not at first in Chast opinion
Hers: All this art shall not make me finde my leggs
Rox: I prethee: wilt thou willfully Confound me
Hers: Well Ime Content for this time to recouer
To saue thy Creddit, and byte in my paine,
But if thou ever failst me, I will fall
And thou shalt neuer gett me vp againe
Rox: Agreed twix't you and I s^{r}, see my Lord
A poore maids w^{rk}: the Man may pass for health now,
Amongst thee Cleerest bloodes and whose are nicest.
Vort: I haue heard of woemen bring men on there knees
But few that ere restord 'em. how now Captaine
Hers: My Lord me thinks I Could doe things past Man
I am soe renewd in vigor, I Long most
For violent excersise to take me downe
My ioyes so high in Blood, I am aboue frailtie
Vort: My Lord of Kent
Heng: Yo^{r} Loues vnworthy Creature
Vort: Seast thou this faire Chaine, think vpon ye meanes

[Fol. 16, *verso*]

To keepe it Linckd for euer
Heng: Oh my Lord
Tis many degrees sundred from y^{t} hope
Besides yor Grace has a young vertuous Queene
Vort: I say think ont, thinke ont?
Hers: And this wind hold!
I shall euen fall to my old desease againe {*flourish*

270 ou *of* thou't *superimposed on other letters in L;* thou art *P;* th'art *Q* 273 w^{t} *L;* whats spretious *P;* what is most precious, *Q;* yet once more *omitted in Q;* more *L* 274 opinion *is a minim short in L* 275 me feel my Legs. *Q* 276 wilt thee *P;* do not wilfully *Q;* the *deleted before* me *in L* 277 I am *Q* 283 Among *Q;* and those *Q; the position of the dot over the* i *in the last word of the line makes it look like* incest *in L* 284 brought *Q* 285 euer stord 'em. *L,P;* e're restor'd them, *Q* 286 o *of* doe *altered from* e *in L* 287 I'me *Q;* 289 I'me *Q;* fralitie *L* 291 your Lordes *P* 292 Faire Chaire, *L,P;* Chain? *Q;* meane< *L* 294–5 *all as one line in L; line-division that of Q* 295 my hope, *Q* 297 I say think on it. *Q* 298–9 hold! I / shall *L;* If this wind hold I fall to my old disease. *Q;* flourish Cornets *omitted in Q;* flourish Cornets E *after 299 and* Exeunt: *after 301 in P*

Vort: Theirs no fault in thee But to Come so late,
All els is excellent; I Chide none But ffate. { *Cornets Exe:*

Actus Tertius Sce Pr^{a}: Enter Hersus: Roxena: [III, i]

Roxe: I haue no Conceit now that yo^{u} euer loude me
But as lust held yo^{u} for the time
Hers: Soe soe;
Rox: Doe yo^{u} pine at my advancement sir
Hers: Oh Barrennes
Off vnderstanding, what a right loue is this
Tis you that fall, I that am reprehended,
What height of honno^{rs} emynence and fortune
Shold rauish me from you,
Rox Who Can tell that s^{r}, whats he Can iudge
Of a Mans appetite, before he sees him eate,
Who knowes ye strength of anyes Constancye
That neuer yet was tempted. we Can Call
Nothing our owne; if they be deeds to Come,
They are only ours when they are past and don?
How blest are you aboue yor apprehension
If yor desire would lend you soe much patience,
To examine ye adventurous Condition
Of our affections, wch are full of hazard,
And draw in ye times goodness to defend vs:
First this bold Course of ours Cant last long
Or neuer does in any without shame,

[Fol. 17, *recto*]

And that you know Brings danger, and the greater
My ffather is in Blood, as hees well risen,
The greater will ye storme of his rage bee,

301 else *is inserted above the line over a caret mark in P;* Chide) *so Q;* Chid *L,P*
III. i. *heading*) Actius *L;* ACT. 3. SCENA 1. *Q;* r *of* Enter *over* e *in L;* Hersus & Roxena *P;* Horsus and Roxena. *Q* 2 led you *Q* 3 See, see. *Q* 5–7 *line-division that of Q;* oh Barrennes, . . . loue is / this tis . . . *L* 7 reprehended *L* 8 honour *P;* honours, eminence of fortune *Q* 10–12 Who . . . Sir? / What's . . . appetite / Before . . . constancy / That *Q* 13 Ca *of* Call *over* te *in L* 14 own, if *Q; one minim too many in* Come *in L* 15 Th'are *Q* 17 desires *P* 18 T'examine *Q;* Condition, *L;* Conditions *P* 20 vs *L* 21 yours Cant *P;* cannot *Q* 22 Nor ever *Q;* a *of* any *over* e *in L* 24 danger *L;* greate< *L* 25 he is *Q*

Gainst his Bloods wronging: I haue Cast for this,
Tis not advancement that I loue alone
Tis loue of shelter to keepe shame vnknowne.
Hers: Oh were I sure of thee, as tis impossible
Their to be ever sure, wheir thers noe hold,
Yo^{r} pregnant hopes shold not be long ariseing
Rox: By what assurance haue yo^{u} held me thus farr
W^{ch} you found firme, despaire you now in that
Hors True, that was good security for ye time
But admitt a Change of state: when y'are advancde
You woemen haue a french toy in yor pride
You make your friend Come Croutching, or perhapps
To bow ith hams the Better, he is put
To Complem^{t} three houres with yor Cheife Gentlewoeman,
Then perhaps not admitted, nay nor neuer
Thats ye more noble fashion: fforgettfulnes
Tis the pleasingst vertue any one Can haue
That rises vp from no thing, ffor by ye same
Forgetting all, they forget from whence they Came
An excellent propertie for obliuion.
Rox: I pitty all ye fortunes of poore gentlewoemen
Now in myne owne vnhappinesse, when we haue giuen
All that wee haue to men, whats their requitall,
An Ill facde Iealousy, wch resembles much
The mistrustfullnes of an insatiate theife,
That scarce beleiues he has all, though he has stripd
The true man naked, and left nothing on him
But the hard Cord that bindes him: so are wee

[Fol. 17, *verso*]

First robbd and then left bound with Iealousie;
Sure he that findes vs now has a greate purchase

27 Blood *L,P;* Against his bloods *Q;* riseing *deleted before* wronging *in L;* Cast f< *L* 28 loue) *so Q;* haue *L,P* 29 *first* n *of* unknowne *over* r *in L* 30 weere *altered from* heere *in P* 31 hold *L* 32 hopes, *L;* soe long *P;* long in rising. *Q* 34 not in that. *Q* 35 true *L* 36 But in a change *Q;* advan'd *P* 38 perhapp< *L* 39 in th'hams *Q* 40 Gentlew< *L;* chief woman, *Q* 41 no nor ever, *Q* 42 more nobler *P* 43 Is the most pleasing vertue they can have *Q* 44 That do spring up *Q* 45 forget whence *Q;* Can< *L* 46 of oblivion. *Q* 47 poor women *Q* 48 Now *omitted in Q;* my *Q;* giu< *L* 49 our requital? *Q* 50 Ill facde) *so Q;* faide *L,P;* that resembles *Q* 52 stri< *L* 53 and lefe *L* 55 by jealousie. *Q;* Iealousie *L* 56–63 *marked for omission in L,P by a line across the page after line 55 and a line from the edge of the margin after line 63 as far as the word* both; *a vertical line in the margin connects the two horizontal lines; Q omits from the beginning of line 56 to* both *in line 63*

And well he gaines that buildes anothers ruines?
Yet man ye only seed thats sowne in envy
Whom Little would suffize as any Creature
Either in food or pleasure; yet tis knowne
What wold giue ten enough Contents not one.
A strong diseasd Conceit, may tell strang tales to you
And so abuse vs both: take but th'opinion
Of Common reason, and youle finde't impossible
That yo^{u} shold loose me in this kinges advancem^{t}
Who heares a vsurper, as he has ye Kingdome
So shall he haue my loue by vsurpation,
The right shall be in thee still; my ascension
To Dignitie is but to wafte ye vpward
And all vsurpers haue a falling sickness
They Cannot keepe vp long,
Hers: May Credulous man
Putt all his Confidence in So weake a bottome
And make a saueing voyage
Rox: Nay as gainefull
As euer Man yet made,
Hers: Goe take thy fortune,
Aspire wth my Consent, so thy ambition
Will be sure to prosper; speake ye faire Certainty
Of Brittaines Queene home to thy wishes
Rox: Speake
In hope I may but not in Certaintye
Hers: I say in both, hope and be sure, Ile quickly
Remoue her that standes betweene thee and thy glorye
Rox: Life is loue;
If lost virginitie Can wyne such a day
Ile haue noe daughter but shall learne my way *Exit Rox*

57 gaines) *so P;* games *L* 59 z *of* suffize *over* c *in L;* sustize *P* 63–4 *Q hides all traces of the half line left by the cut by reading* Take reasons advice, and you'l find it impossible 64 *L has* findet *with the* t *over an original* s 65 you loose *P;* For you to lose *Q* 66 Who's an Usurper here, and as the Kingdom *Q* 68 they right *L;* still *L* 69 vpward *written over something else, now illegible, in P;* thee higher, *Q* 70 have the *Q* 75–6 *line-division of Q; all one line in L,P* 77–82 goe . . . Consent / so . . . prosper / speake . . . Queene / home . . . wishes / speake . . . Certaintye *L;* Go . . . fortunes, / Aspire . . . prosper. / Speak . . . Queen / Home . . . wishes. / Speak . . . may / But . . . certainty. *Q* 76 did *deleted after* man *in P* 77 fortunes, *Q* 78 Consent *L* 79 prosper *L;* certainties *Q* 80 of a Queene, *P* 83–4 both, / Hope . . . I'le soon remove the Lett that stands / Between thee and thy Glory. *Q* 84 betweene thy glorye *L,P* 85 loue *L;* Life of Love! *Q* 87 Exit. *Q*

Hers Twill be good worke for him y^{t} first instructs em

[Fol. 18, *recto*]

May be som son of mine, got by this woman too;
Mans scattered Lust brings forth most strange events,
Ant twere but strictly thought on; how many brothers
Wantonly gott, through ignorance of there Births
May match with their owne sisters: peace tis hee
Enter Vort:
Inuention faile me not, tis a gallants Creditt
To marry his whore brauely.

Vort: Haue I powre
Of life and death and Cannot Comãnd ease
In myne owne Blood: After I was a King
I thought I neuer shold haue felt paine more,
That there had beene a ceasing of all passions
And Common stings which subiects vse to feele,
That were Created with a patience fitt
For all extremityes; but such as wee
Know not ye way to suffer, then to doot
How most prepostrous tis: whats all o^{r} greateness
Iff we y^{t} prescribe bovndes to meaner men
Must not passe these ourselues, oh most ridiculous,
This makes ye vulger merry to endure,
Knowing our state is strict, and less secure;
Ile breake thourgh Custome, why shold not ye mind
The nobler part that's of vs, be allowed
Change of affections, as our bodyes are
Still Change of foode and rayment; Ile haue't soe;
All fashions appeare strange at first production
But this wold be well followed: o Captaine

Hers My Lord I greiue for you, you scarse fetch breath
But a sigh hangs at end ont, this is noe waye
If youle giue way to Councell,

88 them, *Q* 89 too, *L* 90–92 *omitted in Q* 90 Lusts *P;* strange *above the line over a caret mark in L* 91 brother< *L* 92 Births)< *L;* Enter *altered from* Exit *in P* 93 pish tis hee *P;* Vor< *L* 94 gallant *P,Q* 95 ones Whore *Q* 96–7 *line-division as in Q; all one line in L* 97 Comã< *L* 98 my own *Q* 99 more *L* 100 ceasing, *L,P* 102 patient *L* 103 extremityes, *L* 104 do it *Q* 105 prepostruous *P;* prepost'rous 'tis? tush, riddles, riddles. *Q* 105–9 whats all . . . less secure *omitted in Q* 106 bovndes *altered from* bonds *in L* 107 ridiculou< *L* 109 secure *L* 111 noble *P;* is *deleted after* part *in L* 113 Still *omitted in Q;* have it *P,Q;* soe< *L* 116 I scarse *L,P,Q* 117–8 at the end of it, but this / Is not the way, if youl'd *Q*

Vort Sett me right then
And quickly s^{r} or I shall Curse thy Charitye
For lifteing vpp my vnderstanding to me

[Fol. 18, *verso*]

To shew that I was wrong, Ignorance is safe,
I slept happilye, if knowledge mend me not
Thou hast Comitted a most Cruell sinne
To wake me into Iudgment, and then leaue mee:
Hers: I will not leaue yo^{u} soe sir that were rudely
First y'haue a fflame to open and to violente
W^{ch} like blood guiltiness in an offendor
Betrays him, when none Can, out wth it sir
Or let some Cuning Couerture be made
Before our practise enters, 'twill spoyle all els
Vort: Why looke you sir I Can be as Calme as Silence
All ye whiles musick plays, strike on sweete frend,
As mild and merry as ye heart of Innocence,
I prethee take my temper, has a virgin
A heate more modest,
Hers: He does well to aske me
I cold haue told that once: why heers a gouerm^{t},
Theirs not a sweeter amitye in friendship
Then in this frendly leauge twixt yo^{u} and health
Vort: Then since thou findst me Capable of happiness
Instruct me with the practise
Hers: What wold you say my Lord
Iff I ensnare her in an act of Lust
Vort: Oh there were Art to ye life, but thats impossible
I prethee flatter me noe further with't;
Fye, soe much syn as goes to make vp that
Will neere preuaile wth her; why I tell ye sir
Shees so syn-killing modest, that if only
To moue the question were enough adultery

119–20 Set me right then, or I shall heavily curse thee / For *Q* 122 safe *L* 123 I then slept *Q* 125 wake) *so Q;* make *L,P* 126 you, Sir, that were rudely done, *Q* 127 you haue *P;* violente *altered from* violate *in L* 129 when nought else can: *Q* 130 u *of* Cuning *altered from* a *in L;* Coueture *P* 131 Before your *Q* 133 while *P,Q* 134 Innocence) *so Q;* Ignorance *L;* Inorance, *P* 138 I told haue told *L;* told him *Q;* gouerm^{t} *L* 140 this League *Q* 141 Then since / Thou *Q* 142 the *altered to* thy *in P* 143 What will *Q* 144 action of lust? *Q* 145 *prefix omitted in Q;* but 'tis *Q* 146 farther *Q* 147 Fye, soe) *so Q;* fly soe *L,P* 148 never *Q;* I'le tell *Q;* you *P,Q* 149–50 only / To) so *Q;* only to / moue *L*

To cause a seperation, theirs noe gallant
So Brassye impudent, durst vndertake
The wordes that shold belong toot,
Hers Say you soe s^r,

[Fol. 19, *recto*]

Theirs nothing made ith world, but has a way toot,
Though some be harder then the rest to finde,
Yet one there is, thats Certaine, and I thinke
I haue tooke ye Course to light ont
Vort: Oh I pray fort
Hers: I heard you lately saye: ffrom whence my Lord
My practise receiud light first, that yor Queene
Still Consecrates her time to Contemplation,
Takes solitary walkes
Vort: Nay late and early sir
Commandes her weeke gaurd from her, wch are but woemen
When tis at strongest
Hers: I like all this well my Lord
And now yor grace shall know what nett is vsd
In many places to Catch modest women
Such as will neuer yeilde by praiers or guifts;
Now their are some will Catch vpp men as fast
But those shee fowlers nothing Concernes vs
Their Birding is at windows, ours abroad
Wheir Ring-doues should be Caught, thats marryed Wiues
Or Chaste maides, w$^{t.}$ y^e appetite has a mind too,
Tis practisd often, theirfore worth discouerye
And may well fitt the purpose;
Vort: Make no pawse then
Hers: Y^e honest Gentlewoman, wheir ere she bee
When nothing will prevaile, I pitty her now
Poore soule shees enticd forth by her owne sex,
To bee betrayd to man; who in som garden house
Or remote walke takeing his Lustfull time
Bindes darkeness on her eyes, surprizes her

153 the woundes that *P;* that shall *Q* 155 in the *Q* 157 is *L* 158 on it. *Q* 161 life first *Q* 164 sir *omitted in Q* 165 woe< *L* 165–6 but / Women at strongest. *Q* 166 when they are at *P;* stronest *L* 167 this, my Lord, *P,Q* 168 now, Sir, you shall *Q* 170 guifts *L* 171 there be *Q* 172 concern *Q* 174 marryed < *L* 175 maides *L* 176–7 *omitted in Q* 176 often *L;* theire forth *P* 179 wheir ere she bee *omitted in Q* 183 on remote *L* 184 on her eye-lids, *Q*

And haueing a Coach readye turnes her in
Hurryeing her where he list for ye sins safety

[Fol. 19, *verso*]

Makeing a rape of hono^{r} without wordes
And att ye low ebbs of his Lust, perhaps
Some three days after, sendes her Coach'd agen
To thee same place, and wch wold make most madd
Shees spoild of all, yet knowes not where she was robd
Wise deare pretious mischeife
Vort: Is this practisd
Hers: Too much my Lord to be so little knowne
A spring to Catch a Maidenhead after sunsett
Clipp it and send it home againe To'th Cittie
Their twill be never perceiud,
Vort: My raptures want expression, I Conceit
Enough to make me fortunate, and the greate
Hers: Practise it then my Lord,—I knew twold take {*Exevnt*

Scena 2^{a} Enter Castiza A Booke: two Ladyes: [III, ii]

Castiza: Methinks yo^{u} liue strange liues, when I seet not
The less it grieues mee, you know how to ease me then,
If you but knew how well I loude yor absence,
You would bestow't vpon me without asking.
1 Lady Fayth for my part, were it not more for Ceremonye
Then tis for Loue, you should walke long enough
For my attendance, soe thinke all my fellowes
Thoug they say nothing: Bookes in woemens hands
They are as much against ye haire methinks
As to see men work stomachers and nightrayles?

186 her *omitted in P;* safely *P* 188 ebb *P,Q;* Lust perhaps, *L* 189 after *L;* Coach *L* 191 robb'd of all, *Q;* where she's *Q;* d *of* robd *over* b *in L* 192 There's the dear *Q* 195 A Sprindge *Q* 196 to the *Q* 197 'twill ne're be *Q* 198 p *of* expression *over* v *in L* 198–9 expression, / I . . . great. Exit. *Q* 200 I practisd it *P;* I praisd it *L;* I praise it *Q;* take. Exit. *Q*

III. ii. *heading*) ACT. 3. SCENA 2. / [rule] / Enter Castiza (with a Book) and two Ladies. *Q* 1 see it *Q* 2 It grieves me less, you *Q* 4 would *altered from* well *in P;* bestow it *Q* 5 noe more *with* more *added above the line over a caret mark in P;* no more *Q* 5–14 *the whole speech is divided arbitrarily up into verse in Q* 6 then for Love, *Q* 7 without my attendance, / And so *Q* 9 They *omitted in Q* 10 see men *added above the line over a caret mark in P;* wear stomachers, or night rayles; *Q*

She y^t has ye greene sickness and should follow her Councell
wold dye like an ass, and goe toth wormes like a sallett;
not I as long as such a Creature as man is made, shees
a foole that will not know what hees good for ——— {*Ex: Ladyes*

[Fol. 20, *recto*]

Cast: Though amongst liues elections that off virgin
I speake noblest, yet't'has pleasd Iust heauen
To send me a Contented Blesedness
In this of marriage wch I euer doubted:
I see the Kings effection was a true one
It Lasts and holdes out long, thats noe meane vertue *Enter*
In a Com̃anding Man, thoug in greate feare ——— *Vort: & *
At first I was inforcd to venture ont, *Hersus*

Vort: Alls happy Cleere and safe,

Hers: The rest Comes gently then,

Vort: Be sure you seize on her full sight at first
For feare of my discouerye

Hers: Ile not miss it

Vort: Now fortune and I am sped

Cast: Oh help Treason Treason

Hers: Sirrah how stand yo^u, prevent noyse and Clamor
Or death shall end thy seruice

Vort: A sure Cuning

Cast: Oh rescew

Hers: Dead her voyce, away, make speed ——— *Ex^t & enter againe*

Cast: Noe help noe succour

Hers: Lowder yet, extend
Yo^r voice to ye last wrack, you shall haue leaue now,
Yare farr from any pittye,

Cast: Whats my sin

Hers: Contempt of man and hees a noble Creature
And takes it in ill part to be dispisd

Cast: I neuer dispisd any

Hers: Noe? you hold vs

12 to the *P,Q;* sallett *L* 13 so long *Q;* She is *Q* 14 that knows not *Q;* he is *Q* 15 among *Q* 16 I did speak noblest of; yet it has pleas'd the King *Q* 18 In that of *Q;* Enter Vortiger / and Horsus / disguised. *after this line in Q* 20 that *L;* E< *L* 21 Man *L;* Vort: < *L* 22 Hers< *L;* on it. *Q* 24 gently on. *Q* 27 *omitted in Q* 28 *prefix*) Hor. *Q* 29 Oh help *omitted in Q* 30 yo^u *L;* a *of* Clamor *over* i *in L* 33 Oh rescue, rescue. *Q* 34 voyce away *L;* aga< *L; stage-direction omitted in Q* 36 extend) *so Q;* entend *L,P* 36–38 *line-division as in Q;* Lowder . . . wrack, / you shall . . . any < *L* 43 noe *L;* vs, *L*

Vnworthy to be Loude, what Call you that.

[Fol. 20, *verso*]

Cast: I haue a Lord disproues you,
Hers: Pish yor Lord,
Yo^{r} bound to loue yor Lord, thats noe thanks to yo^{u},
Yo^{u} should loue those you are not tyde to Loue,
Thats ye right tryall of a Womans Charitye
Cast: I know not what yo^{u} are nor what my fault is
But if't be life you seeke, whatere you bee,
Vse noe im̃odest wordes, and take it from me:
You kill me more in talkeing sinnfullye
Then acting Cruelly, be soe farr pitifull
To end me without wordes;
Hers: Long may you liue
The wish of a good subiect, 'tis not life
That I thirst after, loyaltie forbid
I should Com̃itt such Treason, you mistake me
I haue noe such bloodye thought, onely yor Loue
Shall Content me
Cast: What sayd yo^{u} sir
Hers: Thus, thus, plainely
To strip my wordes as naked as my purpose,
I must and will enioy yo^{u}; gon already!
Looke to her, Beare her vpp, she goes apace;
I feard this still, and therefore Came prouided,
Theirs that will fetch life from a dyeing spark
And make it spred a furnace; shees well straight,
It kept a Lord 7 yeares aliue together
In spight of nature, that he lookd like one
Had leaue to walke out of a graue to aire himselfe,
Yet still walkd Lord; pish let her goe, she stands
Vppon my knowledge, or els she Counterfeits,

[Fol. 21, *recto*]

I know ye vertue;
Cast: Neuer did sorrowes in afflicted Woman

47 Y'are *Q;* that is *Q* 50 nor what you *Q* 51 But *omitted in Q;* if it *Q* 52 vse more modest wordes, *P* 53 sinnfullye *one minim short in L* 54 acting Cruelty; *Q* 57 'Tis the wish *Q* 63 Thus plainly, *Q* 65 enjoy thee: *Q;* already *L* 66 apace *L* 68 soule *deleted after* dyeing *in L* 69 furnance *P* 70–3 It kept . . . walkd Lord; *omitted in Q* 71 Like *altered from* fitt *in P* 73–5 Pish, . . . knowledge, / Or . . . vertue. *Q*

Meete with such Cruelltye, such hard-harted wayes
Humaine invention never found before:
To Call back life to liue, is but ill taken
Of some departing soule, then to force mine back
To an eternall act of death in lust,
What is it but most excrable.

Hers: Soe Soe
But this is from ye buisness, list to me
Here you are now farr from all hope of frendship
Saue what you make mine, scape me you Cannot
Send yor soule that assurance; that resolud on
You know not who I am, nor neuer shall
I need not feare you then; But giue Consent
Then wth ye faithfulnes of a true friend
Ile open myselfe to yo^{u}, fall yor servant
As I doe now in hope, proud of submission
And seale ye deed vp wth eternall secresye
Not death should pick it open, much less the kings
Authoritye or Torture,

Vort: I admire him

Cast: Oh sir, what ere yo^{u} are, I teach my knee
Thus to requite you, Be Content to take
Only my sight as ransome for myne hono^{r},
And where you haue but mockd myne eyes wth darkeness
Pluck em out quite, all outward light of bodye
Ile spare most willingly, But take not from me
That wch must guide me to another world
And leaue me dark for ever, fast wthout
That Cursed pleasure wch would make two soules

[Fol. 21, *verso*]

Endure a famine everlastingly:

Hers This almost moues

Vort: By this light heele be taken

Hers Ile wrastle downe all pittye, will you Consent;

77 cruelties, *Q;* way< *L* 78 inuentions *P* 80 By some *Q* 82 excreable. *P* 84 my business, *Q* 86 make in me, scape *Q;* Canno< *L* 87 resolue on *P* 88 ever shall, *Q* 90 a *altered from* u *in L* 93 *second* e *of* deed *over* a *in L* 94 shall pluck it from me, much *Q;* the *omitted in L,P* 94–5 *line-division that of Q;* much less / kings authoritye *L* 98–9 *line-division that of Q;* take only / my sight *L,P* 99 my *Q* 100 my *Q* 100–1 *line-division that of Q;* wth / darkness pluck *L* 101 them quite out; *Q;* lights *Q;* of < *L* 102 hut take *Q* 105 will make *Q* 109 pity, what, will *Q*

Cast: Ile neuer be soe guiltye
Hers: Farewell wordes then
You here noe more of me, But thus I Ceize thee
Casti: Oh if a power aboue be reuerencd in thee
I bind thee by that name, by manhood, nobleness
And all ye Charmes of hono^{r} ——— *Ex^{t} vort: Castiza*
Hers: Heers one Caught
For an example; never was poore Ladye
So mockt into false terror: wth what anguish
She lyes with her owne Lord, now she Could Curse
All into barrenness and beguile herselfe by't;
Conceyts a powerfull thing, and is indeed
Placde as a pallat, to tast greife or loue
And as that relishes, so we approue;
Hence it Comes that ou^{r} tast is soe beguilde
Changeing pure blood, for som thats mixt, and soyld
Exit

Scena 3^{a} Enter Hengist [III, iii]

Heng: A faire & fortunate Constelation raignd
When we set footeing here; from his first guift
Which to a Kings vnbounded eyes seemd nothing,
(The Compass of a hide) I haue erected *A noyse*
A strong and spatious Castle, yet Conteynd myselfe
Wthin my limits without Checke or sensure:
Thither wth all ye obseruance of a subiect
(The liuelyest witness of a gratefull minde) *Barbor & Taylor wthin*
I purpose to inuite him and his Queene

[Fol. 22, *recto*]

And feast em nobly.

112 seize you. *Q* 113 *no prefix in P, but marked off by a stroke as a separate speech;* poure *P;* reuerencd) *so Q;* reuerend *L,P;* by thee, *Q* 115 *stage-direction in Q:* Vort. snatches / her away. 116 *no prefix in P, but marked off by a stroke as a separate speech;* Ah ha, here's *Q* 120 by it. *Q* 123 approue *L* 124 Hence comes it *Q* 126 Exeunt. *Q*

III. iii. *heading) in the left margin the sign* ⛢ *appears in L;* ACT. 3. SCENA 3. / [rule] / Enter Hengist. *Q* 2 set foot here, for from *Q* 4 *stage-direction omitted in Q* 7 th'observance *Q;* e *of* subiect *above the line over a caret mark in L; stage-direction omitted in P,Q* 9 *a letter deleted before the beginning of* inuite *and* u *altered from* i *in L and P* 10 them *Q*

Bar: We will enter sir;
Tis a state buisness of a twelue month Long
The Chooseing of a Maior
Heng: What noyse is that
Tay: Sir we must speake with ye good Earle of Kent;
Though we were nere brought vp to keepe a doore
We are as honest sir as som that doe — *Enter Gentleman*
Heng: Now whats ye occasion of their Clamo^{rs} sir
Gent: Please you my Lord a Company of townsmen,
Are bent against all denyalls and resistance
To haue speech wth yor Lordship, and that yo^{u}
Must end a diference, which none els Can doe
Heng: Why then theirs reason in their violence
W^{ch} I never lookd for; let in first but one, — *Exit Gent*
And as we relish him, the rest Comes on,
Twere noe safe wisdome in a riseing Man
To slight of such as these, nay rather these
Are ye foundation of a Lofty worke;
We Cannot build without them and stand sure;
He that ascends vp to a Mountaines topp — *Enter Gent*
Must first begin at foote, now sir who Comes
Gent: They Cannot yet agree my Lord of that
Heng: How
Gent: They say tis worse now for em then euer 'twas before
For wheir ye difference stood but betweene two
Vppon this Coming first, they are at odds,—
On sayes sir he shall loose his place at Church by't
Another heele not doe his wife that wrong,
And by their good wills, they would Come all at first,
The strife Continues in most heate my Lord

11 sir *L* 15 Kent *L* 16 never *Q* 17 Gentl< *L* 18 Clamor *P;* Now, Sir, what's *Q;* sir *omitted after* clamours *in Q* 23 *no prefix in P, but marked off by a stroke as a separate speech* 24 ne're *Q;* em *deleted after* let *in P;* first let in but *Q* 25 come *Q* 26 'Tis no *Q;* ariseing *L,P* 27 slight such *P* 28 foundations *Q;* Enter Gent *after this line in P;* worke *L* 29 em *P;* sure *L* 30 He that first ascends *L,P,Q;* ascends first *Bullen;* a *deleted before* first *in P;* vp *omitted in Q;* Enter < *L* 31 Must begin at the foot. *Q;* Enter Gent. *after this line in Q;* Comes *altered from* loues *in L* 33 *omitted in Q* 34 *prefix omitted in Q;* now then it was *Q;* befor< *L* 35 difference was *Q;* stood, *L* 36 they are) *so P;* they're *L;* th'are all at *Q* 36–7 *line-division that of Q;* odds,—on sayes <> / he *L* 37 sir *omitted in Q;* in the Church *Q* 38 Another will not *Q* 39 Come both at / first, *P;* would all come first. *Q;* firs< *L*

[Fol. 22, *verso*]

Betweene a Contry Barbor and a taylor,
Of ye same parish, and wch yor Lordshipp names
Tis yeelded by Consent that one shall enter.

Heng: Heers noe sweete coyle, Ime glad theire growne soe reasonable
Call in ye Barbor, if ye tale be long
Heele Cut it short I trust, thats all ye hope ont
Now sir are you ye Barbor

Enter Barbor

Bar: Oh most Barbarous: a Corecto^{r} of enormities in haire
my Lord, a promoter of vpper lipps, or what yor Lo^{pp}.
in ye neateness of yor discretion shall vouchsafe to Call it.

Heng: Very good: I see this yo^{u} haue wthout Booke,
But whats yor Buisnes now,

Barb: Your Lo^{pp}: Comes
To a high point indeed, ye buissnes s^{r}
Lyes all about ye head

Heng: Thats worke for you

Barb: No my good Lord; their is a Corporation a kind of bodye, a bodye.

Heng: The Barbors out at bodye, let in ye Taylo^{r},
This tis to reach beyond yor owne profession;
When yo^{u} let goe yor head, you loose yor memorye,
You haue noe buisnes wth ye bodye

Barb: Yes, sir I am a Barbor surgeon, I haue had something to
doe with't in my time my Lord, and I was never soe out
oth body as I haue beene heere of late; send me good luck;
Ile goe marry som whore or other But Ile get in againe.

Heng: Now s^{r} a good discouerye Come from yo^{u}
That we may know ye inwardes of ye Buisnes

Enter Taylor

Tayl: I will ripp vp the linings to yor Lordshipp

42 parish) *ed.;* same, and *L,P;* same Town, and *Q* 43 he shall *Q* 44 sweete toyle *L,P;* sweet quoyl, I am glad they are so reasonable, / Call *Q;* soe / reasonable Call *L;* Heng: *altered from* Hers: *in L* 46 hopes *P;* ont *omitted in Q* 47 you *omitted in L* 48 *this and all the succeeding tradesmen's speeches in this scene are arbitrarily cut up into verse in Q;* Barbarous *altered from* Barborus *in L* 50 shall think fit to call me. *Q* 51 see you have this *Q;* booke, But / what *L* 52 now *omitted in Q* 53–5 *as prose in L,P* 53 His *deleted in front of* Lordship *in P* 54 a very high *Q* 55 lyes about *P,Q;* about *altered from* barbor *in P* 56 Thats) *so Q;* that worke *L;* that works *P* 57 A Body, a kind of Body. *Q* 58 is out *P,Q;* at the Body, *Q;* bodye *L;* Taylo^{r} *L* 59 profession *L* 60 memorye *L* 62 Barber-Chirurgeon, *Q;* had *inserted above the line over a caret mark in P* 63 with it *P,Q;* I was *altered from* Ile as *in P* 64 of the body *Q;* late *L* 65 I'le marry *Q;* whore / But *Q* 66 *stage-direction omitted in Q* 67 *omitted in Q* 68 ripp vp) *so Q;* vp *omitted in L,P*

And show what stuff tis made on, for ye Bodye
Or Corporation
Heng: Their ye Barbor left indeed
Tayl: Tis peecd vp of two factions
Heng: A patchd towne ye whilst

[Fol. 23, *recto*]

Tayl: Nor Can we goe through stich my noble Lord
The Collar is soe greate in the one partye,
And as in linsey woolsey wooue together
One peece makes seuerall suites, so vpright Earle
Our linsey woolsey hearts makes all this Coyle.
Heng: Whats all this now
Enter Glouer &c.
Call in ye rest Ime nere ye wiser yet
I should Commend my wit Could I but guess
What this would Come to, now sirs what are yo^u
Glou: Sir reverence of yor Lordshipp I am a glouer
Heng: What needes that then
Glou: Sometimes I deale with doggs Leather
Sir reverence all that while
Heng: Well to the purpose iff their be any towardes
Glou: I were an ass else, saueing yor Lordshipps pleasure, we haue
a bodye but our Towne wants a hand, a hand of Iustice,
a worshipfull Mr Maior.
Heng: This is well handed yet,
A man may take som hold on't, you want a Maior
Glou: Right, but theirs two at fisty Cufs about it s^r
As I may say at daggers drawing sir
But that I Cannot say because they haue none
And yo^u being Earle of Kent, the Towne does saye
Yo^r Lordshipps voice shall Choose and part ye fraye.
Heng: This is strange worke for me, well s^r what be they

69 made of; *Q* 72 two fashions. *P,Q* 74 we) *so Q;* Can goe *L,P* 75 choler *Q;* this one *P* 76 Link't together *P* 78 make *Q* 79 *stage-direction omitted in P,Q; L has* Enter Glouer Bu<tton:> Brazier *but see the direction at ll. 120–121* 80–2 What's all this now? I am ne're the wiser yet, call in the rest: / Now, Sirs, what are you? *Q; in some copies of Q* the rest: *has dropped out* 83 Sir, reverence on your *Q* 85–6 *all as one line in Q;* in dogs leather, Sir, reverence the while. *Q; in some copies of Q the* ile *of* while *has dropped out* 88 pleasure, < *L;* Lordships presence; *Q* 89 T *of* Towne *over* tw *in L;* Ius< *L* 91 handled *P,Q* 91–2 this . . . hold <> / you . . . *L;* hold / On it. You *Q;* on't *omitted in P* 93 right *L* 94 sir *omitted in Q* 96 our Town *Q* 97 and end the fray. *P;* shall part and end *Q;* fray< *L* 98 be th< *L*

Glou: The one is a Tanner
Heng: Fye I shall be two partiall
I owe two much effection to that trade
To put it to my voice: what is his name
Glou: Symon sir
Heng: How symon too

[Fol. 23, *verso*]

Glou: Nay tis but Symon one s^{r}: the very same Symon
That sold yor Lo^{pp}: the Hide
Heng: What sayst thou
Barb: Thats all his glory s^{r}, he gott his M^{rs} widdow by't presently
after, a rich tanners wife, she has sett him vpp, he was her
foreman a long time in her other husbandes dayes
Heng: Now let me perish in my first aspireing
If the pritty simplicity of his fortune
Does not most highly take me, tis a presage methinkes
Off bright succeeding happines To myne
When my fates glow-worme Casts forth such a shine:
And whats ye other that Contendes wth him
Tayl: Marry my noble Lord a fustian weauer —— *Enter Symon & Oliuer*
Heng: How, will he offer to Compare with symon
He a fitt match for him
Barb: Hark, hark, my Lord *fellmonger Brazier Buttonmunger*
Here they Come both now in a pelting Chafe
From ye Towne house
Symo: How, before me, I scorne thee,
Thou watle facde singd pigg
Oliuer Pigg, I defie thee,
My vncle was a Iew and scornd ye motion.
Sym: I list not brook thy vaunts, Compare with mee
Thou spindle of Concupiscence, tis well knowne
Thy first wife was a flax wench.

102 to his voice *P;* what is *Q;* whats *L,P* 103 sir *omitted in Q* 106 a Hide *Q* 108 *prefix)* Glo. *Q;* by it *Q* 109 after *omitted in Q;* wife *L;* a foreman *P* 112 simplitity *L* 113 Do not *Q* 116 other Contendes *P;* what are those that do contend *Q* 117–21 *stage-direction omitted in Q* 117 my Lord *P* 118 how *L;* How, he offer / To . . . him! *Q* 120 *prefix)* Tail. *Q* 120–1 *all as one line in Q;* fellmongers Braziers / Buttonmongers *P;* B *of* Brazier *over* R *in L* 121 now *omitted in Q* 122 Towne Hall. *P* 123–6 *line-division as in Q; as prose in L,P* 123 How,) *so Q, omitted in L,P;* me *L* 124 facde) *so Q;* faide *L,P* 125 Pigg *L* 126 that motion. *P* 127 r *of* brook *over* o *in L* 129 flax [whench] wench *L;* flax whench. *P*

Oliu: But such a flax wench
Would I might never want at my most need
Nor any friend of mine, my neighbours knew her,
Thy wife was but a hampen halter to her
Symon Vse better wordes, Ile hang y^{e} in my yeare else,
Let whose will Choose ye afterwardes

[Fol. 24, *recto*]

Glou: Peace for shame,
Quench yor greate spirrits, doe yo^{u} not see his Lo^{pp}
Heng: What Mr Symonides
Symo: Symonides what a fine name he has made of Symon; then
hees an asse that Calls me Symon againe; Ime quite out of loue
with't.
Heng: Giue me thy hand; I loue thee and thy fortunes,
I like a man that thriues.
Symo: I tooke a Widdow my Lord to be the best peece of ground to thriue
on, and By my faith theirs a young Symonides like a greene
onion peepeing vpp alreadye
Heng: Th'ast a good luckie hand
Sym: I haue somewhat sir
Heng: But why to me is this election offerd
The Chooseing of a Maior goes by most voices
Symo: True sir but most of our townsmen are soe hoarse wth drinking
theirs nere a good voice amongst em all $\overset{t}{y}$ are now here in this
Companye
Heng: Are you Content both to putt all to these then
To whom I liberally resigne my interest
To prevent Censure
Sym: I speake first my Lord
Oliu Though I speake Last, I hope I am not least,

131 at my need, *Q* 132 mine *L;* her *L* 135 *the foot of the page is cropped and only the upper part of this line is visible in L;* Let who will chuse thee *Q* 136–7 *all as in one line in L, with* Lo^{pp} *above the line through being crowded out at the end of the line; line-division that of Q* 137 spirit, do not you see *Q;* yo^{u} no< >Lo^{pp} *L* 138 my Symonidees *P;* there hees *P* 139 a fair name hath he made *Q;* Symon< *L;* Then *Q;* there *P* 140 againe *L;* I am *Q;* ou< *L* 141 with it. *Q* 142–3 *all one line in L;* hand, / I *Q* 143 love thy fortunes, and like *Q;* a m< *L* 144 ground < *L* 145 faith, my Lord, there's *Q;* like < *L* 147 thou hast *P* 151 a *of* hoarse *over* r *in L;* w^{th} < *L* 152 there's not a good voice among them all. *Q;* $\overset{t}{y}$ . . . Companye *omitted in Q;* here i< *L* 154 content to put it to all these then? *Q* 156 censures. *Q* 158–61 *as prose in L* 158 last, my Lord, I am *Q*

If they will Cast awaye a Towne borne Child
They may, tis but dying some fortye yeares or soe
Before my tyme

Heng: Ile leaue yo^{u} to yor Choice awhile ——— *Exit Hengist*

all — Yo^{r} good Lordship

Symo: Looke yo^{u} neighbors vew vs both well ere yo^{u} be too hastye, let
Oliuer the fustian Weauer stand as faire as I doe, & the
Diuell giue him good ont

Oliuer I doe thou vpstart Callimoocher I doe, tis well knowne to
the I haue beene twice Alecunner, thou mushrump, that
shott vp in one night wth Lyeing wth thy M^{rs}

[Fol. 24, *verso*]

Sym: Faith thou art such a spiney Baldrib, all the
Mistrisses in ye Towne would never gett the vpp

Oliu: I scorne to rise by a Woeman as thou didst:
My wife shall rise by me

Sym: The Better for som of thy neighbors when yo^{u} are asleepe

Glouer I pray Cease of yor Communication we Can doe nothing
ells.

Oliuer I gaue that Barbor a fustian suit, and twice redeemd
his Cittron, he may remember me

Sym: I feare noe false measure but in that Taylor, ye glouer
and the Buttonmonger are both Cocksure,
That Collyers eye I like not,
Now they Consult, the matter is abrewing
Poore Gill my wife lyes Longing for this news,
Twill make her a glad mother

all A symon, a symon, a symon, a symon.

Sym: My good people I thank yo^{u} all.

Oliue: Wretch that I am; Tanner thou hast Curryde fauour

Symo: I Currye; I defye thy fustian fume

159 they) *so Q;* he *L,P;* will <> awaye *L;* Townes borne *P* 160 It is *Q;* dying <> fortye *L;* dying forty *P;* years before *Q* 162 I leave *Q* 164 Neighbours, before you be too *Q;* hastye, < *L* 165 th< *L* 166 Do him good *Q* 167 Callimoother *L,P;* Callymoocher, *Q;* know< *L* 168 to the Parish I *Q;* mushrump, < *L* 169 shot'st up in a night, / By lying *Q* 171 Mistrisis *P;* T *of* Towne *over* C *in L;* will never *Q* 172 lye *deleted before* rise *and* e *of* Woeman *obscured by a blot in L* 172–3 *line-division that of Q;* didst: my / wife *L* 173 thee *deleted before* me *in L* 174 *omitted in Q* 175 I pray leave your *Q* 177 o *of* Barbor *over* a *in L* 178 Cittern *Q* 180 Button-maker *Q* 181–2 *line-division as in Q; as prose in L* 181 eye *omitted in P* 182 in brewing, *Q* 183 the news, *Q* 185 A Symon *twice only in Q* 186 My *omitted in Q* 187 tc *of* wretch *obscured by a blot in L*

Oliu: But I will proue a rebell all thy yeare
And raise vp the seauen deadly sinns against the —— *Ex^{t}*

Sym: The deadly sins will scorne to rise with thee
And they haue any breeding—as Commonly they
are well brought vpp, tis not for every scabb
to be acquainted with em; But leaueing scabs, to yo^{u}
good neighbours now I bend my speech first to say
more then a Man Can say, I hold it not soe fitt
to be spoken, But to say what man ought to saye
theire I leaue you alsoe; I must Confess that yor
loues haue Chosen a weake and vnlearnd man, that
I Can neither write nor reade yo^{u} all Can witness,
yet not all together soe vnlearnd, but I Cold set my
mark to a bond, if I would be so simple, an excellent

[Fol. 25, *recto*]

Token of gouerment; Cheere yo^{u} then my harts, yo^{u} haue
don you know not what, theirs a full point, you must all cough
and hem now,

All: hum hum hum Cough

Symo: Now touching our Common adversary the fustian weauer who
threatneth he will raise the deadly sins amongst vs, which as
I take it are 7 in number, let em Com, our towns bigg
enough to hold em, we will not much disgrace it; Besides you know
a deadly sinne will lye in a narrow hole, But when they think
themselues safest and ye webb of their iniquitye wouen, with
the horse strenght of my Iustice Ile breake the loomes of their
Concupiscence, and let the weauer goe seeke his shuttle, here
you may hem againe iff youle doe me ye fauour

All: Cough and hem

189 Reble in thy yeare *P* 190 sinns *is one minim short in L;* against you *P* 191 with you *P;* by thee, *Q* 192 If they *Q;* breeding as *L* 194 them; *Q;* leaving the scab, *Q;* scabs *L* 195 now) *so Q;* no *L;* lo *P* 196 not fit *Q;* fitt *originally* fitting, ing *having been deleted, in L* 197 a man *Q* 198 confess your *Q* 201 Can set *Q* 202 be so < *L* 203 yo^{u} < *L* 204 point. There you *Q;* must a< *L* 205 now *omitted in Q* 206 *Q alters this into a stage-direction:* Here they all cough and hem. 207 *prefix omitted in Q;* weau< *L* 208 threatens . . . among *Q;* vs, < *L* 208–9 which . . . number *omitted in Q* 209 t *of* let *over* f *in L;* are in number seuen, *P;* Let them *Q;* Com *L;* Town is *Q; only the tails of the two* g's *in* bigg *are visible in L* 210 hold them, *Q;* em *L;* not so much *Q;* it *L;* Beside< *L* 210–11 besides your deadly sins *P;* besides you know / A deadly sin *Q* 211 they < *L* 212 iniquitye noue< *L;* iniquity best woven, *Q* 213 I will break through the / Loom *Q;* loomes < *L* 214 and make the *Q;* shut< *L* 215 may cough and hem *Q* 216 *Q alters this into a stage-direction:* They cough and hem again.

Symo: Why I thanke yo^{u}, and it shall not goe vnrewarded: now for the 7 deadly sins, first for pride wch alwayes sitts vppermost and wilbe placd wthout a Church-warden, Being a syn that is not like to be Chargable to ye parish, I slipp it ouer and think it not worthy of punishment: now yo^{u} all know that sloth does not any thing, this place you see requires wisdom, how Can a man in Conscience punish that which does nothing: Envy a poore leane Creature that eates raw liuer, perhapps it pines to see me Chosen, and that makes me the fatter wth laughing, if I punish envy then I punish mine owne Carkas, a great syn against authoritye: for wrath, the less we say, ye better tis, a scurvy desperate thing it is that Commonly hangs itselfe and saues Iustice many a halter by't; now for Couetuousnes and Gluttony, Ile tell yo^{u} more when I Com out of myne office, I shall haue time to try what they are: Ile proue em soundly,

[Fol. 25, *verso*]

and if I find Couetuosnes and Gluttony to be directly syns, Ile bury on ith bottom of a Chest, and thother ith end of my garden, But sirs for Letcherie, I meane to tickle that home; nay Ime resolud vpont, I will not leaue one whore in all ye towne.

Bar: Som of yor neighbors may goe seeke their wiues ith Contry then

Symo: Barbar be silent, I will Cut thy Comb else; to Conclude, I will learne ye villanies of all trades, myne owne I know alreadye, if their be any knauery in the Baker I will bowlt it out, if in ye Brewer I will tast him throughly, and then piss out his iniquitye in his owne

217 *prefix omitted in Q;* thank you all, *Q;* now for seuen *P;* vnrewarded: n< *L; Q reads* Now for the deadly sins, Pride, Sloth, Envy, Wrath; as for / Covetousness *i.e. it omits* first for (*line 218*) *down to* halter by't (*line 230*) 218 vpperm< (*with only two minims of* m *visible*) *L* 219 l *of* wilbe *over* b *in L;* syn th< *L* 220 ouer < *L* 221 kn< (*with only one minim of final* n *visible*) *L* 222 see req< *L* 223 punish tha< *L* 224 that eat< *L* 225 pins *P;* that < *L* 226 then I < *L* 227 Carkas *L;* authoritye: < *L;* for *omitted in P* 228 authoritye: wrath, the Lessen say, *P;* c *of* scurvy *over* n *in L;* thing it < *L* 229 man< (*with only one minim of final* n *visible*) *L* 230 Ile < *L* 231 my Office; *Q;* hau< *L* 232 I will prove them *Q;* proue em < *L* 233 Gluttony and Covetousness *Q* 234 bury the one in the . . . And the other in the *Q* 235 sir *L,P;* Sirs, for Leachery, / I'le tickle that home my self, I'le not leave a Whore in the Town. *Q* 236 home *L* 238 sin of *P;* must seek *Q;* in the *Q* 241 villany *Q;* my own *Q* 244 throughily, *P;* and piss *Q;* at his *Q*

sinckhole; in a word I will knock out all enormities
like a Bullock, & send the hide to my fellow tanners.

Enter Hengist & Roxena

All: A Symonides a true symonides indeed.
Heng: How now how goes yor choise
Taylo: Heeres hee my Lord
Sym: You may proue I am the man, I am bold to take
the vpper hand of yor Lo^{pp}: a little, Ile not loose an
inch of myne hono^{r}
Heng: Hold sirs theirs som few Crownes to mend yor feast
Because I like yor Choise
Barb: Ioy bless yor Lo^{pp}:
Weele drinck yor health wth trumpetts
Symo: I with sackbuts
Thats the more solleme drinking for my state
No mault this yeare shall fume into my pate

Exevnt

Heng: Continues still that fervor in his Loue
Rox: Nay wth increase my Lord the flame growes greater
Though he has learnd a Better art of late
To set a skreen before it.

Enter Vort: & Hersus

Heng: Canst speake low
Hers Heard every word my Lord

[Fol. 26, *recto*]

Vort: Plainely
Her: Distinctly;
The Course I tooke was dangerous but not fayleing
For I Conveyd my selfe behind the hangings,
Euen first before her entrance.
Vort: Twas well venturd
Hers: I had such a womans first and second longing in me
To heare how she would beare her mockd abuse
After she was halfe returnd to priuacye,
I Could haue fasted out an ember weeke
And never thought of hunger to haue heard her:
She fetchd three short turnes, I shall neere forget em,

245 suck-hole: *Q;* knock down *Q* 246 like a Butcher, *Q* 247 t *of* true *a later addition in L* 249 This is he, *Q* 250 To prove I am *Q* 251 a little *omitted in Q* 252 my honour. *Q* 255–6 *as one line in L;* bless you, Sir, / We'le *Q* 259 fume our pate *P;* Exit cum suis. *Q* 260 Continue *Q;* that fauour *P,Q* 262 he *omitted in L* 263 *omitted in L,P* 264 Canst) *so P;* Can *L;* Heng. Speak lower. *Q* 267 distintly *P;* distinctly *L* 269 seffe *L;* hangins *L,P* 270 Even just before *Q;* her) *ed.*; his *L,P,Q* 272 c *of* second *over* n *in L;* in m< *L* 273 hear her how *Q* 274 was return'd *Q* 277 neuer *P*

Like an emprisond larke that offers still
Her wing at libertie and returnes checkt,
Soe would her soule faine haue bene gon, & even hung
Flittering vpon ye barrs of poore mortallitye,
Which ever as it offerd, droue her backe againe
Then Came yor holy Lupus and Germanus,
Vort: Oh two holy Confessors
Hors: At whose sight
I Could perceiue her fall vpon her Breast
And Cruelly afflict her selfe with sorrow:
I never heard a sigh till I heard hers,
Who after her Confession pittying her
Putt her into a way of patience,
W^{ch} now she holdes to keepe it hidd from yo^{u},
Theirs all ye pleasure that I tooke int now
When I heard that my paines was well remembred
Soe with applying Comforths and releife
They haue brought it low now to an easie greife.

[Fol. 26, *verso*]

But yet the tast is not quite gon. ———— *Enter Castiza:*
Vort: Still fortune
Sitts bettering our invention
Hers: Here she Comes
Cast: Yonders my Lord: oh Ile returne againe
Methinks I should not dare to looke on him
Hers: Shes gon againe
Vort: It works the kindlyer sir
Goe now and Call her back: she windes her selfe
Into the snare soe prettily, tis a pleasure
To set toyles for her,
Cast: He may read my shame,
Now in my blush
Vort: Com y'are soe linckt to holynes
Soe taken vpp wth Contemplatiue desires
That the world has you, yet enioyes yo^{u} not
You haue bene weepeing too

277–82 *omitted in Q* 284 Oh *omitted in Q* 285 At whose first sight *Q* 289 C *of* Confession *over* c *in L* 293 remem< *L* 295 lower, to an *Q* 297–8 *line-division that of Q; as one line in L* 298 inventation *altered from* inuitation *in L;* inuitation *P;* Inventions. *Q* 304 now *omitted in L,P* 307–8 *line-division as in Q; all one line in L* 310 ta'ne with *Q* 311 hus you, *P*

Cast: Not I my Lord
Vort: Trust me I feare you haue: y'are much to blame
And yo^{u} should yeild soe to passion without Cause,
Is not theire time enough for meditation,
Must it lay title to yor health and Beautie,
And draw them into times Consumtion too.
Tis too exacting for a holye facultie;
My Lord of Kent, I pray wake him Captaine
He reades himselfe asleepe sure
Hers: My Lord
Heng: Yo^{r} pardon s^{r}
Vort: Nay Ile take away yor Booke, and bestowt here,
Ladye, yo^{u} that delight in virgins storyes
And all Chast workes, heeres excellent readeing for yo^{u},
Make of that booke, as raisd men make of fauor
W^{ch} they grow sick to part from; and now my Lord

[Fol. 27, *recto*]

You that haue soe Conceitedly gone beyond me
And made such large vse of a slender guift
Which we never minded, I Commend yor thrift
And for yor buildings name shall to all ages
Carry ye stamp and impress of yor witt
It shalbe Cald thong castle
Heng: How my Lord
Thong castle their yor Highness quits me kindlye
Vort: Tis fitt art should be knowne by her right name,
You that Can spredd my guift Ile spred yor fame
Heng: I thank yor grace for that sir
Vort: And lou'de Lord
So well we doe accept thy invitac̄on
With all speed weele set forward
Heng: Your loue hono^{rs} me ——— *musique Exevnt Omnes*

315 To yield so much to passion *Q* 316 theire) *so P;* yor *L;* some *Q* 317 Beautie,: *L* 320 pray work *L,P;* prithee wake *Q* 323–4 *these two lines are transposed in Q* 325 *prefix* Vor. *in Q;* Ladye that yo^{u} that *L,P;* virgin storyes *L,P* 326–8 *line-division that of Q;* readeing / for yo^{u}, make . . . make of / fauor . . . from and < / Lord you . . . *L* 327 as made men do of favours, *Q* 328 wth ye grow sick, to part from and < > / Lord *L;* with the grow sick, to part from, *P* 329 u *of* haue *a minim short in L;* beyond m< *L* 330 so large *Q* 331 ne're *Q* 332 And that your Building may to *Q* 334 shall be *Q* 336 your Grace quitts *Q* 337 its right *Q;* name *L* 339 sir *omitted in Q* 341 your Invitation, *Q* 342 forwards. *Q* 343 loues honours *P;* Your Honour loves me. Exit. *Q*

Actus Quartus Scena Prima: Enter Vortiger Castiza two Ladyes Roxena Devon: Staff: at one Doore Symon And his Brethren at the other [IV, i]

Sym: Loe I the Maior of Quinborough towne by name
Wth all my Brethren, saueing one thats Lame
Are Come as fast, as fyerie milhorse gallopps,
To meete thy Grace, thy Queene and thy faire trollops:
For reason of or Coming doe not Looke
It must be don, I found it ith towne Booke,
And yet not I my selfe, I scorne to reed
I keepe a Clark to doe theise iobbs for need;
And now expect a rare Conceit before thong castle see thee
Reach me ye thing to giue ye King, ye other too I prethee
Now here they be for Queene & thee, ye gifts all steele & leather,

[Fol. 27, *verso*]

But ye Conceite of mickle weight, & here they're Come together,
To shew two loues must ioyne in one, or towne prsents to ye
This gilded scabberd to the Queene, this dagger vnto thee:
Vort: Forbeare yor tedious and rediculous duties
I hate em as I doe ye rotten rootes of you
You inconstant rabble, I haue felt yor fits,
Sheath vp yor Bountie wth yor Iron wits
And get you gon ——— *musique* *Exevnt King Lordes*
Sym: Looke sirs is his back turnd
All Tis tis
Sym Then bless ye good Earle of Kent say I
Ile haue this dagger turnd into a pye
And eaten vp for anger every Bytt ont

IV. i. *heading*) ACT. 4. SCENA 1. *with catchword* Actus *at foot of previous page in Q;* e *of* Scena *a later insertion by the scribe in L;* Casti< *L;* Sy< *L;* Enter Symon and all his Brethren, a Mace and Sword before him, meeting Vortiger, Castiza, Hengist, Roxena, Horsus, two Ladies. *Q* 1 *the sign* ȸ *in the left margin after the prefix in L;* towne *inserted above the line over a caret mark in L;* towne *omitted in Q* 4 To greet *Q;* her fair *Q;* trollo< *L* 6 find *Q;* k *of* Booke *over* e *in L* 7 I cannot read, *Q* 8 those iobs *P,Q* 9 see thee) *so Q;* soe thee *P;* so< *L* 10 I pr< *L* 11 gift *Q;* & le< *L* 12 they come *Q* 13 tow loues *P;* to thee *P;* by me *Q* 14 Queene *L* 16–7 I hate them, as I do the roots of your / Inconstant Rabble, *Q;* of your / inconstant *P, the* r *of* your *being a later addition* 17 rable *deleted before* fits *in L;* fits *L* 18 Bounties *Q;* Iror *L; stage-direction in Q:* Exit cum sociis. 19 *omitted in Q;* king and Lordes *P* 20 sirs) *so Q;* sir *L,P* 21 It is, it is. *Q*

[IV, i]

& when that pye is new Cut vpp by som rare Cuning pyeman
They shall all lamentably sing put vp thy dagger symon

Exevnt

Hoboys the King and his traine mett by Hengist and Hersus they salute & Exevnt; while the Banquet is Brought forth Musique plays, Enter Vortig: Hors, Dev: Staff: Castiza Roxena and two Ladies [IV, ii]

Heng: A Welcom mightie Lord may appeare Costlier
More full of talke and toyle, shew and Conceit,
But one more stoard wth thankfull loue and truth
I forbid all ye sons of men to boast of

Vort: Why here's a Fabrick that implies eternitye,
The Building plaine but most substantiall,
Methinks it looks as if it mockt all ruin
Saue that greate M^{r}peece of Consumation,
The end of time, wch must Consume even ruin
And eate that into Cinders

Heng: Theirs no Brass
Would last yor praise my Lord; 'Twold last beyond it,

[Fol. 28, *recto*]

And shame o^{r} durablest mettle

Vort: Hersus

Hers: My Lord

Vort: This is ye time I haue Chosen, heers a full meeteing
And here will I disgrace her

Hers: Twill be sharp my Lord

Vort: Oh twill be best sir.

Hers: Why heers ye Earle her ffather

Vort: I and the Lord her Vncle, thats ye height ont,

25 this pye shall be cut *Q* 26 full lamentably *Q;* sing *has one minim too many in L* 27 Ex. *Q* IV. ii. *heading*) ACT. 4. SCENA 2. / [rule] / Enter Hengist, Horsus, Vortiger, Devonshire, Stafford, / Castiza, Roxena, Ladies. *Q;* Hers, Devo, . . . two Ladyes. *P;* tow Ladies *L* 1 Costllier *L* 2 of toil and talk, *Q* 3 full loue *inserted above a caret mark in P* 5 Why there's a Fabrick that implies eternity, / The *Q;* why thats a welcom that implyes / the *L,P* 6 full *deleted after* plaine *in P;* most *omitted in L,P* 7 ruim *L* 8 Saving that Master-piece of Consummation *Q* 9 ruim *L* 11–13 *line-division that of Q;* theirs . . . my Lord [*end of page*] / 'Twold . . . mettl< *L* 12 Would pass *Q* 14 Vort: *over* Hers *erased in L* 16 a full) *so Q;* of all *L,P* 19 sir *omitted in Q* 21 I and) *so Q;* and I *L,P;* of it, *Q*

Invited both a purpose to rise sicke
Full of shames surfeyt
Hers: And thats shrewd Birladye
It euer sticks Close to ye ribbs of hono^{r}
Greate men are never sound men after it,
It leaues som ach or other in their names still
Which their posterityе feeles at euery wether,
Vort: Mark but ye least p^{r}sentm^{t} of occasion
As such times yeilds enough, and then mark me.
Hers: My observance is all yo^{rs}, you know't my Lord;
What Carefull wayes som take t'abuse themselues,
But as their be assurers of mens goods
Gainst storme or pyratt, which giues venturers Courage,
So such their must bee to make vpp mans theft,
Or their would be noe woman ventuerer left.
See now they find theire seates, what a false knott
Of amitye he tyes about her arme
W^{ch} rage must part, in marriage tis no wonder —— *Musique*
Knotts knitt wth kisses are oft broke with thunder
Musique then I haue don, I alwayes learne
To giue my betters place
Vort: Wheirs Captaine Hersus

[Fol. 28, *verso*]

Hers: My Lord
Vort: Sitt sitt weele haue a health anon
To all good services
Hers: Th'ar poore in these dayes
They had rather haue the Cup then the health my Lord
I sitt wrong now, he heares me not, and most
Great men are deafe on that side.

22 on purpose *Q* 24 b'er lady, *Q* 30 these times yield *Q* 31 observance *originally* observations *in L, but* tions *deleted and* nce *written above the line over a caret mark* 32 to abuse *Q;* themselu< *L* 34 *second* t *of* pyratt *over* e *in L;* pyrates, *P;* storms or Pirates, *Q;* ventuers *L;* ventures *P;* Adventurers *Q;* C< *L* 36 vetuerer *L* 37 the find *L;* i *of* theire *over* e *in L* 39 part in marriage, tis *L,P;* part? in marriage 'tis *Q;* Mu< *L; stage-direction omitted in Q* 40 kisses oft are *Q* 44 *omitted in Q* 45 *prefix omitted in Q* 45–6 *all one line in Q* 47 they are *P,Q* 48 th'had *Q;* the Carp *Q;* my Lord *omitted in Q* 49 I sitt wrong now, *omitted in Q* 47–50 *Q divides this passage as follows:* They are . . . the Carp / Then . . . not, / And . . . side. 49–50 most great men / are *L*

Song

If in musique were a powre
To breath a welcom to thy worth
This should be ye rauishing howre
To vent her spirrits treasure forth;
Welcom oh welcom, in that word alone
Sheeld choose to dwell and draw all parts to one.

Vort: My Lord of Kent I thank yo^{u} for this welcome
It Came vnthought of in ye sweetest languadge
That ever my soule rellisd
Heng: You are pleasd my Lord
To raise my happiness from slight deseruings
To shew what powr's in princes: not in vs
Ought worthy, tis in yo^{u} that makes vs thus
Ime Cheifly sad my Lord, yor Queenes not merry
Vort: Soe hono^{r} bless me, he has found the way
To my greife strangely: is their noe delight,
Cast: My Lord I wish not any, nor ist needefull;
I am as I was euer
Vort: That's not soe
Cast: How oh my feares
Vort: When she writ Mayd my Lord
Yo^{u} knew her otherwise
Deuo: To speake but truth,
I neuer knew her a greate friend to mirth,
Nor taken much wth any one delight
Though their be many seemely & honno^{rble}:
To giue Content to Ladyes without taxeing

[Fol. 29, *recto*]

Vort: My Lord of Kent, this to thy full desart
Which intimates thy higher flow to hono^{r},
Heng: W^{ch} like a riuer shall returne service
To ye greate M^{r} fountaine
Vort: Wheirs yor Lord
I mist him not till now Ladye? and yours,
No marvell then we were soe out oth waye

51–7 *omitted in Q; song unpunctuated in L,P* 59 sweetest *altered from* secretest *in L* 62 for slight *Q* 63 powre is *P* 65 I am *Q* 68 needefull *L* 72 whe she writ f Mayd *L;* who's shee writt *P* 72–3 *line-division that of Q; all one line in L* 73 other ways *P* 79 deserts, *Q* 80 imtinates *L;* imitates *P* 81 servine *L,P;* return in service *Q* 84 now; Lady, and yours? *Q;* Ladyes and yours *L,P* 85 of the way *Q;* waye, *L*

Of all pleasant discourse, they are the keyes
Of humane Musique, sure at their natiuities
Greate nature signd a generall patent to em,
To take vpp all ye mirth in a whole Kingdome,
Whats their imployment now,
1 Lady: Mayt please yor grace
We never are soe farr acquainted wth 'em
Nothing we know, But what they Cannot keepe
Thats even ye ffashion of 'em all my Lord
Vort: It seemes you haue greate faith though in their Constancy,
And they in yours, yo^{u} dare soe trust each other,
2 Lady Hope well we doe my Lord, we haue reason fort
Because they saye Browne men are honestest,
But shees a foole will sweare for any Colour
Vort: They would for yours
2 Lady Troth tis a doubtfull question
And Ide be loth to put mine toot my Lord
Vort: Faith dare yo^{u} sweare for yo^{r}selues y^{ts} a plaine motion.
2 Lady My Lord
Vort: You cannot deny that with hono^{r}
And since tis vrgd Ile put yo^{u} toot in troth
1 Lady Mayt please yor grace
Vort: Twill please me wondrous well

[Fol. 29, *verso*]

And heeres a booke, mine never goes wthout one
Shees an example to yo^{u} all for puritie,
Com sweare, I haue sworne you shall: y^{t} yo^{u} never knew
The will of any man Besides yor Husbandes
2 Lady: Ile sweare my Lord as farr as my remembrance
Vort: How yor remembrance, that were strange
1 Lady: Yo^{r} grace,
Hearing our Iust excuses will not say soe
Vort: Well whats yor Iust excuse, y'are nere without som
1 Lady: Ime often taken wth a sleepe my Lord

88 to them *Q* 91 May it *Q* 92 with them, *Q* 94 that even *L;* of them *Q* 95 y'have great thought in their constancies, *Q;* Con< (*with only one minim of the final* n *visible*) *in L* 97 for it, *Q* 101 Truth 'tis *Q* 102 I'ld *Q; first* t *of* toot *over* C *in L* 103 plain question. *Q;* motio< *L* 106 vrdg *L* 107 may it *P,Q* 108 'Twould please me very well, *Q* 111 all *deleted before* shall *in L;* ne're *Q* 112 ancy man *L* 113 Ille sweare *L;* my re [*end of page*] remembrance *P* 115–6 *line-division that of Q; all one line in L* 116 excuse, *Q* 118 I am *Q*

The lowdest thunder Cannot waken me
Not if a Cannons Burthen were dischargd
Close by mine eare, the more may be my wrong;
Their can be noe infirmitie my Lord
Thats more excusable in any woman
2 Lady And Ime so troubled with ye Mother too
I haue often Cald in helpe, I know not whom
Three at once has bene to weake to keepe me downe
Vort: I perceiue theirs noe ffastening: well fare on then
That nere deceiues faithes Anchor of her hold
Com at all seasons: here: be thou the starr
To guide those erring woemen: show ye way
W^{ch} I will make em follow: why doost start
Draw back and looke soe pale;
Cast: My Lord
Vort: Come hither
Noething but take that oath, thou'lt take a thousand
A thousand, poore, a million, nay as many
As their be Angells registers of oathes:
Why Looke their ouer-holy fearefull Chastitye
That syns in nothing but in to much nicenes

[Fol. 30, *recto*]

Ile begin first and sweare for ye myselfe,
I know ye a perfection so vnstaind
So sure so absolute, I will not pant ont
But Catch time greedilye: by all these blesings
That blowes truth into fruitfulness, & those Curses
That with their barrein Breaths Blast periurye
Thou art as pure as sanctityes best shrine
From all mans mixture, But whats Lawfull: mine.
Cast: Oh heauen forgiue him, has forsworne himselfe,
Vort: Com tis but goeing now my way
Cast: Thats bad enough
Vort: I haue Cleerd all doubts you see

120 nor if *P;* be discharg'd *Q* 121 my ear; *Q;* more be *P;* wrong *L* 122 can *added above the line over a caret mark in L* 122–3 *all one line in Q* 123 Thats *omitted in Q* 124 I am *Q* 126 have been *Q* 127 *no prefix in P;* fare one *Q;* fair one *Dyce* 128 never *Q;* Achor *L* 131 them *Q* 134 *no prefix in P* 135 take *altered from* tat't *in L* 136 thousand! Nay a million, or as *Q* 137 Angells, registers *L,P* 138 ouer holy *with the final* y *altered from* d *in L;* look thee, over-fearful Chastity, *Q* 139 sinn'st *Q;* much inocense, *P* 142 on it, *Q* 143 those blessings *Q* 144 blow *Q* 147 save what's *Q;* Lawfull min< *L* 148 him, he has *Q*

Cast: Good my Lord spare mee
Vort: How, it growes later now, then soe
For modesties sake make more speed this waye
Cast: Pardon me my Lord: I Cannot
Vort: What
Cast: I dare not
Vort: Faile all Confidence
In thy weake kind forever.
Devon Heers a storme
Able to wake all of o^{r} name inhumed
And raise em from their sleepes of peace and fame
To set ye hono^{r} of their Bloodes right here
Hundred yeares after, a perpetuall motion
Has their true glory bene from seed to seed,
And Cannot be Choakd now with a poore graine
Of Dust and earth; we that remaine my Lord
Her vncle and my selfe, in this wild tempest,
As euer robd mans peace, will vndertake
Vppon liues deprivation, landes & hono^{r},
She shall accept this oath.
Vort: You do but call me then
Into a world of more despair and horrour;
Yet since so wilfully you stand engag'd
In high scorn to be touch'd, with expedition
Perfect your undertakings with your fames,
Or by the Issues of abus'd belief
I'le take the forfeit of liues, landes & hono^{r},

[Fol. 30, *verso*]

And make one ruin serue o^{r} Ioyes and yo^{rs}.
Cast: Why heeres a height of misery never reachd yet

153 how *L;* now *L;* later then so, for modesties sake / Make *Q* 155 Lord, / I *Q* 158–9 *all one line in L,P,Q* 158 Confidence, *L* 161 wake) inhumed) *so Dyce;* make . . . inhumid *L,P,Q* 162 sleepes *in italics, possibly a later addition in P;* them *Q* 163 honours *Q* 167 we that remaine my Lord *omitted in Q, whose line-division is as follows:* Of . . . self / Wild . . . peace, / Will . . . deprivation / She 168 in this wild tempest) *suggested by Dyce;* would in this tempest, *L,P;* Wild in this tempest *Q* 170 landes & hono^{r}, *omitted in Q* 171–8 *these lines are supplied from Q, since they are missing in L,P; the omission in the MSS. seems to be due to the fact that a transcriber's eye caught similar words eight lines further on and went on from that point;* landes & hono^{r}, *omitted by Q at line 170, both completes the line, and makes the omission more probable* 178 Honours, *Q* 180 miseries *Q*

I loose my selfe and others
Devon: You may see
How much we lay in Ballance wth yor goodness
And had we more it went, for we p^{r}sume
You Cannot be religious and soe vild
Cast As to forsweare myselfe: tis true my Lord
I will not add a voluntary syn
To a Constraind one, I Confesse greate s^{r}
The hono^{r} of yor Bed has bene abusd
Vort: Oh beyond patience
Cast Giue me heareing sir
But farr from my Consent: I was surprizd
By villaines and soe rauishd
Vort: Heare you that sirs
Oh Cuning texture to enclose adulterye
Mark but what suttle vaile her sinn puts on;
Religion brings her to Confession first,
Then steps in Art, to sanctifie that Lust,
Tis likely you Could be surprizd
Cast: My Lord
Vort: Ile heare noe more, our gaurd: Ceize on those lordes
Devon: We Cannot perish now to fast, make speed
Swift to distruction, he breathes most accursed
That liues so long to see his name dye first *Exevnt*
Hersus: Ha ha, heres noe deare villany
Heng: Let him entreate sir
That falls in saddest greife for this event
W^{ch} ill begins ye fortune of this Building:
My Lord

[Fol. 31, *recto*]

Rox: What if he should Cause me to sweare too Captaine
You know sir Ime as farr to seeke in honestye

182–3 *line-division of Q; all one line in L* 183 with / your good and *P* 184 went. *L; a stroke such as is used to separate speeches after this line in L* 185 soe religious and vild too. *P;* so vile: *Q* 186 'tis truth, great Sir, *Q* 187–8 *omitted in Q* 189 hath *Q* 191 But give *Q; a stroke such as is used to separate speeches after this line in P* 192 'Twas far *Q* 193 rauishd *altered from* rauisd *in L;* so raught. *Q* 196 sinn *is one minim short in L* 201 lordes) wordes *L;* woodes. *P;* Lords: *Q* 202 fast *L* 203 Swift to distruction) swifter distruction *L,P;* To swift destruction; *Q* 204 Ex^{t}evn *L;* Exit *P; no stage-direction in Q* 205 Ha ha, *omitted in Q* 207 suddest *L,P* 208 n *of* fortune *over* r *in L* 208–9 *line-division that of P; all one line in L,Q* 211 know I am *Q*

As the worst here Can be, I shold be shamd too:
Her: Why foole, they sweare by that we worship not
So yo^{u} may sweare yor heart out, and nere hurt yor selfe
Rox: That was well thought on, Ide quite lost my selfe,
Vort: You shall p^{r}vaile in noble suites my Lord
But this—this shames ye speaker
Hers: Ile step in now
Though it shall be to noe purpose: good my Lord
Thinke on yor noble and most hopefull isue
Lord Vortiner ye prince
Vort: A Basterd sir
Oh that his life were in my furye now
Cast: That iniurye stirrs my soule to sweare ye Truth
Of his Conception. here I take ye booke my Lord
By all ye gloryfide rewardes of vertue
And p^{r}parde punishm^{ts} for Consents in syn,
A Queens hard sorrowe never supplide a Kingdome
Wth issue more Ligittimate then Vortiner
Vort: Pish this takes not out the staine of p^{r}sent shame though
To be once good, is nothing when it Ceases,
Continuance Crowns desart, she Can nere goe
For perfect honest thats not alwayes soe
Beshrew this needelesse vrgeing of this oath
'Thas Iustified her somwhat
Hers: To small purpose s^{r}
Vort: Amongst soe many woemen not one here
Dare sweare a simple Chastity, hers an age
To ꝑpogate vertue in, since I haue began't
Ile shame you altogether, and soe leaue yo^{u}?
My Lord of Kent

[Fol. 31, *verso*]

Heng: Yo^{r} Highness
Vort: Thats yor daughter

212 worst) *so Q;* best *L,P* 215 I had *P,Q;* self else. *Q* 217 this this *L;* But this does shame *Q* 219 it should *P* 220 Issue *deleted after* noble *in P* 221 i *of* Vortiner *inserted later in L;* Vortiner *is the normal spelling in L,P, but Q always has the more correct* Vortimer 223 I would his life *Q* 224 *second* i *of* iniurye *a later insertion in L;* inury *P;* to speak the truth *Q;* ru *of* Truth *written over something else in L* 228 ne're *Q* 229 g *of* Liggitimate *written over something else in L, and* a *so badly blotted as to be illegible* 230 pish *and* though *omitted in Q* 231 *omitted in Q* 232 she ne're can *Q* 234 Beshrew thy heart for urging this excuse, *Q* 235 Th'hast *Q* 236 s^{r} *omitted in Q* 237 Among *Q* 239 begun, / I'le *Q* 240 all together, *Q*

Heng: Yes my good Lord
Vort: Though Ime yor guest to daye
And shold be less austeere to yo^{u} or yo^{rs}
In this case pardon me, I will not spare her
Heng: Then her owne goodness frend her: here she Comes my Lord
Vort: The tender reputation of a mayde
Makes vp yor hono^{r}, or ells nothinge Can
The oath yo^{u} take, is not for truth to man
But to yor owne white soule, a mighty Taske;
What dare yo^{u} doe in this,
Rox: My Lord as much
As Chastity Can put a woman too
I aske no fauo^{r}, and t'approue the puritie
Of what my habitt and my time professes,
As also to requite all Curteous sensure
Heer I take oath I am as free from man
As truth from death, or sanctity from staine
Vort: Oh thou treasure, that rauishes the posseso^{r},
I know not where to speed so well agen
Ile keepe thee while I haue thee: heres a fountaine
To spring forth Princes and ye seed of Kingdomes;
Away with that infection of greate Hono^{r}
And those her leprous pledges, By her poyson
Blemisd and spotted in their fames for ever;
Here we'll restore succession with true peace
And of pure virgins grace the poore increase. *Musique*
Hers: Ha ha: hees well prouided now, here struck my fortune *Exevnt*
Wth what an impudent Confidence she swore honest,
Haueing ye advantage of ye oath: the mischeifes

[Fol. 32, *recto*]

That peoples a lost hono^{r}: oh they're infinite
For as at a small Breach in towne or Castle
When one has entrance, a whole Army followes,

245 I am *Q* 246 least austeere *P* 247 case) *so Q;* life *L,P;* I may not *Q* 248 here *omitted in Q;* my *altered from* ny *in L* 250 Makes your *Q* 252 Taske *L* 257 professeth, *Q* 258 As likewise to *Q* 260 from falshood, *Q* 261 posseo^{r}, *P* 264 the seeds *Q;* Kingdomes *L* 265 black honour, *Q* 265–6 Away . . . pledges, *all one line in Q* 266–7 By her . . . ever *omitted in Q* 267 ever *L* 268 here will restore *L,P;* will we store *Q* 268–9 Musique / Eexnt *P;* Exeunt all / but Horsus. *Q* 270 struck) *so Q;* struct *L,P;* fortunes. *Q* 271 an *originally* am *and* i *of* impudent *altered and blotted in L* 272 th'advantage *Q;* Oath! Precious Whore. *Q* 273–9 *omitted in Q* 273 peoples lost *P* 274 for at *P*

In Woman, so abusiuely once knowne,
Thousandes of sins has passadge made with one:
Vice Comes wth tropes, and they that entertaine
A mighty potentate must receiue his traine.
Me thinks I should not here from fortune next
Vnder an Earledome now, she Cannot spend
A night so Idely, but to make a Lord
Wth ease, me thinks & play; the Earle of Kent
Is Calme & smooth, like a deepe dangerous water,
He has som secret way, I know his Blood
The graues not greedier, nor hells Lord more proud
Somwhat will hap, for this astonishing choise
Sriks pale ye Kingdome at wch I reioyce [*Exit*]

Hoboyes *Dumb show* *Enter Lupus Germanus Devon Staffo:* Leading [D.S. iii] *Vortiner* they seate him in ye throne & Crowne him King, Enter *Vortiger* in greate passion and submission, they neglect him, then *Roxena* expressing greate fury & discontent, they leade out *Vortiner,* and leaue *Vortiger* and *Roxena;* she subornes two saxons to murder *Vortiner,* they sweare performance and secresie and Ex^{t} wth *Roxena,* then *Vortiger* left alone draws his sword and offers to run himselfe thereon *Enter Hersus* and prevents him, then ye Lordes Enter againe and Ex^{t} *Hersus,* then is brought in ye Bodye of *Vortiner* in a Chaire dead, they all in amazem^{t} and sorrow take *Vortiger* and vpon his submiss ion restore him, sweareing him against ye saxons, then *Enter Hengist* with diuers saxons: *Vortiger* and ye rest

278 voice Comes *L,P* 279 a *of* traine *over* r *in L* 280 r *of* from *over* e *in L; after this line in L is the fragmentary stage-direction:* Lor<des> / Black<son> / Bri<ggs> 283 of *omitted in L,P* 287 Something will *Q* 288 Exit *omitted in L,P*

Dumb-show. *no margin in P.* 1 Gemanus Deuon & Stafford *P;* Lea< *with* ea *over* ad *in L* 2 in throne *P;* King, < *L* 3 submission *L;* him, < *L* 4 ou< *L* 5 Roxena she suborne tw< *L;* tow Saxons *P;* 6 Vortiner *L;* performanc< *L* 7 dra< *L;* dwraws *P* 8 himselfe through *P;* Hers< *L* 9 Hersu< *L* 10 the< *L* 11 his su< *L* 12 t< *L* 13 ye re< *L* *Q has:* Dumb show. Enter Lupus, Germanus, Devonshire, and Stafford, leading Vortimer, and Crown him: Vortiger comes to them in passion, they neglect him. Enter Roxena in fury expressing discontent, then they lead out Vortimer; Roxena gives two Villains gold to murther him, they swear performance and go with her: Vortiger offers to run on his sword, Horsus prevents him, and perswades him; the Lords bring in Vortimer dead; Vortiger mourns and submits to them, they swear him, and Crown him. Then Enters Hengist with Saxons, Vortiger draws, threatens expulsion, and then sends a Parley, which Hengist seems to grant by laying down his weapons, so all depart severally. / Enter Raynulphus.

[D.S. iii]

[Fol. 32, *verso*]

wth their swordes drawn threaten their expulsion: whereat
Hengist amazd, sendes one to entreate
a peaceable parly, wch seemeing to be granted by laying down
there weapons *Exevnt seuerally* *Enter Raynulph.*

Ray: Off Pagan Blood a Queene beeing Chose [Chor. iv]
Roxena hight, ye Brittaines rose
And *Vortiner* they Crowned King;
But she soone poysoned that sweete spring;
Then to rule they did restore
Vortiger and him they swore
Against the saxons, they Constraynd
Begd peace-treaty—& obtaind:
And now in numbers equally
Vppon ye plaine nere salsbury
A peacefull meeteing they decreen
Like men of loue no weapon seene.
But Hengist that Ambitious Lord
Full of guile Corrupts his word;
As ye sequell too well proues
On that yor eyes, on vs yor Loues. *Exit*

Enter Hengist Gentleman & Saxons [IV, iii]

Heng: Iff we let slip this oppertunefull howre
Take leaue of fortune, Certainty or thought
Of ever fixing: wee are loose at roote
And ye least storme may rend vs from ye bosome
Of this Landes hopes for ever: But deere saxons
Fasten we now, and o^{r} vnshaken firmnesse
Will assure affter ages

14 sw *of* swordes *over* wth *erased in L* 15 with diuers saxons *deleted after* Hengist *in L* 16 laying by their *P*

Chor. iv.) 1 Choose, *P* 2 hight *L* 3 the Crowned *L,P;* For Vortimer, and crown'd him King, *Q;* King *L* 4 spring *L* 5 unto Rule *Q* 8 Peace, Treaty, *Q* 10 vppon, y^{e} *L;* of Salsbury, *P* 14 guil, *Q* 15 t *of* too *over* v *in L* 16 Loues *L*

IV. iii. *stage-direction*) Gentlemen *P;* Enter Hengist with Saxons. *Q* 5 hoopes *P* 7 Will endure *Q*

Gent: We are resolud my Lord
Heng: Obserud yo^{u} not how Vortiger ye King

[Fol. 33, *recto*]

Base in submission threatned o^{r} expulsion,
His arme held vpp against vs? ist not time
To make o^{r} best p^{r}ventions, what should Checke mee?
'Has perfected that greate worke in our Daughter
And made her Queene, she Can ascend noe higher,
Nor Can ye insestant fflow of his Loues praises
W^{ch} yet still swayes, take from y^{t} height it raises:
Shees sure enough: what rests then but that I
Make happy mine owne hopes; and policie
Forbidds noe way, noble or trecherous ended,
What best effects is of her best Commended:
Therefore be quick, dispatch, here every man
Receiue into thee service of his vengeance
An instrument of steele, wch will vnseene,
Lurke like ye snake vnder ye innocent shade
Of a spread sommers leafe; and as greate substance
Blocks itselfe vp into lesse roome in gold
Then other mettles, and less Burthensome
So in ye other hand lyes all Confinde
Full as much Death as ever changd mankind;
Tis all ye same time that a small watch showes
As greate Church dialls, & as true as those,
Take hart ye Commons Loues vs: those remoude
That are his nerues, our greateness standes improud
Gent: Giue vs ye word my Lord, and we are perfect
Heng: Thats true the word, I loose my selfe, nemp yor Sexes,
It shall be that,
Gent: Enough s^{r} then we strike
Heng: But the Kings mine, take heed yo^{u} touch not him

8 *prefix*) Sax. *Q;* resolud *inserted above the line over a caret mark in P* 9 Observe *Q* 11 Is it *Q* 12 prevention? *Q;* p^{r}ventions *L* 13 has *L;* He has *Q;* worke: in *L* 14 she has ascend *P* 15–20 *omitted in Q* 15 Loue *L,P* 16 height raises: *P* 17 rest then that but I, *L,P* 19 ffobidds *L;* ended *L* 21 quick *L* 22 ee *of* thee *over* is *in L* 23 *first* e *of* steele *a later insertion in L, and* l *written over* k 24 shade *deleted between* the *and* snake *in P;* a snake *Q* 25 Summer-leaf, there fly you on, / *Q;* and of greate *P* 25–31 and as . . . those, *omitted in Q* 28 so in *omitted in P;* orther *P* 29 mankind *L* 32 love *Q* 33 the nerves, *Q* 34 *prefix*) Sax. *Q* 35–6 *line-division that of Q;* thats . . . selfe, / nemp . . . that, *L* 37 *prefix*) Sax. *Q* 38 touch him not. *Q*

Gent: We shall not be at leysure never feart
We shall haue worke enough of our owne my Lord [*Enter Vortiger & British Lords*]

[Fol. 33, *verso*]

Heng: They Come, Calme lookes But stormy soules possess yo^{u}
Vort: Wee see yo^{u} keepe yor word in all pointes firme
Heng: Noe Longer may we boast of so much Breath
As goes to a words makeing, then of Care
In ye preserueing of it when tis made
Vort: Y'ar in a vertuous way my Lord of Kent
And since w'are both sides well mett like sons of peace
All other armes Layd by in signe of fauour
If our Conditions be imbracd,
Heng: Th'ar th'ar
Vort: Weele vse noe other but these only here
Heng: Nemp yor sexes
Br: Lordes Treason Treason
Heng: Follow to'th hart
My Trusty saxons, tis yor libertye
Yo^{r} wealth & honno^{r}; soft y'ar myne my Lord
Vort: Take me not Basely when all sence & strength
Lyes bound vpp in amazem^{t}, at this trecherye,
What Diuell hath Breathd this euerlasting part
Of falshood into thee?
Heng: Let it suffice
I haue yo^{u} and will hold yo^{u} prisoner
As fast as death holdes your best props in silence:
We know ye hard Conditions of o^{r} peace,
Slauery or diminution wch we hate
Wth a ioynt loathing: may all perish thus
That seeke to subiugate or lessen vs.

39 *prefix*) Sax. *Q;* fear it, *Q* 40 her *deleted after* of *in L;* Lor< *L; stage-direction added from Q; omitted in L,P* 41 They Come *omitted in Q;* Come *L;* posseses *L;* you all. *Q* 42 your words *Q* 43 Breath *altered from* Birth *in L* 44 word *L,P* 47 sides met together / like *P;* since both sides are met *Q* 48 others *P;* armyes *L,P;* signs *Q* 50 their their *L,P;* They are: (*only once*) *Q* 51 these heere, *P* 53 *prefix*) Vort: *P;* Brit. *Q* 54 to the *P,Q* 54–5 Follow it to . . . Saxons, / It is . . . you are . . . Lord. / *Q* 55 saxons *L* 58 vp *deleted after* lyes *in P* 61 & w *erased after* suffice *in L* 62 yor prisoner *L,P* 64 ye hard ye hard *L;* the hard the hard *P* 65 w^{ch} *originally* wch *but the last two letters have been erased and the* w *of* we *written over the original* h *in L*

Vort: Oh you strange nookes of guile & subtiltie
Where man soe Cuningly lyes hid from man
Who Could exspect such treason from yor brest

[Fol. 34, *recto*]

Such Thunder from yor voice: or take you pride
To imitate the faire vncertaintye,
Of a Bright day that Teemes the sodainst storme,
When ye world least expects one: but of all
Ile neuer trust faire skye in man againe
Theirs ye deceitfull weather: will you heape
More guilt vppon yo^{u}, By detaineing me,
Like a Cupp taken after a full surfeyt,
Euen in Contempt of health, & heauen together?
What seeke yo^{u}

Heng: Ransom for yor libertye
As I shall like of, or yo^{u} neere obtain't

Vort: Heres a most headstrong dangerous ambition;
Sow yo^{u} ye seedes of yor aspireing hopes
In Blood and treason, & must I pay for em.
Haue not I raisd you to this height.

Heng: My Lord
A worke of mine owne merritt since yo^{u} enforce it

Vort: Theirs even ye generall thankes of all aspirers:
When they haue all ye hono^{rs} Kingdomes Can impart
They write aboue it still there owne desart

Heng: I haue writt myne true my Lord

Vort: Thats all their sayeinges
Haue I not raisd yor daughter to a Queene

Heng: Why y'haue ye harmony of yor pleasure fort
Y'haue Crownd yor owne desires; whats that to me.

68 the strange *Q;* guil or *Q* 69 When man *Q* 70 yor) y^{e} *L;* the *P;* thy *Q* 71 thy voice? *Q;* your pride *L,P;* takest thou pride *Q* 73 a sudden storm, *Q* 75 ne're *Q;* in a man *Q* 77 yo^{u} *deleted after* detaineing *in L* 78 a sore surfeit *Q* 79 Contempt, *L;* heauen *written above* euer *deleted in P* 82 obtain it. *Q* 83 most headlong *Q;* ambition *L* 85 them? *Q* 86 *prefix* Heng. *before this line instead of line 87 in Q;* Have not I *Q;* this height of pride? *Q; second* h *of* height *inverted in some copies of Q* 87 Heng: *over* Vort: *erased in L;* My Lord *omitted in Q* 87–8 *as one line in L* 88 my own *Q;* enfo< *L* 89 aspirers *L* 90 all a Kingdom can *Q;* impar< *L* 91 writte *L;* write about it *P;* still, *L* 92 I *badly blotted and* d *of* Lord *over* e *in L* 94 Haue not I *P;* thy daughter *Q;* to Queene *L,P* 95 Why *omitted in Q;* You have *Q;* byt *deleted after* pleasure *in L;* for it, *Q* 96 You Crown *Q*

Vort: And what will Crowne yo^{rs} sir
Heng: Faith things of reason,
I demand Kent
Vort: Why y'haue ye Earledom on't
Heng: The Kingdome ont I meant, wthout Controll,
Y^{e} full possession
Vort: This is strange in you

[Fol. 34, *verso*]

Heng: It seemes y'are not acquainted wth my blood yet
To Call this strange;
Vort: Never was King of Kent yet
But who was generall King
Heng: Ile be ye first then,
Euerything has begining
Vort: No lesse title
Heng: Not if you hope for libertie my Lord
So deere a hapiness would be wrongd by slighting
Vort Well tak't, I resign't
Heng: Why I thank yor grace
Vort: Is yor greate thirst sufficd yet
Heng: Faith my Lord
Theirs yet behind a paire of teemeing sisters
Norfolke & Suffolke, & I haue don wth yo^{u}
Vort: Y'haue got a fearefull thirst my Lord of late
How ere you Came byt
Heng: It behoues me then
For my Bloodes health to seeke al meanes to quench it
Vort Them too
Heng: Theirs nothing willbe abated sir.
Put yor assurance int
Vort: You haue ye advantage,

97 sirs *L,P* 98–9 *line-division that of Q; all one line in L,P* 98 reason S^{r}: *P* 100 of it. *Q* 101 of't *Q;* mean, *Q* 101–2 *line-division that of P,Q; all one line in L* 102 controul, / In full *Q;* poss< *L* 104 yet *omitted in Q* 106 yet *omitted in Q* 108–9 *line-division that of Q; as one line in L* 112 would not be wrong'd with *Q* 113 Very well, take it, I resign it. *Q* 115 thirst sattisfied. yet. *P;* thirst yet satisfied? *Q* 117 there is *P* 119 a dangerous thirst of late, my Lord, *Q* 120 by it. *Q* 122 all *deleted before* seeke *in P* 123 *this and the next four speeches (i.e. till the foot of the page) lack prefixes in P, though the speeches are separated by strokes* 124–5 *all one line in L;* There will nothing be abated, I assure you. *Q* 126–8 *line-division in L:* you . . . whom / ffate . . . em, / 126 have me at advantage, *Q*

He whom ffate Captiuates must yeilde to all
Take em,

Heng: And yo^{u} yor libertie and peace my Lord
Wth our best loue and wishes: heres an howre
Begins vs Saxons, in wealth fame & powre. —— *Exit*

Vort: Are these the noblest fruites & fairst requitalls
From workes of our owne raiseing;
Methinks ye murder of Constantius
Speakes to me in ye voice on't, and ye wrongs
Of our late Queene slipt both into one Organ
Here is noe safetye for me, but whats most doubtfull
The Ranck rowt loue me not, & ye strength I had —*Enter Hersus*

[Fol. 35, *recto*]

This fowle devoureing Treachery has demollishd;
Ambition, hell, mine owne vndooing Lust,
And all ye broode of plauges Conspire against mee
I have not a friend left me.

Hers: My Lord he dyes
That saies it But yor selfe, wert that theife King
That has soe boldly stolne his honno^{rs} from yo^{u},
A Treason that wrings teares from honest manhood

Vort: So rich am I now in thy loue and pittye
I feele no loss at all; But we must part
My Queene & I to Cambria

Hers: My Lord
And I not namde that haue vowde Lasting seruice
To liues extremest minute to yor fortunes?

Vort: Is my ruind fate blest with soe deere a friend

Hers: My Lord not space in Earth, nor Breadth in sea
Shall devide me from you.

Vort: Oh faithfull treasure

127 fate / Does captivate *Q;* Captuates *P* 128 them. *Q* 129 u *of* yo^{u} *over* r *in L* 131 Exit cum suis. *Q* 135 of it, *Q* 137–40 *omitted in Q* 137 heers *P* 138 R *of* Ranck *over* r *in L;* loues *P; the stage-direction comes after line 136 in Q and after line 141 in P* 139 H< *L* 140 devourering *L,P;* demollishd, *L* 141 my own undoing, lust, *Q* 143 *added from Q; omitted in L,P* 145 no *deleted before* that *in P* 146 boldly, *L* 149 o *of* loss *over* e *in L* 151–3 My . . . nam'd, / That . . . minute? /; my lives *Q;* to yor fortunes *omitted in Q* 154 tis my *P;* my sick fate *Q;* so pure a *Q* 155 no space of Earth, nor breadth of Sea *Q;* a *of* sea *over* e *in L* 157–8 *line-division that of Q; all one line in L, with stage-direction crowded in under the end of the line;* is mad< *L;* E< *L*

All my lost happiness is made vp in thee. *Exit*

Hers: Ile follow yo^{u} through ye world, to Cuckold yo^{u}
Thats my way now; euery one has his toye
While he liues here: some men delight in Building,
A tricke of Babell & will nere be left,
Some in Consuming what was raysd wth toyleing
Hengist in getting hono^{r}, I in spoyleing —— *Exit*

Actus Quintus Scena p^{ra}: Enter Symon: Clark Glouer fellmonger etc: graz Musique [V, i]

Sym: Is not that Rebell Oliuer ye fustian weauer
That Traytor to my yeare p^{r}hended yet
Clark: Not yet soe please yor worship
Sym: Not yet sayst thou;
How darst thou say not yet, & see me p^{r}sent,

[Fol. 35, *verso*]

Thou malapart Clark,
Thats good for nothing but to write & reade,
Is his loome Ceizd on.
Clark: Yes and it like yor worship
& sixteene yards of fustian
Sym: Good; let a yard be saude to mend me betweene ye leggs, y^{e}
rest Cut in peices & giuen to ye poore, tis heretick
fustian & shold be burnt indeed, But being worne
threed bare, the shame will be as greate, how think yo^{u}
neighbors *Enter foot:*
Glou: Greater methinks ye Longer it is wore

162 tr *of* tricke *retouched and* t *of* left *over* s *in L;* Babel, which will *Q* 163 some *altered from* sone *in L; catchword* Actus *at foot of page in Q*

V. i. *heading*) fell< *L;* graz & Musique. *P;* ACT. 5. SCENA 1. / [rule] / Enter Symon and his Brethren, Aminadab his Clerk. *Q; the symbol* ♅ *appears to the left of the rule under the heading in L* 1 ye fustian weauer *omitted in Q* 1–2 weauer that / Traytor *L* 3 *prefix*) *here and elsewhere in this scene the prefix to the Clerk's speeches in Q is* Ami. 4–8 *as prose in L, the page ending with* see *in line 5; as in previous scenes the tradesmen's speeches are arbitrarily cut up into verse in Q, but it is of little help in distinguishing true verse from prose* 5 durst *Q* 6–7 Clark thats, good *L;* malapert, that art good *Q;* i *of* write *a later addition in L* 8 seiz'd upon? *Q* 9 if it like *Q* 9–10 *all as one line in L* 11 leggs *L* 15 *stage-direction* Enter a / Footman *after line 18 in Q* 16 worne *L,P;* wore, *Q*

Wheir beeing once Burnt, it Can be burnd noe more
Sym: True wise and most sencelesse, how now sirrah
Whats he approaching here in dusty pumps
& greasie haire
Clark: A footeman s^{r}. to ye greate King of Kent
Sym: The King of Kent, shake him by the hand for me
Footeman, thou'art wellcom, lo my deputy shakes thee;
Come when my yeares out and Ile doot my selfe,
Ant twere a dogg Come from ye King of Kent,
I keepe those officers wold shake him I tro;
And whats ye news wth thee thou well stewd footeman,
ffoote: The king my M^{r}
Sym: Hah
foote Wth a few saxons
Intends this night to make merry wth you
Symo: Merry with me, I shold be sorry else fellow
And take it in euill part, soe tell Kents King
Why was I Chosen Maio^{r}, But that greate men
Shold make merry with mee, thers a Iest indeed
Tell him I lookd fort, & me much he wrongs
If he forgett symon that Cutt out his thongs.
foote: Ile run with yor worshipps answere [*Exit*]

[Fol. 36, *recto*]

Symo: Do I prithee;
That fellow will be roasted against supper,
Hees halfe enough already: his browes baste him:
The King of Kent, ye King of Kirsondom
Shall not be better welcom to me,
For you must immagine now neighbors this is
The time y^{t} Kent stands out of Kirsondom

18 wisse *L* 19 pumps. *L* 20 & greasie hair *added in another hand in L, but omitted altogether in P,Q* 19–20 *all as one line in L* 22 Kent *L; P has* shaken *with the last two letters deleted* 23 Th'art welcome, Footman, *Q* 23–5 shakes / thee; . . . my / selfe, ant . . . *L* 24 year is out, I'le *Q* 25 If 'twere a Dog that came *Q* 27 thou) *so Q; omitted in L,P* 31 intend *L,P;* y *of* merry *added later in L* 32 *second* r *of* merry *over* e *in L* 33 in ill part, *Q* 34 chosen, but *Q* 35 there is *Q* 37 forget Sym *Q* 38 *stage-direction from Q; omitted in L,P* 39–70 *as prose in L,P and as rather uncertain verse in Q; the division into lines, which is sometimes doubtful, is mostly that of Q as amended by Dyce and Bullen* 39 *omitted in L,P* 41 brewes *L;* halfe e< > / already *L* 42 Kent *L;* K< > / Kirsondom *L* 43 to me *omitted in Q* 44 ffor y< > / immagine *L* 45 when Kent *Q;* Ken< > / out *L*

For he thats King there now was neuer Kirsond;
This for yor more instruction I thought fit
That when y'are dead you may teach yor Children witt
Clark
Clark At yor worshipps elbow
Symo: I must turne you
From ye hall into ye Kitching tonight,
Giue order that twelue Piggs be roasted yellow,
Nine geese and som 3 Larks for pidling meate,
But twenty wood Cocks, Ile bid all my neighbors:
Giue Charge ye mutton Come in all blood raw;
Thats Infidell meate? the King of Kents a Pagan
& must be serud soe; and let those officers
That seldome or never goe to Church bring't in,
Twill be well taken; run: Com hither yo^{u} now;
Take all ye Cushions downe & thwack em soundly
After my feast of millers; for their Buttocks
Has left a peck of flowre in em, Beate em Carefully
Ore a bolting hutch, their'l be enough
For a panpuding as yor dame will handle it;
Then putt fresh water into both the bow pots,
And burne a little Iuniper ith Hall Chimney,
Like a beast as I was I pissd out ye fire Last night
& never thought of ye Kings Coming: how now
Returnd so quickly.
Clark Please yor worship thers a Certayne Company of players.
Symo: Hah players

[Fol. 36, *verso*]

Clark: Country Comedians, Enterluders sir, desire yor worships
leaue and fauor to enact in ye Towne Hall

46 here now *Q;* was < > / Kirsond *L* 48 you are *Q;* Children < > / Clark *L* 49 C erk *Q* 52 to the *Q;* ton< > / giue *L* 54 nine < > / and *L* 55 And twenty *Q;* w< > / Cocks *L* 56 ye m< > / Come *L* 57 that is Infidels *Q;* Kin< > / Kents *L;* Kent is *Q* 58 thos< > / that *L* 59 it in, *Q* 60 'twill be the better taken. *Q;* tw< > / well *L;* Run, run, come you hither *Q* 61 y< > / Cushions *L;* all my *Q;* them *Q* 62 my f< > / of *L* 63 Have *Q;* flow< > / em, *L;* in them . . . them *Q* 64 Over *Q;* their< > / enough *L;* there will *Q* 65 as you dame will order it: *P;* handl< > / then *L* 66 Bough-pots, *Q* 67 bur< > / little *L;* in the *Q* 68 as I < > / I *L;* fire *added above the line over a caret mark in L in another hand* 69 And never dreamt *Q;* Kings < > / ing *L* 71 here are / A *Q;* pl< *L* 73 desirs *L,P* 74 favour / And leave *Q*

Symo: Ith towne hall: tis ten to one I neuer grant it, Call
em before my worship, if my house will not serue
their turne I wold faine see ye proudest hee lend a
Barne to em: now sirs are you Comedians

Enter Cheaters

2 Chea: We are anything sir: Comedians Tragedians
Tragicomedians, Come-tragedians, pastorallists
humorists, Clownists & saterists, we haue em sir
from ye smile to ye laugh; from ye laugh to the handkercher

Symo: You are very strong ith wrists: and shall these good
parts y'are indud withall, be cast away among ped
lars and maultmen,

1 cheat: For want of better Company and't please yor wo^{pp}.

Symo: What thinke you of me my maisters: haue yo^{u}
audacitie enough to play before so high a person:
will not my Countenance daunt yo^{u}, for if you play
befor me I shall often looke at you: I giue you that
warneing Before hand, take it not ill my Masters,
I shall laugh at yo^{u}; and truely when Ime least offended
wth you; my humo^{r} tis, but be not you abashd.

1 Chea: Sir we haue plaid before a Lord ere now,
Though we be Country Actors

Symo: A lord, hah hah,
Youl finde it a harder thing to please a maior

1 Chea: We haue a play wherein we vse a horse

Symo: Fellowes you vse noe horse play in my house,
My roomes are rubd, keepe it for hackney men

1 Chea: We will not offer't to yor wo^{pp}: sir

Symo: Giue me a play without a beast I Charge yo^{u}

2 Cheat: Thats hard, wthout a Cuckold or a drunckard

75 *no prefix in P, but the speech is separated from the previous one by a stroke;* In the *Q;* grant them that; *Q* 76 them *Q* 77–8 lend them a barn: *Q* 78–9 *the stage-direction comes three lines earlier in Q* 79 We are Sir, Comedians, *Q;* g *of* Tragedians *over* d *in L* 80 Pastorists, *Q* 81 & *omitted in Q;* them *Q* 82 *after* sir *Q continues* From the hug to the smile, from the smile . . .; handkerchief. *P,Q* 83 strongists wrists *L,P;* Y'are very strong in the wrist methinks; / And must all these *Q;* goods parts *P* 84 parts be cast away / Upon *Q* 85 Malt-men, ha? *Q* 86 1 chet: *L;* if it please *Q* 87 Masters? / Hum; have *Q* 88 person as myself? will *Q* 89 Countenance, daunt yo^{u} for *L* 90 on you, *Q* 92 I am *Q* 93 you; / It is my humour, but *Q;* abas'd. *P* 94–5 *line-division that of Q; as prose in L* 96–7 *line-division that of Q; all as one line in L* 97 pelease *L;* Thou'lt finde *Q* 98 *prefix)* 2 Cheat. *Q* 99–100 *line-division that of Q; as prose in L* 100 rubd *in L, with* d *over original* b 101 We'le not offer it to your Worship. *Q* 103 hard *L*

[Fol. 37, *recto*]

Symo: Oh those Beasts are often ye best men ith ꝑish & must not be kept
out But which is yor merryest play now, that wold I harken after.
2 Chea: Why yor wo^{pp}: shall here ye names all ore & take yor Choise
Sym: And thats plaine dealeing trust me Com begin sir
2 Chea: The whirlegig, ye whible, Carwidghin
Symo: Hey day what names are these
2 Chea: New names of Late:
The wildgoose Chase
Sym: I vnderstand ye now
2 Cheat: Gull vpon gull
Sym: Why this is somwhat plaine yet
2 Chea: Woodcocke of our side
Symo: Gett you farther off then
1 Cheat: The Cheater & ye Clowne
Symo: Is that Come vp againe
That was a play when I was prentise first
2 Cheat: I but ye Cheater has learnd more tricks since sir
And guls ye Clowne with new aditions
Sym: Then is Clowne a Coxscombe; wch is hee
Clow: I am ye Clowne sir
Sym: Fye, fye, your Company must fall upon him and beat him,
hees too faire to make ye people laugh
1 Chea: Not as he may be drest sir
Symo: Faith dress him how you will, Ile giue him that guift, heele
never looke halfe scurvily enough: oh ye Clownes that I haue
seene in my time, ye very peepeing out of em wold haue
made a young heire laugh if his father had layen a dyeing;
A man vndon in Law the day before; ye saddest Case that Can
be; might for his two pence haue burst himselfe with
laughing & ended all his miseryes: here was a merry world
my Maisters, som talke of things of state, of puleing

104 in a Parish, *Q;* be< *L* 105 now *omitted in Q;* That I would *Q;* harke< *L* 106 Why *omitted in Q;* Their names, and take *Q;* Chois< *L* 107 Symo: *written over* 2 Ch *in P;* trust me *omitted in Q* 108 whirregig, *P;* Carwidgham. *P;* the Carwidgen. *Q* 110–11 *line-division that of Q; all one line in L* 114 plaine now. *P;* somewhat yet. *Q* 115 1 Cheat. *Q* 116 Get thee further *Q* 117 2 Cheat. *Q* 120 tricks of late, / And *Q* 122 is your Clown *Q;* Coxscombe *L* 123 1 Cheat. This is our Clown, Sir. *Q* 124 *This line, which is omitted from L,P is added from Q* 125 fiare *in P, the* i *being a later insertion;* too fair y'faith / To *Q* 127 He will *Q;* guift, < *L* 128 that < *L* 129 of one of them *Q;* wold h< *L* 130 laugh, though his Father lay *Q;* a dy< *L* 131 Case < *L* 132 himselfe < *L* 133 merry w< *L* 134 M *of* Maisters *over* m *in L;* state *L; only the tail of the final* g *is visible in L*

[Fol. 37, *verso*]

Stuff, theirs nothing in a play to a Clownes part, if he
haue ye grace to hitt on't, thats ye thing indeed:
Y^{e} King showes well But he sets of ye King
But not ye King of Kent I meane not soe
The King I meane, is one I doe not knowe,
2 Chea: Yo^{r} wo^{pp}: speakes with safety like a rich man
& for yor findeing fault our hope is greater
Neither wth him ye Clowne, nor me ye Cheater. *Exevnt Cheaters*
Symo: Away then shift Clowne to thy motley Crupper
Weele see em first, ye King shall after supper.
Glo: I Commend yor wo^{pps}: wisdome in that Mr Maior
Sym: Nay tis a point of Iustice ant be well examined not to
offer ye King worse then Ile see my selfe; for a play may
be dangerous, I haue knowne a greate man poysond in a play
Glou: What haue yo^{u} Mr Maior
Symo: But to what purpose many times I know not
fell: Me thinks they shold destroy one another soe
Sym: No no, he thats poysond, is allwayes made priuy too it
Thats one good order they haue amongst em;
What ioyfull throat is that Aminadab
What is ye meaneing of this Crye *showte*
Clark The Rebells tane *Enter Oliuer*
Symo: Oliuer ye puritane
Clark Oliuer puritan & fustian weauer altogether
Symo: Fates I thank yo^{u} for this victorious day
Bonefires of peese straw burne, let ye bels ring
Glou: Theirs two amending sir yo^{u} know they Cannot
Sym: Las ye tenors Broken, ring forth the treble
Ime ouercloyd with Ioy, welcom thou Rebell
Oliuer I scorne thy welcome

[Fol. 38, *recto*]

Symo: Art thou yet soe stowt

135 a Clown, / If *Q* 136 on it, *Q* 136–7 indeed: ye King / showes *L* 139 King is one, I mean, I *Q* 141 our hopes are *Q* 142 withim *P; stage-direction*) Cheater *L,P;* Ex. Players. *Q* 144 them *Q* 146 if it be *Q* 149 G *of* Glou: *over* S *in L* 151 *prefix*) Felt. *Q* 152 Oh no no, *Q; second* o *of* too *added later in L;* too't, *P* 153–5 *all as prose in L* 153 among them. *Q* 155 *apparently a second* e *has been inserted in* meaneing *in L so as to make it* meaneeing; A shout / within. *Q* 156 Rebel is taken. *Q; stage-direction* Oliver is / brought in. *after line 162 in Q* 161 in mending, and you *Q* 162 ring out *Q* 163 I am *Q* 164 welcome, I. *Q*

Wilt thou not stoope for grace, then gett ye out.
Oliuer I was not Borne to stoope but to my loome
That Ceizd vpon my stoopeing days are doon,
In plaine termes if thou hast anything to say to me send me away
quickly, this is no bideing place, I vnderstand thers players
in ye house, dispatch me I charge the in ye name of all the
Bretheren
Sym: Nay now proud Rebell, I will make ye staye
& to thy greater Torment see thee Playe
Oliue: Oh Devell I Coniure thee by Ansterdam
Sym: Our word is past
Iustice may winck awhile But see at Last
The play begins; hold stopp him, stopp him
Oliu: Oh oh that prophane Trumpett
Sym: Sett him downe theire I charge yo^{u} officers
Oliu: Ile hide myne eares, & stopp mine eyes.
Sym: Downe wth his golls I Charge you
Oliue: Oh tirrany, reveng it tribulation
Sym: For rebells their are many Deaths; but sure ye only way
To execute a Puritan is seeing of a Playe,
Oliue: Oh I shall swound
Symo: But iff thou doost, to fright thee
A players Boy shall Bring thee Aquauite *Enter: 1 Cheat:*
Oliuer Oh Ile not sound at all fort, though I dye
Sym: Peace heers a rascall, list and edifie
1 Cheat I say still hees an ass, that Cannot liue by his wits
Symo: What a bold rascalls this; he Calls vs all asses at first
dash; sure none of vs liues by o^{r} witts $neighbo^{rs}$, vnless it
Be Oliuer y^{e} Puritane

166 *first* o *of* stoope *a later insertion in L* 167 thy loome *P* 168–9 *line-division that of Q;* doon, in plai< > / termes *L* 169 aw< *L* 170 no) *so Q;* not *L,P;* place *L;* there are *Q;* thers p< *L* 171 house *L;* thy house, *Q;* charge *written above* pray *deleted in L;* th< *L* 174 a Play. *Q* 175 *first* e *of* Devell *over* i *in L* 178 begins *L* 179 Oh that prophane trumpet! oh, oh. *Q* 181 my ears . . . my eyes. *Q;* my eyes. *P;* eares *deleted before* eyes *in L* 182 this golls *L* 183 Oh tyrrany, tyranny, revenge *Q* 184 *prefix omitted in Q;* Death; *L* 186 *prefix omitted in Q* 187 S *of* Symo: *over* P *partially erased in L;* Which if *Q;* doost *L;* to spite thee, *Q* 188 Aquanite *L,P;* 1 C< *L* 189 swound *Q* 191 Cannot *altered from* Camno *in L;* wi< *L* 192 this *L;* at fi< *L* 193 dash *L;* r *of* sure *over* e *in L;* live *Q;* $neighbo^{rs}$ *omitted in Q;* vnless < *L; a stroke such as usually separates speeches after this line in L*

Oliuer I scorne as much to liue by my wits, as y^{e} proudest on yo^{u} all

Symo: Why yo^{u} are an ass for Company Oliuer & soe hold yor prateing

Enter 2 Cheater

2 Chea: Fellowes in armes welcom, ye news ye news

Symo: Fellowes in armes quotha, he may well Call em fellowes in armes, for they are all out oth elbowes

1 Che: Be liuely my hart be liuely, ye Bootyes in hand: hees but a foole of a yeamons eldest son, he Comes ballanst on both sides, Bully hees goeing to pay rent wth th'one pocket, & buy household stuff with th'other

2 Chea: And if this be his Last day my Chucke, he shall forfeyt his lease quoth th'one pocket, & eate his meate ith old wooden platters quoth th'other

Sym: Faith then hees not so wise as he ought to be, if he let such taterdemalians gett th'vpper hand on him ——

Enter Clowne

1 Che: He Comes he Comes

2 Chea: I but doe yo^{u} mark how he Comes; small to o^{r} Com forth, wth both his handes ins pockets, how ist possible to pick a Lock when the key's oth inside oth doore

Symo: I heers ye part now neighbors that Carrys away ye play, if the Clowne miscarry, ffarewell my hopes for ever, ye plays spoild

Clow: They say thers a foolish thing Cald Cheaters abroad, that will gull any yeamons son of his purse, & laugh ins face like an Irishman, I would faine

195 scorne to liue *P;* of you *Q;* all *originally written at the beginning of a fresh line in L, but accidentally deleted by the stroke separating this speech from the next, and rewritten in a very small hand at the end of the previous line* 196 y'are *P;* Why then y'are *Q;* company, so *Q* 197 Enter Cheater *L; stage-direction omitted in P;* Enter second / Cheater. *Q* 198 Fellow *Q;* quotha *deleted after* armes *in L* 199 Fellow in armes, quoth he? *Q* 199–200 call him fellow in arms. / I am sure th'are both out at the Elbows. *Q* 201 *prefix)* 2 Cheat. *Q;* Booty is at hand, *Q* 202 yeamons son, *P;* He's ballanc'd *Q* 203 the one *P* 204 and household *P* 203–4 going to buy houshold-stuff / With one pocket, and to pay rent with the other. *Q* 205 *prefix)* 1 Cheat. *Q;* c *of* Chucke *over* i *in L* 206 the one *Q;* in wooden *Q* 207 the other. *Q;* th'other pocket. *P* 208 be, to let *Q;* such, *L* 209 gett, *L,P;* the upper hand of him. *Q* 210 *second* he Comes *omitted in Q* 211 Comforts, *P;* I, but smally to our comfort, with both his hands in / His pockets; how is it *Q* 212 in his *P* 213 when ye Key when the key's oth inside dore *L;* o'the inside the doore. *P;* Key / Is on the inside of the Door? *Q* 214 Oh neighbours here's the part now / That carries *Q* 216 ever *L;* the pay is spoild. *P* 217 there is a foolish kind of thing call'd a Cheater *Q* 218 o *erased after* son *in L* 219 in his face *P,Q;* fame *L*

meete wth one of those Cheaters; Ime in as good
state to be guld now as ever I was in my Life, ffor I
haue 2 purses at this time about me, and Ide
faine be acquainted wth that rascall y^{t} wold but take one of

[Fol. 39, *recto*]

em now.
Sym: Faith thou mayst be acquainted wth two or three, y^{t} will doe
their good wills I warrant yo^{u}
1 Chea: That ways to playne, too easie Ime afraid
2 Che: Come Come s^{r} yor familiar Cheates takes best
They show like naturall things & least suspected
Giue me a round shilling quicklye
1 Che: Twill but fetch one of his handes neither, if it take
2 Che: Thou art to Couetuous, lets haue one at first prethee
Thers time enough to ffetch out thother after
Thou Lyest tis Lawfull mony, Currant monye [*They draw.*]
1 che: I: so is Copper in som Countryes sir
Clow: Heers a fray towardes, But Ile hold my handes
Let who will part em
2 Chea: Copper I defye thee
And now I shall disprooue thee: looke yo^{u} sir,
Heere Comes an honest yeamons son oth Contrye
A man of Iudgment
Clow: Pray be Couerd s^{r}
I haue eggs in my Capp and Cannot put it off.
1 che: Will you be tryde by him
2 Che: I am Content sir
Symo: They looke rather as if they would be tryde next sessions
1 che: Pray giue yor Iudgment of this peece of Coyne sir
Clow: Nay ant be Coyne yo^{u} striue about lets seet,

220 some of these Creatures, / I am in *Q* 222 I would *Q* 223 would take *Q* 224 them *Q* 225 accquainted *L* 226 warrant thee. *Q* 227 that was to plaine, *P;* I am *Q* 228 *one* Come *omitted in Q;* your most familiar Cheats take best, *Q* 231 It will fetch / But one *Q* 232 so Couetuous *L,P;* too covetous, *Q;* one out first, *Q* 233 the other *P* 234 lawful currant money. *Q; stage-direction added from Q, being omitted in L,P* 235 som Centry Country sir *L;* Contry *P;* I say 'tis Copper in some Countries. *Q* 236 Here is *Q;* I will *Q* 237 who) *so Q;* whose *L,P;* them. *Q* 239–40 Looke you, here's an *Q* 240 of the *Q* 242–3 *line-division that of Q; all one line in L* 242 Pray you be *Q* 243 Cann< *L* 244 *prefix*) 2 Cheat. *Q* 245 *prefix*) 1 Cheat. *Q* 246 session< *L* 247 g *of* Iudgment *added above the line over a caret mark in L* 248 Nay if it *Q;* Let me see it, *Q;* see it, *P* 248–9 *all as one line in L*

I loue to handle money
1 che: Looke ont well sir [*They pick his pocket.*]
2 che: Let him doe his worst sir
clow: Y'ad need to weare Cutt Cloathes, gent,
Yare both soe chollerick.
2 che: Nay rubbe it and spare't not sir
Clow: Now by this siluer Gentlemen tis good money
Would y'ad a hundred of em
2 che: We hope well sir,
Th'other pocket now and we are made men. [*Exevnt*]
Sym: Oh neighbors I begin to be sick to see

[Fol. 39, *verso*]

This foole so Cosend, I wold make ye Case mine owne
Clow: Still would I faine meet wth this thing Calld Cheaters
Sym: A horson Cockscombe they haue mett wth thee,
I Can endure him noe Longer wth patience
Clow Oh my rent my whole yeares rent
Sym: A murren on yo^{u}
This makes vs Land Lordes stay soe long
Wthout our money
Clow: The Cheaters haue beene here
Sym A scurrvy hobby horse that Cold not leaue his mony wth
me haueing such a Charg about him, a poxe on the for
an asse, thou play a Clowne! I will Committ
thee for offering ont, officer away wth him
Glou: What means your Worship? why you'l spoil the Play, Sir.
Sym: Before the King of Kent shall be thus serv'd,
I'le play the Clown my self, away with him.
Clow: Wth me ant please yor wo^{pp}: twas my part
Sym: But twas as foolish a part as ever thou plaidst in thy

249 I love money. *Q;* handl< *L* 250 Look on it well, Sir. *Q; stage-direction added from Q, being omitted in L,P* 252–3 *all as one line in L;* Y'had both need wear cut clothes, y'are so *Q* 253 choll< *L* 254 rubbd *L,P;* spare not, *Q;* spare it not *P* 255 It is *Q* 256 would I had *Q;* them. *Q* 257–8 *all as one line in L* 258 pocket / And *Q;* made < *L; stage-direction added from Q; omitted in L,P* 259–60 sick of this fool, / To see him thus couzen'd, I would make his case my own. *Q; as prose in L* 261 I meet with these things *Q* 262–3 *as prose in L; line-division that of Q* 263 I can no longer endure him *Q* 265–7 *as prose in L* 266–7 so long for our *Q* 268 Cheaters) *so Q;* Cheater *L,P* 271 asse *L;* Clowne *L* 272 offering it; Officers. *Q* 273–5 *these lines are supplied from Q, since they are omitted in L,P* 276 me? if it *Q* 277 'twas a foolish part as ever *Q*

Life, and Ile make thee smoke fort, ile teach the to
vnderstand to play a Clown, thou shalt know every
man is not borne toot: looke thee, away wth him
quicklye heele haue the other pocket, I heard him sayt
with mine owne eares, see hee Comes in another
disguise to Cheate the agen. *Ex^{t} with Clowne*

2 Che: Pish whether goes he now, he spoiles all my part [*Enter 2 Cheater*]

Sym: Come on sir letts see what yor knaueship Can doe at me
now, you must think now rascall yo^{u} haue noe foole
in hand: the foole I haue Committed for playing
ye part soe like an ass, [*He throws off his Gown, discovering his doublet with a satten forepart and a Canvas back.*]

2 che: Whats here to doe

Glou: Fy good sir Com away:
Will yor wo^{pp}: base yor selfe to play a Clowne

Sym: Away Brother tis not good to scorne anything: a man
does not know what he may Come too; every one

[Fol. 40, *recto*]

knows his ending but not his begining, ꝑceed varlett, doe
thy worst, I defye thee:

2 che: I beseech yor worship lets haue o^{r} owne Clowne, I know not
how to goe forward else

Sym: Knaue play out thy part wth me, or Ile lay the by thee heeles all the
days of thy life els: why how now my Maisters who's that laughd now;
Cannot a man of wo^{pp}: play ye Clowne a little for his pleasure
but he must be laughd at; doe yo^{u} know who I am: is ye Kings
deputye of no better accompt amongst yo^{u}: was I Chosen to
be laughd at, wheirs my Clark

Clark Here ant please yor worship

Symo: Take a note of all those that laugh at me, that when I haue don

278 life, / I'le *Q;* for it, *Q* 279 Clown *L;* a Clownes part, thou *P* 280 to it, away with him quickly, Exit Clown. *Q;* him. *L* 281 quicklye *has one minim too many in L;* other Pocket pickt else, I heard them say it *Q;* heere him *L,P* 282 my own *Q;* he's come in *Q* 284 now *L;* he spoiles all my part *omitted in Q; stage-direction omitted in L,P;* Enter second Cheater. *Q* 285 letts what *L,P;* let us see what *Q* 286 now *L;* must not think you have a Clown in hand, *Q* 286–9 *stage-direction from Q; omitted in L,P* 287 committed too, for *Q* 288 soe like an ass *omitted in Q* 290–1 *as prose in L; line-division that of Q* 292–5 *omitted in Q* 293 ones *L* 294 knowes there ending but not their begining *P;* varlett< *L* 296 let us *Q;* know < *L* 297 forwards *Q* 298 *parts of* y *of* by *and* t *of* thee *obscured by a large blot in L* 298–9 thee foo< > / days *L;* foole all days *P;* heels all the days *Q* 299 els *omitted in Q;* who *L;* that *added above the line over a caret mark in L;* who's that *P;* who is *Q;* laug< *L;* laugh'd now Cannot *P;* laugh'd at me? / Cannot *Q* 300 a Clowne *P;* his p< *L* 301 is *altered from* if *in P;* ye K< *L* 302 noe other *P;* among *Q;* Chose< *L* 304 if it please *Q* 305 I hau< *L*

I may Committ em, lett me see who dares doot now: & now
to yo^{u} once againe s^{r} Cheater; looke yo^{u} heeres my purse
strings I defy yo^{u}:
2 che: Good sir tempt me not, my part is soe written, y^{t} I should
cheat yor wo^{pp}: and yo^{u} were my father.
Sym I shold haue much ioy to haue such a rascall to my son
2 che: Therefore I beseech yor wo^{pp}: pardon me, ye part has more knaue
ry then when yor wo^{pp}: saw it at first, I assure you youle be deceiud
int sir, ye new additions will take any mans purse in Kent or
Kirsondom.
sym: And thou Canst take mine now, Ile giue't thee freely
& doe thy worst, I charge yo^{u} as thoult answert
2 *Che:* I shall offend yor wo^{pp}:
Sym: Knaue doot quickly [*Throws meal in his face, takes his purse, &*]
2 che: Say you soe then, theirs for you & heers for me then {*Exit*
Sym: Oh bless me neighborrs I am in a fogg
A Cheaters fogg I Can see no bodye
Glou: Run follow him officers

[Fol. 40, *verso*]

Sym: Away let him goe, for heele haue all yor purses & he com back;
a pox of yor new additions, they spoile all ye plays that
ever they Com in, ye old way had no such rougery int, I
remember; Call you this a merry Comedye, when
as a mans eyes are put out, Brother Honnisuckle.
Graz: What sayes yor sweete wo^{pp}:
Symo: I make yo^{u} my deputy to rule ye Towne, till I Can se againe
wch I hope will be wthin nine days at furthest: nothing
greues me but that I heare Oliuer ye rebell laugh at me;
a pox of yor puritane face, this will make yo^{u} in

306 them. *Q;* dare do it *Q;* & < *L;* and note to *P* 307 here are my *Q;* my p< *L* 308 I do defie thee. *Q* 309 temp me *P;* shoul< *L* 310 if you *Q* 312 more < *L* 313 Knavery in it then *Q;* the when *with* t *of* then *over something else in L;* first I assure, you, *L;* be < *L* 314 in it, *Q;* Kent < *L;* Kent sir Kirsendom. *P* 316 2 Che: *deleted before* sym: *in L;* If thou canst take my purse, I'le give it *Q* 317 charge thee; *Q;* thou wilt *P;* answer it. *P,Q* 319 do it *Q* 320 so? then there's *Q;* here is for me: *and final* then *omitted in Q; Stage-direction from Q;* Exi< *only in L and* Exit *in P* 324 go, / He will *Q;* purses, if he *Q;* back *L* 325 A pox on *Q;* a *over* to *erased in L;* a *omitted in P* 326–7 roguery in it; / Calls you *Q;* int remember; *L,P* 327–8 when a mans *Q;* put out in't? / Brother *Q* 329 *prefix)* Felt. *Q* 330 you Deputy *Q* 331 Which will be within these nine *Q;* farthest. *Q* 332 *first* me *added above the line over a caret mark in L;* me now, but *Q;* at me *L* 333 a pox on *Q;* p *of* pox *over* x *in L*

loue wth playes ever hereafter, we shall not keepe yo^{u}
from em now

Oliuer In Cinseritye I was neuer better edifyde at an
exersise

Sym: Neighbo^{rs} w^{t} Couller is thee rascalls dust he threw in my face

Glou: Tis meale ant please yor wo^{pp}.

Sym: Meale Ime glad ont, Ile hang ye miller for selling
ont

Glo: Nay ten to one ye Cheater never bought it,
He stole it Certainly

Sym: Why then Ile hang ye Cheater for stealing ont, & y^{e}
miller for being out of the way when he did it

ffellm: I but yor wo^{pp}: was in ye fault yor selfe,
Yo^{u} bad him doe his worst

Sym: His worst thats true,
But he has don his best, ye rascall,
For I know not how a villaine cold put out a mans eyes
better, & leave em ins head, then he has don ——

Enter Clark

Clark Wheirs my Masters wo^{pp}:

Sym: How now Aminadab, I here the though I see ye not

Clark Y'ar sure Cosend sir, they are all Cheaters ꝑfest

[Fol. 41, *recto*]

They haue stolne 3 spoones too & ye Clowne tooke his heels
wth all Celeritye: they only take ye name of Contry
Comedians to abuse simple people, wth a printed play or two
They bought at Canterbury last weeke for six pence,
& wch is worst they speake but w^{t} they list ont
& frible out ye rest

Sym: Heers no abuse to th Common wealth *Enter Hengist*
If a man Coold see to looke intoot

334 loue, *L;* Plays as long as you live, / We *Q;* keepe the *P* 335 them *Q* 336 better pleasd edifyde at *L,P;* better pleas'd at an exercise. Ha, ha, ha. *Q* 338 ee *of* thee *over* is *in L;* this *P;* colour was the dust / The Rascal threw *Q* 339 'Twas meal, if it *Q* 340 I am glad of it, *Q;* selling it. *Q* 342–3 *as prose in L* 344 stealing it, *Q* 346 *prefix*) Felt: *Q* 346–7 *line-division that of Q; as prose in L* 347 You bid *Q* 348–9 *all as one line in L;* true, / But the Rascal hath done his best; for *Q* 349 best *L* 351 e *of* em *over* f *erased in L;* them in his head, / As he has done mine. *Q; stage-direction omitted in Q* 352 Where is *Q* 354 *this speech lacks a prefix in P, though it is marked off by a stroke from the previous one;* You are *Q;* Cheaters and profest, *P;* all professed Cheaters, *Q* 355 stoln two silver spoons, and *Q* 357 play < *L* 358 Which they *Q;* last weeke *omitted in Q* 359 And what is worse, *Q;* list of it, *Q* 361 to the *Q;* Hengi< *L* 362 Could looke *P;* into it, *Q*

But mark ye Cunning of these Cheateing slaues
First they make Iustice blind, then play ye knaues
Glou: Odspretious Brother ye King of Kent's new lighted
Sym: Y^{e} King of Kent where is he where is he
Oh that I shold liue to this day, & yet not liue to se
To bid him welcom
Heng: Now wheirs symonides our frendly host
Sym: As blind as one y^{t} had bene foxt a sennight
Heng: Why how now man
Sym: Faith practising a Clowns part for yor grace
I haue practisd both mine eyes out
Heng: What need yo^{u} practise that
Symo: A mans never to old to learne: yor grace will say soe
when yo^{u} heere all ye villany, the truth tis my Lord I
meant to haue bene merry, & now tis my Luck to
weepe water & Oatmeale But I shall se agen at supper
time I make no doubt ont ——— *Enter Gentleman*
Heng: This is strange to me sirs
Gent: Arm arme my Lord
Heng Whats that
Gent: Wth swiftest speed,
If ever youle behold ye Queene yor daughter
Aliue agen

[Fol. 41, *verso*]

Heng: Roxena
Gent: Their Besidgd
Aurelius Ambrose & his brother Vther
Wth numbers infinite in Brittaine fforces
Besett there Castle, & they Cannot scape
Wthout yor speedy succour
Heng: For her safety
Ile forgett food & rest—away

363 slaues) *actually* sllaues *altered from* knaues *in L* 364 *after this line Q has:* Heng. Where's Mr. Mayor? 365 Kent is newly alighted. *Q* 366–7 Kent? where is he? / That I should *Q* 367 not see *P* 367–8 *all as one line in L;* him we< *L* 369 Heng. Where is *Q* 370 Ah blind *Q;* foxt a night. *P;* snnight *L;* sevenight. *Q* 373 my eyes *P,Q* 375 A man is *Q* 376 hear the jest of it; the truth is, *Q* 377 it is *Q;* Luck < *L* 378 But *omitted in Q;* at su< *L* 379 time *omitted in Q;* of it. *Q;* Enter a Gentleman. *Q* 383–5 wth . . . ever / youle . . . agen / *L;* With . . . behold / The Queen *Q* 387 They are *Q* 387–8 Aurelius, / Ambrose, *Q* 389 Brittaines / fforces *P;* of British Forces, *Q* 392–3 *as one line in L,Q* 393 rest away *P*

Symo: I hope
Yo^{r} grace will here ye Iest afore yo^{u} goe
Heng: The Iest, torment me not, set forward
Symo: Ile follow yo^{u}
To wales wth a dogg and a bell but Ile tell't yo^{u}
Heng: Vnreasonable folly ——— *Exit*
Symo: Tis signe of war when greate ones disagree
Looke to ye Rebell well till I Can see
& when my sights recouerd,
Ile haue his eyes putt out for a fortnight
Oliuer Hang thee: myne eyes, a deadly sinn or two
Shall pluck em out first, thats my resolution *Exevnt omnes*

Scena 2^{a} Enter Aurelius and Vther wth Souldiers [V, ii]

Vther My Lord the Castle is so fortifide
Aur: So fortifide—lett wild fire ruin it
That his destruction may appeare to him
Ith figure of heauens wrath at ye Last day;
That murderer of our Brother, hast away
Ile send my hart noe peace till't be Consumd,
Vthe: There he appeares agen: behold my Lord *Vortiger Horsus on ye walls*
Aur: Oh that ye zealous fire on my souls alter
To the high birth of vertue Consecrated,
Would fitt me with a lightning now to blast him,

[Fol. 42, *recto*]

Even as I looke vpon him.

395 your Worship *Q;* e're you go. *Q* 394–5 *all as one line in L,P,Q* 396 Iest *L;* set forward *omitted in Q; both L and P have* Exevnt *after this line* 397–8 *all as one line in L* 398 I will tell it you. *Q* 399 Unseasonable *Q;* Exit cum suis. *Q* 400 Warrs *P;* great men *Q* 402 sight is *Q* 403 putt out (*with* putt *altered from* plvckt) *above the line over a caret mark in a second hand in L;* putt out *omitted in P;* I will have / His eyes pull'd out for *Q* 404 the mine eyes *P;* sinn *is a minim short in L;* My eyes? hang thee, / A . . . pluck them out first, / That is my resolution. Ha, ha, ha. *Q* 405 Exvnt: *P;* Exeunt. *Q*

V. ii. *heading*) ACT. 5. SCENA 2. / [rule] / Enter Aurelius and Uther with Soldiers, (Vortiger and Horsus above.) *Q* 2 So fortifide *omitted in Q;* fortified lett *L* 4 In the *Q;* day *L* 5 brother hast *P;* Hence away, *Q* 6 till it *Q* 7 *stage-direction omitted in Q* 8 om *L* 10 lightning) *so Q;* a sighting *L, the* t *being a later addition;* sighing to *P;* w *of* now *over* t *in L*

Vther: Good my Lord
Yo^{r} anger is to noble & to pretious
To wast it selfe on guilt so fowle as his,
Let ruin worke her will.
Vort: Begirt all round
Hers: All all my Lord: tis folly to make doubt ont;
You question things that horror long agon
Resolud vs on.
Vort: Giue me leaue *Hersus* though
Hers Doe what yo^{u} will sir question em agen
Ile tell em ouer to you.
Vort: Not soe sir:
I will not haue em told agen
Hers: It rests then
Vort: Thats an ill word putt in when thy hart knowes
Their is noe rest at all, But torment makeing.
Hers: True, my hart findes it that sitts weepeing blood now
For poore Roxenas safetie, youle Confesse my Lord
My loue to yo^{u} has brought me to this danger;
I could haue liud lik hengist King of Kent,
& London yorke Lincolne & winchester
Vnder ye power of my Command, ye portion
Of my most iust desart, it fell toot: enioyd now
By pettier deseruers;
Vort: Say you soe sir
And youle Confess since you begin Confession
(A thing I should haue dyed before Ide thought on.)
Ime out of yor loues debt, ith sam Condition,
Y'haue marrd ye fasshion of yor affection vtterly

[Fol. 42, *verso*]

In yor owne wicked Councell; theire yo^{u} paid mee,
You Could not but in Conscience loue me afterward,

12 *a stroke such as separates speeches partially erased after this line in L* 14 selfe *added from Q; omitted in L,P;* his *L* 16 Aure: *deleted in the margin and* Vort: *added before it in L* 17 ont *L;* of it, *Q* 18 ago *Q* 21 him *deleted and* em *written above it in L;* them *Q* 22 them to you. *Q* 23–4 *line-division that of Q; all one line in L* 24 them *Q* 25 rest's *L* 26 im *L* 27 makeing) *Bullen would read* waking 28 true *L;* it now that *P;* blood n< *L* 29 x *of* Roxenas *over* o *in L;* Lor< *L* 30 danger *L* 32 & *omitted in Q* 33 of my my Command y^{e} *L* 34 iust *added from Q; omitted in L,P;* it fell toot *omitted in Q* 35 pettier *from Q preferred to* lesser *in L on account of the metre;* less *P* 37 began *Q* 38 dyd *L,P;* e're I had *Q* 39 *omitted in Q;* ith som *L;* it some *P* 41 mee *L* 42 You were bound in conscience to love me after, / You were bound to't, *Q;* afterward *L*

You were bound to Doot, as men in honestie
That vitiate virgins to giue doweries to 'em,
My faith was pure before to faithfull woman

Hers My Lord my Councell

Vort: Tis the mapp now spred
That shewes me all my miseryes, & discouers
Strange new found ruin to me, all these obiects
That in a dangerous ring Circle my safetye,
Are yo^{rs}, and of yor ffasshoning

Hers: Death mine:
Extremitie breedes ye wildness of a desart
Into yor soule; and since, y'haue lost yor thankfullness
W^{ch} is ye noblest part in King or subiect;
My Councell doot,

Vort: Why Ile be iudgd by those
That knitt death in their Browes, & think me now
Not worthy ye acception off a flaterye;
Most of those faces smild, when I smilde once
My Lordes

Vthe: Reply not Brother

Vort: Seedes of scorne
I mind you not; I speake to those alone
Whose force makes yo^{rs} a powre, wch els were none:
Shew me ye maine foode of yor hate, my Lords
W^{ch} Cannot be ye murder of Constantius
That Crawles in your revenges, ffor yor Loue
Was violent Long since that

Gent: And had bene still
If from that pagan woman, thoudst slept free
But when thou fledst from heauen we fled from thee

Vort: Was this yor Councell now

[Fol. 43, *recto*]

Hers: Mine, twas ye Councell

43 D *of* Doot *over* l *in L* 44 vitiates *P;* them; *Q* 45 to a faithful *Q* 47–56 *omitted in Q* 50 n *of* dangerous *added later above the line in L* 52–6 *as prose in L* 53 extremities *P* 57 Iudg *P;* these *Q* 58 knitt death in) *so Q;* knitt in teach their *L,P;* and hold me *Q* 59 Not worth the acception *Q;* exception *L,P;* flaterye *L* 60–1 *all one line in L,Q* 60 of whose *Q* 61 my Lord *P* 63–7 Seeds . . . not, / I . . . power, / Which . . . hate / Which . . . *Q* 64 to them *Q* 65 makes you *P;* were nowie, *P;* none *L* 66 manie food *P;* my Lords *omitted in Q* 68 n *of* in *inverted in some copies of Q;* your) *so Q;* their *L,P;* loves *Q* 69 Were *Q* 70–1 *line-division of Q; as prose in L* 70 *prefix*) 1 Lo. *Q* 71 paga *L;* Pagan wound th'hadst kept thee free, *Q;* thou hadst *P* 73 This was *Q*

Of yor owne Lust & blood; yor appetite knowes it
Vort: May thunder strike me from these walls my Lords
& leaue me many leauges off from yor eyes,
If this be not ye man whose stigian soule
Breathd forth that Councell to me, & sole plotter
Off all these false iniuryous disgraces
That haue abusd ye vertuous patience
Of our religious queene
Hers: A diuell in madnes
Vort: Vpon whose life I sweare their sticks no staine
But whats most wrongfull: & wheir now she thinks
A rape dwells in her honno^{r}, onely I
Her rauisher was, & his ye policye
Aur: Inhumane practise
Vort: Now yo^{u} know ye truth
Will his death serue yor ffurye
Hers: Mine my death
Vort: Will't doot
Hers: What if it would
Vort: Say will it doot
Hers: Say they should say it would
Vort: Why then it must
Hers: It must
Vort: It shall: speake but ye wordes my Lord,
He shall be yeilded vp.
Hers: I yeilded vpp,
My Lordes beleeue him not, he Cannot doot,
Vort: Cannot
Hers: Tis but a false and base insinuation
For his owne Life, & like his late submission
Vort: Oh sting to hono^{r}, aliue or dead thou goest [*stabs him*]
For y^{t} wordes rudeness only
Gent: See sin needes
Noe more distruction then it breedes

76 my L< *L;* Lords, *Q;* Lord *P* 77 u *of* leaue *one minim short in L* 80 those *Q* 81 *what is apparently an accidental stroke across the top of the* u *of* abusd *in L makes the word look like* abasd 85 think< *L* 86 on her *Q* 91 Hor. My death? *Q* 92 will it *P* 92–3 *omitted in Q* 94 will't *P;* do it? *Q* 95 Say they should say 'twould doe't? *Q* 98–9 *all one line in L,Q;* but the word, it shall *Q;* yeilde< *L* 100–1 *all one line in L; Q omits* I yeilded vpp, my Lordes; do it. *Q* 105 *stage-direction added from Q; omitted in L,P* 107 *prefix)* 1 Lo. *Q* 107–8 *as one line in L;* No other *Q; Bullen inserts* what *before* it *for the sake of the metre*

In it owne Bosome
Vort: Such another brings him
Hers: What, has thy wild rage stampt a wound vpon me,
Ile send one to thy soule shall never heale fort
Vort: How to my soule
Hers It shall be thy M^{r} torm^{t}
Both for ye paine & ye everlastingnes
Vort: Ha ha
Hers Dost laugh, take leaue ont, all eternitie
Shall never see the doe so much agen
Know thou art a Cuckold
Vort: What
Hers: You Change to soone sir
Roxena whom thast raisd to thyne owne ruine
She was my whore in Germany
Vort: Burst me open,
Yo^{u} violence of whirlewindes
Hers: Heere me out ffirst
For her embrace wch yet my flesh sitts warme in
I was thy friend & follower
Vort: Deaffen me
Thou most imperious noise y^{t} starts ye world
Hers: & to serue both o^{r} Lusts, I practisd wth thee
Against thy vertuous Queene
Vort: Bane to all Comforthes
Hers: Whose faithfull sweeteness, too pretious for thy blood,
I made thee Change for loues hyppocrisie
Vort: Insufferable
Hers: Onely to make my way to pleasure ffeareles
Free & fluentt
Vort: Hells trump is in that throat
Hers It shall sound shriller [*They stab each other. Rox. enters in fear.*]

109 its *Q* 111 what *L;* hasty wild *P;* thy vile *Q;* me *L* 116 Ha *three times in Q* 117 leave of it, *Q* 119 th'art *Q* 121–2 Roxena *comes at the beginning of line 121 instead of 122 in L,P; the text has been altered to conform with Q* 122 thou hast *P;* thy own *Q* 124 open; *L* 125 yo^{u} violence is whirlewindes *L;* you violent whirlwindes *P;* the violence of whirlwinds! *Q* 124–5 *as one line in L,Q* 127 flesh yet sits *Q;* flesh is *P;* a *of* warme *altered from* e *in L* 129–30 *line-division that of Q; as prose in L* 131 serue both o^{r} Lusts,) *so Q;* serue o^{r} Lust, *L;* Lusts *P* 134–5 *line-division that of Q;* whose . . . sweeteness / too . . . Change / for *L* 135 C *of* Change *over* st *in L* 137–8 *all one line in Q;* pleasure / ffeareless free *L* 139 trumpet *P* 140 *stage-direction added from Q; omitted in L,P*

[Fol. 44, *recto*]

Vort: Ile dam it vp with Death ffirst
I am at thy hart I hope
Hers: Hold out Breath
And I shall finde thee quickly
Rox: Oh for succor
Whose neere me, help me, saue me, ye flame followes me,
Itts ye figure of poore Vortiner ye Prince
Whose life I tooke by poyson
Vort: Ile tugg out
Thy soule here
Hers: Doe monster
Rox: Vortiger
Vort: Monster
Roxe: My Lord
Vort: Slaue
Roxe: *Hersus Hersus*
Hers: Murderer
Roxe: My Lord
Vort: Toad Pagan
Hers: Viper Christian
Roxe: Here me, help me,
My loue my Lord, Ime scortchd, what all in Blood
Oh happy men, that ebb shews yor neere falling,
Haue you Chose that way yo^{r}selues rather to dye
By yor owne swordes, then feele fires keener Torment
& will not kill mee, y^{t} most needes that pittye,
Captaine, my Lord, send me som speedier death
And one less painefull, I haue a womans sufferings,
Oh thinke vppon't, goe not away soe easily
And leaue ye harder Conflict to my weakeness:
Most wretched; Ime not worth soe much distruction
As wold destroy me quickly, & turne Back

143 *omitted in Q* 144–5 *this speech comes between lines 149 and 150 in Q; all one line in L,Q* 146–8 *as prose in L* 147 me . . . me . . . *L; third* me *omitted in L,P;* flam< / followes *L* 148 'Tis in the figure of young Vortimer, *Q* 150 tug thy soul out *Q* 150–1 *all one line in L,P,Q* 156–9 *omitted in Q* 162 *Q reads:* Oh hear me, / Oh help me, my Love, my Lord, 'tis here, / *i.e. Q omits from* Ime scortchd *in line 163 to* my Lord *in line 174; in L and P there is a vertical line in the margin indicating omission from line 162 to 176, and a horizontal line after line 176 ending at* Consumd *to indicate the extent of the cut* 164 men *L* 166 Tormen< *L* 167 me; *L* 169 sufferin< *L*

I Cannot, oh tis here, my Lord, tis here
Hersus looke vp if not to succor me

[Fol. 44, *verso*]

To see me yet Consumd, oh what is Loue
When Life is not regarded
Vort: What strength's left,
Ile fix vppon thy throate [*Both stab, Hor falls*]
Hers: I haue som force yet
Rox: No way to scape; is this ye end of glory
Doubly besett wth enemyes wrath and fire;
See, for an arme of Lust, Ime now embracde
W^{th} one that will destroy me, wheir I read
The horror of dishonest actions, guile
& dissemblance: it comes neerer now, riuers
And ffountaines fall: teares weare now a blessing
It sucks away my breath, I Cannot giue
A Curs to syn, & hear't out whilst I liue:
Oh help help help [*She falls.*]
Vort: Burne burne, now I Can tend thee,
Take time wth her in torments, Call her Life
Affarr of to thee, dry vpp her strumpet blood
& hardly parch ye skyn, let one heate strangle her
Another fetch her to her sence agen,
& ye worst paine be only her reviueing
Follow her eternally: giue her not ore
But in a bitter shape: I shalbe Cold
Before thy rage reach me: oh mysticall harlott
Thou hast thy full due, whom Lust Crownd queene before
Flames Crowne her now, ffor a trivmphant whore.
& that end Crownes em all ——— *falls*
Aure: Our peace is full now

175 succor *over a caret mark above* suffer *deleted in L* 178–9 *all one line in L,Q;* left yet, Ile *P; stage-direction from Q; omitted in L,P* 181 scape *L* 182 doubtfully beset *P;* enemyes, wrath *L,P;* fire *L* 183 see *L* 183–6 *Q omits* See . . . dissemblance 185–7 the horror of dishonest actions / it was neerer now, riuers and ffountaines / guile & dissemblance: teares . . . *L,P;* weare *deleted after* ffountaines *in L; Q reads* fire: / It comes nearer, rivers and fountains fall, / It sucks . . . 188 breath *L* 189 heart out *L* 189–90 *all one line in L,Q;* while I live. Help, help. *Q; stage-direction from Q; omitted in L,P* 191 burne now *L* 192 torment, *Q* 194 hard y *in some copies of Q* 197–9 giue her . . . reach me: *omitted in Q* 199 oh my mysticall *P* 201 now a most triumphant *Q* 202 ende *P;* them all. He falls. *Q* 203 now *omitted in Q*

In yond vsurpers fall; nor haue I knowne
A iudgment meete more ffearefully:
Here take this Ring, deliuer ye good Queene

[Fol. 45, *recto*]

And those graue pledges of her iniurd honor,
Her worthy father & her noble vncle,
Too long, too much abusd: whose Cleere eyd ffames
I reuerence wth respect to holynes due,
A spotles name being sanctity now in few;
How now my Lordes ye meaneing of thes soundes,

Devon Staff: leading Hengist prisoner

Heng: The Consumer has bene here, shes gon shees Lost,
In gloweing Cinders now lyes all my ioyes,
Ye headlong fortune off my rash Captiuitye
Strikes not soe ferce a wound into my hopes
As thy deere Loss
Aure: Her ffather & her Vncle
Gent: They are indeed my Lord
Aure: Part of my wishes
What ffortunate powre has prvented me
And ere my Loue Came, brought 'em victorye.
Gent: My wonder sticks in Hengist king of Kent,
Devon: My Lord to make that plaine wch now I see
Fixt in astonishment, the only name
Of yor returne & being, brought such gladnes
To this distracted kingdom, that to express
A thankfullnes to heauen, it grew greate
In Charitable actions, from wch goodnes
We tasted libertie, that lay ingagd
Vppon ye innocence of womans honnor,
A kindnes that even threatned to vndoe vs,
& haueing newly But inioyd ye benefitt
And fruites of our enlargment, twas or hapiness,
To entercept this monster of Ambition,

204 yon *Q;* that *P* 205 *something seems to have dropped out of this line, which is the same in all three texts; Bullen adds* the bad *after* meete 206 deliuert the *P* 207 iniurd *altered from* inured *in L;* her ruind honour, *P;* her murthered honour, *Q* 208 vncle *L* 209–11 *omitted in Q* 209 too, long too *L;* Cleered fames, *P* 210 due *L;* Staff:< *L;* Enter Hengist, / Devon. Staf. / & Soldiers. *after line 212 in Q* 211 name, *L;* few *L;* priso< *L* 212 my Lordes *omitted in Q* 213 there *L* 214 now *added from Q, but omitted in L,P;* lye *Q* 216 so deep *Q* 219 *prefix*) 1 Lo. *Q* 222 them *Q* 223 *prefix*) 1 Lo. *Q* 226 returne; *L* 230 taste our liberty, who liv'd engag'd *Q* 231 honnor *L* 234 enlargements *P*

Bred in these times of vsurpation,

[Fol. 45, *verso*]

The ranckneś of whose insolence & treason
Grew to such height twas armd to bid yo^{u} battaile,
Whom as our ffames redemption, on our knees
We p^{r}sent Captiud.

Aure: Had it needed reason
You rightly Came prouided, what is hee

Gent: My Lord that trecherous *Hengist* King of Kent

Aure I vnderstand not yor desart till now my Lordes;
Is this that Germane Saxon, whose least thirst
Could not be satisfied vnder a province

Heng Had but my fate directed this bold arme
To thy Life, the whole Kingdome had bene mine
That was my hopes greate aime, I haue a thirst
Cold never haue bene full quenchd, vnder all;
The whole land must, or nothing

Aure: A strange drowth
& what a little ground shall death now teach yo^{u}
To be Content wthall.

Heng: Why let it then
For none else Can, y'haue namd the only way;
When Ime Content, it must be when Ime claye.

236 *the last three letters of* vsurpation *are obscured by a large blot in L* 237 Insolent treason, *P* 238 to bid yo^{u} bid yo^{u} *L* 239 *one minim too many in* m *of* ffames *and* d *of* redemption *over* n *in L* 240 Captive. *Q* 242 You richly *Q* 242–3 what . . . Kent *omitted in Q* 243 treacherous king *P* 244 *prefix omitted in Q;* I understood / Not . . . deserts . . . my honoured Lords, / *Q;* desarts *P;* Lordes *L* 245 thrist *P* 248 nine *P* 249 thrist *P* 250 all *L* 251 whole must doe't or *Q* 252 draught! *Q* 253 teach / you, *P;* yo^{u}, *L* 256 way *L* 257 *Q omits from this line to the end of the play, and concludes it as follows:*

. . . the only way
To limit my Ambition, a full cure
For all my fading hopes and sickly fears;
Nor shall it be less welcome to me now
Then a fresh acquisition would have been
Unto my new built Kingdoms; Life to me,
('Less it be glorious) is a misery.
Aur. That pleasure we will do you; Lead him out,
And when we have inflicted our just doom
On his usurping head, it will become
Our pious care to see this Realm secur'd
From the Convulsions it hath long endur'd. *Exeunt omnes:*

FINIS.

257 n *of* when *altered from* m *in L*

Aure: My Lordes ye best requitall yet we giue yo^{u}
Is a ffaire inward ioy, Speake to yor ffames
Gloryes vnblemishd, ffor ye Queene yor Daughter
Enter Castiza a Gent
Liues firme in hono^{r}, neither by Consent
Or act of violence staind, as her greife iudges;
Twas her owne Lord abusd her honest feare
Whose ends shamde him, onely to make her Cleere
Devon: Had yor grace giuen a Kingdome for a guift
It had not bene soe welcom
Aure: Here she Comes
Whose vertues I must reverence

[Fol. 46, *recto*]

Cast: Oh my Lord
I kneele a wretched woman,
Aure: Arise wth me
Greate in true ioy and honno^{r}
Heng: This sight splits mee
It Bringes Roxenas ruin to my memorye.
Cast: My Lord it is to greate a ioy for Life
Aure: Tis truth, and that I know you ever ioyd in,
His end Confest it
Cast: Are you returnd soules Comforths
Aure: Nay to approue thy purenes to posteritie
The fruitfull hopes off a faire peacefull Kingdom
Here will I plant
Cast: Too worthles are my merrits
Aure: Their speakes thy modestye, and to the ffirmness
Of Truths plantation in this Land for ever,
W^{ch} always grones vnder som Curse wthout it,
As I begine my rule with the distruction
Of this ambitious Pagan, so shall all
Wth his adulterate faith distaind, and soild,
Either turne Christians, dye, or liue exild.
Omnes *A Blessing on those Vertues:*
fflorish Exevnt:

Finis
Hengist King off Kent

262 act or *L,P; final* e *of* greife *over* u *in L;* iudges *L* 267–8 *all one line in L;* t *of* vertues *over another letter in L* 269–70 *all one line in L* 274 at Bringes *L* 275 tis *P* 276 truth *L;* know. *L;* in *L* 280 hopes, *L; only two minims of the last letter of the line are visible in L* 283–4 ffirmness of / Truths *L* 288 whi *deleted before* with *in P;* adulterous *P* 289 liud *P*

[Fol. 46, *verso*]

Enter Raynulph [Chor. v]

For story of Truth Compact
I chose theis tymes, these men to act,
As Carefull now to make yo^{u} glad
As this were the first day they plaid—
And though som that giue none their due
Please to mistake em; doe not yo^{u}
Whose Censures haue bene ever kind;
We hope tis good, But if we find
Yo^{r} grace and loue, by pleasd signes vnderstood
Wee cease to hope for then we know tis good. *Exit*

Musique

the whole of the Epilogue is omitted in Q and is in italics in P 4 as theye were *P* 7 kind *L*

NOTES

DRAMATIS PERSONÆ

14. *Symon a tanner.* Simon's name is linked with his profession on scriptural authority. There are references to "Simon a tanner" with whom the Apostle Peter lodged in *Acts,* ix, 43 and x, 6 and 32.

CHORUS I

The rhymed choruses and the two songs in the play are written in the rather stilted and artificial complimentary style which Middleton adopted for his civic shows and entertainments, and which is easily distinguishable from the more direct and natural style of his plays.

The first and last choruses constitute the prologue and epilogue, and are different in kind from the other choruses, which are commentaries on the dumb-shows. In the latter Raynulph appears as the presenter of the dumb-shows; in the former as the presenter of the play.

Enter Raynulph. Raynulph Higden (d. 1364) was a Benedictine monk in the Abbey of St. Werburg at Chester. His *Polychronicon*—his best known work—was a universal history from the beginnings down to his own times. Though it had little original value and was almost entirely a compilation, it enjoyed great popularity during the later Middle Ages, and a translation of it into English was printed by both Caxton and Wynkyn de Worde. Raynulph appears in the play as a typical chronicler of olden times.

5–6. There is some doubt from the references in the play as to the type of theatre in which it was originally performed. These lines suggest a public theatre, but the Buttonmonger's words at I, ii, 34–35 ("the roome was not halfe so light as this") suggest an indoor theatre, lit by artificial light. Since the play is known to have belonged to the King's Men, it can only be presumed that it was given both at the Globe and the Blackfriars, although the title-page of the quarto of 1661 merely states that it had "Been often Acted with much Applause at *Black-Fryars.*"

8. *too poore howres.* This, and the many other authorities for the two-hour performance of Elizabethan plays (e.g., "the two houres traffique of our Stage," prol. to Q1 of *Romeo and Juliet,* "these two short howers," prol. to *The Alchemist,* "two short houres," prol. to *Henry VIII*) are discussed in full by A. Hart in "The Time allotted for Representation of Elizabethan Plays" (*R.E.S.,* viii [1932], 295–413). Mr Hart estimates the length of the quarto version of this play as 2249 lines, which, he says, would easily permit of its being acted without any abridgment in "two poor hours." He makes no mention, however, of the dumb-shows, which must have taken up some extra time, and Professor Max Förster has very reasonably protested ("Shakespeare and Shorthand," *P.Q.*, xvi [1937], at 27–28) against taking "the 'two hours traffic of our stage' too literally and too rigorously."

ACT I, SCENE I

2. *Lyn,* cease (*O.E.* linnan). The word is not in the *N.E.D.*, although "blin" (*O.E.* blinnan, be-linnan), which has the same meaning and survived until the eighteenth century, is recorded. "Lin" is also found in Drayton's *Nimphidia,* 305.

14. *seauen yeares Bondage.* Seven years was the normal period of apprenticeship to a trade.

26. *straighter.* There may be a deliberate ambiguity here: (1) more direct, (2) more narrow.

29–175. "Constantius sonne of Constãtine, by meane of Vortigernus was made kinge of Britayne, in the yere of our Lord .iiii. hundred and .xliii. This as before is touched, for so muche as his father thought he was not very apt to take so great a charge as to gouerne the lande after hym, was made a religious man in the monasteri before named. Or as some writers meane, the sayde Constante of pure devociõ that he had to God & saynt Amphiabyl made him selfe a monke, vnweting the kinge his father, and other hys freendes.

"But how or in what maner so euer he became a monke, trouth it is that Vortigerus or Vortigernus after the death of Constãtine founde such meanes that he was taken out of the abbey, and crowned Kynge of Britayn. By meane wherof the sayd Vortiger had all the rule of the lande, so that Constante had but onely the name."

Fabyan, *Chronicle* (ed. 1559), 68.

"After that Constantine was murthered (as before ye haue heard) one Vortigerus, or Vortigernus, a man of great authoritie amongst the Britains, wrought so with the residue of the British nobilitie, that Constantius the eldest sonne of their king the fore-remembred Constantine, was taken out of the abbie of Winchester where he remained, and was streightwaies created king, as lawfull inheritour to his father."

Holinshed, *Historie of England* (ed. 1587), 76–77.

63–64. After mentioning the growth of Pelagianism in Britain, Fabyan states (p. 72) that "For the whiche two holy Bishops named Germanus & Lupus, as of Gaufride is witnessed, came into Britayne to refourme the people y^t erred from the way of truth." Germanus, or St. Germain (378?–448), Bishop of Auxerre, is supposed to have visited Britain in 429 and 447. Lupus, who was also canonised, was his companion on these two journeys.

78. *efection* (spelling variant of "affection"), disposition.

103. *require* is used in the Latin sense of "seek" or "ask for."

112. "He [Constantinus] begat of his wife three sonnes (as the British historie affirmeth) Constantius, Aurelius Ambrosius, and Vter surnamed Pendragon."

Holinshed, *Historie of England,* 76.

114. Vortiger speaks this line to those beside him who are holding the crown, ready to place it on the head of Constantius.

118. It is not clear when Aurelius entered; apparently various courtiers and attendants were meant to come on at the same time as the procession of monks, and doubtless he did so too. One would expect Uther to be on the stage as well, as there can be little doubt that Constantius would point to them both as he spoke line 113.

133–134. As Bullen has pointed out, these lines are quoted by Lamb in *The Superannuated Man,* with the deliberate alteration of "rough" in line 134 to "green."

136–152. "Ye haue heard how Constantius was made a moonke in his fathers life time, bicause he was thought to be too soft and childish in wit, to haue anie publike rule committed to his hands: but for that cause speciallie did Vortigerne seeke t'aduance him, to the end that the king being not able to gouerne of himselfe, he might haue the chiefest swaie, and so rule all things as it were vnder him, preparing thereby a way for himselfe to atteine at length to the kingdome as by that which followed was more apparentlie perceiued."

Holinshed, *Historie of England,* 77.

144. *laws still ending and yet neuer Dun.* A reference, presumably, not to Acts of Parliament, like the later Mutiny Act, but to proclamations and ordinances of the Privy Council, which were to take effect for a limited period only, but which were constantly renewed and extended.

163. *blowne vpp* means not "inflated," but "exploded" or "shattered."

189–194. "This Constantius then the sonne of Constantine, by the helpe (as before ye haue heard) of Vortigerne, was made king of Britaine, in the yere of our Lord 443. But Constantius bare but the name of king: for Vortigerne abusing his innocencie and simple discretion to order things as was requisite, had all the rule of the land, and did what pleased him."

Holinshed, *Historie of England,* 77.

200. *inclosures.* There is a pun here, and the word is made to refer not only to the clothes of the graziers, which reveal their occupation, but also to the use of the word "inclose" in line 197.

DUMB-SHOW I

1. *ffortune is discouered vppon an alter, in her hand a golden round full of Lotts.* Middleton has evidently been influenced by the accounts of the classical goddess Fortuna, which had become a commonplace during the Middle Ages (see H. R. Patch, *The Tradition of the Goddess Fortune,* Smith College Studies in Modern Languages, iii and iv). In Roman times there was a temple and statue of the goddess at Praeneste. A derogatory passage in Cicero (*de Divinatione,* ii, 41) makes clear the manner in which the oracle was consulted, and the facts are admirably summarised by Sir James Frazer in his edition of Ovid's *Fasti,* iii, 259:

> The responses of the goddess were inscribed in archaic letters on oaken tablets, which were kept in a chest of olive wood. When anybody inquired of the

oracle a boy thrust his hand into the chest, shuffled the tablets about and drew out one at haphazard. The writing on it purported to be the answer to the question.

Middleton's reasons for making Fortune a Germanic goddess are not so clear, unless he was influenced by a passage in Fabyan (see p. xxxix of the Introduction) and by a recollection of the *Germania* of Tacitus (see Appendix, p. 131).

It is interesting to compare with this dumb-show II,ii of *Alphonsus, Emperor of Germany,* and especially the opening direction of the scene: "Enter Isabella, the Empress; Hedewick, the Duke of Saxon's daughter, apparelled like Fortune, drawn on a globe, with a cup in her hand, wherein are bay-leaves, whereupon are written the lots. A train of ladies following with music" (*Tragedies of Chapman,* ed. T. M. Parrott, 418). Another parallel is furnished by the last scene of Heywood's *Golden Age* (*Works,* ed. Pearson, iii, 79) where the following direction occurs: "Sound a dumbe show. Enter the three fatall sisters, with a rocke, a threed and a paire of sheeres; bringing in a Globe, in which they put three lots."

The symbolism of the dumb-show would thus have been fairly familiar to Middleton's audience. The globe or wheel had been one of Fortune's attributes from earliest times; cf.

> haec dea non stabili, quam sit levis, orbe fatetur,
> quem summum dubio sub pede semper habet.
> Ovid, *Ex Ponto,* IV, iii, 31–32.

Most of this symbolism is to be found in Dürer's famous engraving, known as "Der grosse Gluck," which shows Fortune above the clouds, standing on a globe and bearing an urn in one of her hands.

3. *they Draw Lotts and hang them vp.* Why the lots should have been hung up as an offering to Fortune it is difficult to say, unless Middleton has confused them with the votive tablets of classical times.

DUMB-SHOW I AND CHORUS II

Vortiger "caused the leders of thē to be brought vnto his presence, freyning of thē the cause of their landing and of their nacion and countrey. The which answered vnto the kinge and sayd, they were of the countrey of Germanie, and put oute of theyr countrey by a maner sorte or lot, at sundrie times vsed within the sayde lande, the whiche was vsed for muche as the people therin encreased so faste, that without such prouision had, the countrey shuld not suffice for the people, the whiche was suche as followeth.

"At sondrie times when ye saide countrey was replenished of people, the Princes and rulers therof wolde assemble at a certayn place & cal before them the lustie yonge folkes. Of the which they wolde chose out a certayne nomber, and appoynte to them certayne dukes or leders, with all thing necessary to the warre. And them so garnyshed, wolde commaunde to serche their aduenture, and to wynne some lande by theyr knighthode, where they might inhabite them selfe. By whiche vse and custome thus longe vsed, now was fallen to their lotte, to doo as their fore fathers had done before them.

"Wherefore sins fortune hadde brought them to this lande, they besoughte the king that he wolde take them to his seruice, and they wolde be redie to fight for the defence of him and his countrey. And when the king had enquired further: he found that they had two leders named Hengistus and Horsus, and thei and theyr people were called Saxons."

Fabyan, *Chronicle,* 70.

"Some have written that the Saxons were not sent for, but came by chance into the Ile, and the occasion to be this. There was an ancient custome among the English Saxons a people in Germanie, as was also at the first among other nations, that when the multitude of them was so increased, that the countrie was not able to susteine and find them, by commaundement of their princes, they should choose out by lots a number of yoong and able personages fit for the warrs, which should go foorth to seeke them new habitations: and so it chanced to these, that they came into great Britaine, and promised to serue the king for wages in his warres."

Holinshed, *Historie of England,* 78.

ACT I, SCENE II

Stage-direction. *felmonger.* Q has "Feltmonger" here. The *N.E.D.,* however, does not record the word, and the usual term for a maker of and dealer in felt was "felter." A fellmonger was, of course, "a dealer in the hides and skins of animals, especially sheepskins," and the *N.E.D.* has a quotation from Defoe's *English Tradesman* which shows that the fellmonger also dealt in wool. The determination of the correct reading and of the nature of the fellmonger's business is of some importance in connection with the interpretation of line 101.

34–35. See note on chor. i, 5–6.

47. This line is explained by the *N.E.D., sub* button, 10: *"pl.* The dung of sheep, etc. Hence in obs. phrase meaning 'to be in great terror.' " Among the quotations is one from Florio's *World of Words,* 1598: *"Il culo gli fa lappe,* his taile makes buttons, his buttocks goes a twitter twatter."

101. *enormitie.* None of the examples of this word quoted in the *N.E.D.* exactly parallels its use here. It originally meant a divergence from a normal standard or type, whence it derived the sense of moral obliquity which it bears today. It was also used to indicate excess in magnitude. It seems to be used here somewhat in this last sense, and the fellmonger is complaining that the wool market is disorganised; because of a glut he cannot dispose of his stocks. For the bearing of this on the date of the play, see Introduction, pp. xiii–xiv.

103. I cherished a hope for a short time that this passage might also help to throw some light on the date of the play, but reference to J. E. Thorold Rogers's *History of Agriculture and Prices in England* soon showed how scanty are the surviving data for forming any conclusions as to the fluctuations in pastoral rents at this period.

119. *a royall deere,* or, more properly, a hart royal proclaimed:

> If *a Stagge* come to be sixe yeeres of age, then hee is *a Hart:* But if the King or Queen doe hunt or chase him, and he escape away aliue, then after such a hunting or chasing, he is called a *Hart Royall.* But if the King or Queene doe hunt or chase a Hart in the Forest, which by chasing is driuen out of the Forest, so farre, that he is not likely to returne to the Forest againe of himselfe, and the King giueth him ouer, either for that he leaueth off from hunting, as being weary, or, for that he cannot recouer him, And because that such a Hart hath shewed the king pastime for his delight, And, is also, as *Budæus* saith, *Eximius Ceruus,* a goodly Hart, & therefore the king would haue him preserued to returne to the Forest againe, He doth cause open proclamation to be made in all Townes and Villages neere vnto the place, where the same Hart is so remaining, that no maner of person or persons shall kill hurt, hunt, or chase him, but that hee shall safely returne to such a Forest againe, from whence he came, and for that cause the King doth appoint certaine Foresters to harbor the said Hart there, for a while, & by degrees to bring him into the forest againe, And then euer after, such a Hart is called *a Hart Royall proclaymed.*
>
> J. Manwood, *A Treatise of the Lawes of the Forest* (ed. 1615), 42–43.

When a hunted stag had been killed, the venison was divided with elaborate ceremony, and the paunch given to the hounds as their quarry. If, however, the stag pursued was found to have been proclaimed, the hunt would have to be abandoned, and the hounds would thus be cheated of their reward.

DUMB-SHOW II AND CHORUS III

"This Vortiger then consideringe the innocencie and mildenesse of the kynge, caste in his mynde how he might be kinge himselfe. And amonge other meanes, founde to haue aboute the kinges person an hundred Pictes, or after some Scottes, the whiche he ordeyned for a gard for the kinges person, whiche done, he bare him in suche wise againe the Pictes by meanes of great giftes and otherwise that they at length had Vortiger in such fauoure, that they feared not to say openly y^t^ Vortiger was more worthy to be the kinge then Constant. In this while Vortyger gat into his possession the kinges treasure, and what was of him commaunded, was doone, thoughe other therat murmured and grudged. And euer in ryght & wronge he fauoured the foresayd Pictes or Scottes. The whiche at lengthe perceiuing his corrupt minde, when they sawe that they had conueniente time, fell vpon ye king, and him slew or murdered.

"After which cruel deede, by thẽ done, they presented the hed of Cõstante vnto Vortiger, then being at London. Wherof when he was ware to the ende that the Britõs should thinke that dede to be done againe his minde and will: wepte and made semblaunce of al sorow and heuinesse, and caused the sayd hundred knightes to be taken in all haste after, and them by dome and law of the lande to be hedded, by reason whereof he was taken not culpable, or innocente of the kinges death. . . .

"Vortigernus . . . was made kinge of Britain in the yere of our lorde .iiii. hundred and .xlviii."

Fabyan, *Chronicle,* 68–69.

"Where vpon first, where there had beene a league concluded betwixt the Britains, Scots and Picts, in the daies of the late king Constantine, Vortigerne caused the same league to be renewed, & waged an hundred Picts, and as manie Scots to be attendant as a gard vpon the kings person, diuers of the which (corrupting them with faire promises) he procured by subtile meanes in the end to murther the king, and immediatlie vpon the deed doone, he caused the murtherers to be strangled, that they should not afterwards disclose by whose procurement they did that deed."

Holinshed, *Historie of England,* 77.

ACT II, SCENE II

1–23. "And ouer that manie and diuerse of the greate of the Britons, perceiuing that the kinge Constant was not murdered all without consent of the said Vortiger, rebelled again him . . . which put the said Vortiger to great vnrestfulnesse, & the more for that, that he wiste not, nor knew not in whom he might putte hys truste and confidence."

Fabyan, *Chronicle,* 69.

"He (doubting least the people would not be ruled by him, for that it was knowen how he would haue made awaie Constantines children) kept him about London, & durst not commit himselfe so much to the sight of a multitude, as to go foorth in that iournie in his owne person."

Holinshed, *Historie of Scotland,* 92.

9. *impostume,* a purulent swelling or cyst.

24–29. "And ouer this the king was so harde beset with the fore named enemies, that he was constreined as affermith Policronica, to sende for paynenis, as the Saxons, to helpe to withstande his enemies and defende his land and also he daylie feared the landing of Aurely and Vter.

"Vortiger thus being beset w[t] many aduersities in visitinge his lande, and then being for diuerse causes him mouing, at Dorobernia or Caunterburie: tydynges came to him of the arryuynge of three longe shippes full of armed men at the ysle of Tenet. Wherof firste he made countenance as though he had bene in doubt whether it had ben the two bretherne of Constant or no. But when the fame was blowen aboute, y[t] they were none enemies: anon he caused the leders of thẽ to be brought vnto his presence."

Fabyan, *Chronicle,* 70.

30–48. "The kinge thus being ascerteined of the maner of these straungers, and that they were of the gentyle or Pagan lawe: sayde he was very heuie & sorie, that they were miscreantes. But he was ioyous and glad of theyr cōminge for so muche as he hadde neede of suche souldyours to defende hym and his land, agayn his enemies. And so receiued them to hys wages and seruice, as is witnessed of Gaufride and other mo writers."

Fabyan, *Chronicle,* 70.

ACT II, SCENE III

1–25. "These Saxons thus arriuing in Britaine, were courteouslie receiued, & hartilie welcomed of king Vortigerne, who assigned to them places in Kent to inhabit, and foorthwith led them against the Scots and Picts, which were entred into Britaine, wasting & destroieng the countrie before them. Heerevpon comming to ioine in battell, there was a sore fight betwixt the parties for a while. But at length when the Saxons called to their remembrance that the same was the day which should either purchase to them an euerlasting name of manhood by victorie, or else of reproch by repulse, began to renew the fight with such violence, that the enemies not able to abide their fierce charge, were scattered and beaten downe with great slaughter."

Holinshed, *Historie of England,* 78.

26–31. "Now Hengistus, being a man of great wit, rare policie, and high wisdome, vnderstanding the kings mind, who wholie trusted to the valiancie of the Saxons, & herewithall perceiuing the fruitfulnesse of the countrie, presentlie began to consider with himselfe, by what wiles and craft he might by little little [*sic*] settle heere, and obteine a kingdome in the Ile, and so establish the same to him and his foreuer.

"Therefore first he indeuored with all speed possible to fense that part of the countrie, which was giuen him and his people, and to inlarge and furnish it with garisons appointed in places most conuenient. After this he did what he could to persuade the king, that a great power of men might be brought ouer out of Germanie, that the land being fortified with such strength, the enimies might be put in feare, and his subiects holden in rest. The king not forseeing the hap that was to come, did not despise this counsell tending to the destruction of his kingdome, and so was more aid sent for into Germanie."

Holinshed, *Historie of England,* 78.

26–46. "Then it foloweth, these Saxõs w^{t} the kinges power beate downe the enemies before said, and defẽded the lande in mooste knightlie wise, so that the king had the saxons in great loue and fauour, whiche fauour Hengistus wel apperceauinge vpon a season when he sawe conuenient time, he asked of the king so much grounde as the hide of a bulle or other beast wold compace, which the kinge to hym graunted. After whiche graunte, the sayde Hengiste to the ende to winne a large ground caused the sayde bestes skin to be cut into a small and slender thonge. And wyth the same mette oute a large and great circuite of groũd vpon the whiche he shortlye after builded and set a large & stronge castel. By reason of which thonge the sayde castell was longe after named Thonge castell."

Fabyan, *Chronicle,* 71.

"In this meane while a new supplie of fiue thousand Saxons, with their wiues and children, came ouer to this land, in eighteene hoies, and amongest other came Hengists wife and his daughter the ladie Roxena. Shortlie after king Vortigerne gaue vnto Hengist & his Saxons a great part of the countrie called Lindseie, with a castell of great strength called Thongcastre. Some haue written that Hengist required of Vortigerne so much ground as he might compas with an oxe hide, and hauing that granted, he tooke a mightie oxe hide, and cut it into small thongs, and so compassing about a right strong plot of ground with those thongs line wise, began there the foundation of a castell, which tooke name of those thongs, wherewith the plot of ground was first measured, and so was it called Thong-castell."

Holinshed, *Historie of Scotland,* 94.

"But common opinion (conceiued vpon report, receiued of the elders by tradition) chalengeth it to *Tong* Castle in this Shyre Sittingbourne: Wherevnto if a man doe adde the first planting, and the chiefe abiding, of *Hengist* and *Horsa* was in *Kent,* and adioyne also the authoritie of *Mathew* of *Westminster,* which writeth plainely, that *Aurelius Ambrose* the captaine of the *Britons* prouoked *Hengist* to battaile at *Tong* in *Kent,* he shall haue cause, neither to falsifie the one opinion lightly, nor to faith the other vnadvisedly. . . .

"The ditch and ruines of this olde Castle do yet appeere at *Tong* Mill, within one quarter of a mile of the parish Church there, and about so much Northward from the highway between *London* and *Canterbury* where you may see the water drayned from the Castle ditch, to serue the corn-Mill."

W. Lambarde, *Perambulation of Kent* (ed. 1596), 244–245.

34–37. Cf. the passage from Fabyan quoted in the note on II, ii, 30–48 above.

53–55. A feeble pun on the two meanings of hide: (i) a skin, and (ii) a measure of area.

90. *Cutt and slasht.* The two words seem to be synonymous here, although, strictly speaking, cutwork was a type of embroidery used mainly for trimming cloths and garments. Slashing, on the other hand, was ornamentation similar to pinking (see note on line 95 below) except that the slits were considerably longer. "To prevent ravelling" slashing, like pinking, "was done on the bias of the material, and the designs were governed by the pinker's imagination. Since such garments were usually lined with material of contrasting colour, they offered rich possibilities for colour effects." (M. C. Linthicum, *Costume in the Drama of Shakespeare and his Contemporaries,* 154.)

Iiggets. The spelling approved by the *N.E.D.* is the French one, "gigot." The word originally meant a leg or haunch of mutton, then a slice or small piece. The *N.E.D.* quotes, beside this passage, "They eat the inwards; then in giggots cut the other fit for meat" (Chapman, *Iliads,* i, 452) and "Cut the slaves to giggets" (Fletcher, *Double Marriage,* III, ii).

93. An additional piece of word-play. As Bullen points out, " 'Cutter' was a cant term for a bully or sharper."

95. *pinckt.* "Pinking was a term applied to the cutting of small holes or slits, one sixteenth to three-fourths of an inch in length, either in the materials or the finished garment. . . . It was not uncommon for a garment to have from one to nine thousand 'pinks' " (M. C. Linthicum, *op. cit.,* 153–154). The *N.E.D.* gives a quotation from Stubbes's *Anatomy of Abuses* (ed. 1882), ii, 37 which shows that leather was a favourite material for pinking: "They [the skins] must be stitched finelie, pincked, cutte, karued."

109. *Bulls pizel,* the penis of a bull, and the name given to an instrument of flagellation.

110–111. The numerical puzzle alluded to in these lines is evidently a very old one. It depends for its effect on a very simple exercise in geometrical progression. A later variant of the same puzzle is alluded to by Mr. Weller senior in his description of Mr. Stiggins:

> "Borrows eighteenpence on Monday, and comes on Tuesday for a shillin' to make it up half a crown; calls again on Vensday for another half-crown to make it five shillin's; and goes on, doubling, till he gets it up to a five-pound note in no time, like them sums in the 'rithmetic book 'bout the nails in the horse's shoes, Sammy."
>
> Sam intimated by a nod that he recollected the problem alluded to by his parent.
>
> *Pickwick Papers,* ch. xxvii.

140–145. The sentiment of these lines is a modern, not an Elizabethan, one, and, as far as I know, this expression of it is unique in Elizabethan and Jacobean literature. It would be interesting to know for certain whether the omission in *Q* of lines 143–145 was originally due to the censor.

172–246. "Then by the sonde of Hengiste, came with .xvi. sayles Ronowen the daughter of the said Hengist, which was a mayden of excellent bewty. After whose comminge, Hengist vpon a day besought the kinge he wolde se his castell, which he had newly edified. To whose request the king was agreable, and at the dai assigned came to the sayde castell, where he was ioyouslie receaued. And there amonge other pastimes the sayde Ronowen wyth a cuppe of golde full of wyne presented the kinge, saluting and saying wassayle. The king which before that time had herde no like salutacion, nor yet vnderstode what she mente, asked of her father what she mẽt by that word wassayle. To whom it was answered by Hengyst that it was a salutacion of good and gladnes, and that the king should drinke after her, ioyning therevnto this answere, drinke hayl, wherfore the kinge as he was infourmed toke the cuppe of the maydẽs hande and dranke: and after he behelde the wenche in such maner, that he was wounded with the derte of the blind god Cupide, that neuer after he coulde w^t^draw his loue from that wenche but lastely by instygation of the deuyll, asked her in mariage of her father. And by force thereof, as wytnesseth Policronica, he put frõ him hys lawful wyfe, of the whiche he had before time receaued .iii. noble sõnes called Vortimerus, Catagrinus, and Pascencius. Then the kinge gave vnto Hengistus the Lordeshyp of Kente."

Fabyan, *Chronicles,* 72.

"Now at this second time there arriued heere 16 vessels fraught with people, and at the same time came the ladie Rowen or Ronix (daughter to Hengist) a maid of excellent beautie and comelinesse, able to delight the eies of them that should behold hir, and speciallie to win the heart of Vortigerne with the dart of concupiscence, wherevnto he was of nature much inclined, and that did Hengist well perceiue. . . .

"A great supper therefore was prepared by Hengist, at the which it pleased the king to be present, and appointed his daughter, when euerie man began to be somewhat merrie with drinke, to bring in a cup of gold full of good and pleasant wine, and to present it to the king, saieng; Wassail. Which she did in such comelie and decent manner, as she that knew how to doo it well inough, so as the king maruelled greatlie thereat, and not vnderstanding what she ment by that salutation, demanded what it signified. To whom it was answered by Hengist, that she wished him well, and the meaning of it was, that he should drinke after hir, ioining thereto this answer, Drinke haile. Wherevpon the king (as he was informed) tooke the cup at the damsels hand, and dranke.

"Finallie, this yoong ladie behaued hir selfe with such pleasant woords, comelie countenance, and amiable grace, that the king beheld hir so long, till he felt himselfe so farre in loue with hir person, that he burned in continuall desire to inioy the same: insomuch that shortlie after he forsooke his owne wife, by the which he had three sonnes, named Vortimerus, Catagrinus, and Pascentius, and required of Hengist to haue his daughter, the said Rowen, or Ronowen in mariage. Hengist at the first seemed strange to grant to his request, and excused the matter, for that his daughter was not of estate and dignitie meet to be matched with his maiestie. But at length as it had beene halfe against his will he consented, and so the mariage was concluded & solemnized, all Kent being assigned vnto Hengist in reward."

Holinshed, *Historie of England,* 78–79.

250–285. Cf. the more elaborate and more farcical test of virginity in *The Changeling,* IV, i and ii.

281. The modern vulgarism "between you and I" is apparently less modern than most people believe.

ACT III, SCENE I

42–45. This "vertue" is one which several of the gallants in Middleton's city comedies possess, e.g.

> *Sale. & Rear.* Master Lethe, sweet Master Lethe.
> *Let.* Gentlemen, your pardon; I remember you not.
> *Sale.* Why, we supped with you last night, sir.
> *Let.* O, cry you mercy! 'Tis so long ago,
> I'd quite forgot you; I must be forgiven;
> Acquaintance, dear society, suits and things,
> Do so flow to me,
> That had I not the better memory,
> 'Twould be a wonder I should know myself.
>
> *Michaelmas Term,* I, i, 173–182.

Cf. also *Your Five Gallants,* II, iii, 83–105.

53. *true man,* honest man. Bullen quotes "A true man or a thief that gallops thus" (*Love's Labour's Lost,* IV, iii).

73. *bottom,* the hull of a ship.

89–93. The subject of incest seems to have exercised a certain fascination over Middleton. He introduces it into the plot of *Women Beware Women* and recurs to it again in *A Game at Chess,* IV, ii, 101–107.

94–95. Without attempting to vouch for real life in Middleton's day, we may at least note that the situation here suggested occurs more than once in his comedies, e.g., *A Trick to Catch the Old One,* and *A Chaste Maid in Cheapside.*

126. The *N.E.D.* cites no authority for the use of "rudely" as an adjective, as it appears to be here, unless some word like "done" is understood or has dropped out.

173. *Their Birding is at windows.* In this connection it is interesting to remember the plans of Allwit and his wife, in *A Chaste Maid in Cheapside,* after they have been cast off by Sir Walter Whorehound:

Mis. All. Let's let out lodgings then,
And take a house in the Strand.
Allwit. In troth, a match, wench!
We're simply stocked with cloth-of-tissue cushions
To furnish out bay-windows; pish, what not
That's quaint and costly, from the top to the bottom.
A Chaste Maid, V, i, 157–162.

195. Cf. Polonius's "springes to catch woodcocks," *Hamlet,* I, iii, 114.

ACT III, SCENE II

Stage-direction. The words "A Booke," not even introduced by "with," seems to have originated as an insertion by the prompter to remind him of a property that had to be brought on to the stage.

9. *against ye haire.* The equivalent modern idiom, "against the grain," is a carpenter's metaphor. We, however, preserve the Elizabethan image in such a phrase as "to rub someone up the wrong way."

10. *stomachers.* "An ornamental, detachable shield worn over the abdomen under the doublet or kirtle body to fill the front opening in these garments. It was made over a foundation of pasteboard, or was stiffened by busks" (M. C. Linthicum, *Costume in the Drama of Shakespeare and his Contemporaries,* 191).

nightrayles, "a cape which hung below the shoulder, to be worn at night," Linthicum, *op. cit.,* 166.

34. Stage-direction. The stage is empty for a moment to indicate a change of scene and a brief passage of time.

67–73. These lines describe one of the attributes of the elixir of the alchemists. Sir Epicure Mammon thus discants upon its powers:

He that has once the flower of the sun,
The perfect ruby, which we call elixir,
Not only can do that, but, by its virtue,
Can confer honour, love, respect, long life;
Give safety, valour, yea, and victory,
To whom he will. In eight and twenty days
I'll make an old man of fourscore, a child.
Surly. No doubt; he's that already.
Mam. Nay, I mean
Restore his years, renew him like an eagle
To the fifth age; make him get sons and daughters,
Young giants; as our philosophers have done,
The ancient patriarchs, afore the flood,
But taking, once a week, on a knife's point,
The quantity of a grain of mustard of it;
Become stout Marses, and beget young Cupids.
The Alchemist, II, i, 46–60.

102–104. Compare with these lines the appeal of the White Queen's Pawn in *A Game at Chess,* II, i, 151–152, when her chastity is somewhat similarly endangered:

Then take my life sir,
And leaue my honor for my guide to heauen.

ACT III, SCENE III

16. Though the *N.E.D.* does not appear to recognise the usage, "to keep a door" had the subsidiary meaning of to pimp, or pander. There is no doubt, for example, of Lysimachus's meaning when he exclaims to Boult in *Pericles,* IV, iv, 126, "Avaunt thou damned door-keeper."

26–31. Compare with these lines the conduct of Bolingbroke as reported by Richard II:

Ourself and Bushy, Bagot here and Green
Observ'd his courtship to the common people:
How he did seem to dive into their hearts,
With humble, and familiar courtesy,
What reverence did he throw away on slaves;
Wooing poor craftsmen with the craft of souls
And patient under-bearing of his fortune,
As 'twere to banish their affects with him.
Off goes his bonnet to an oyster wench,
A brace of draymen bid God speed him well,
And had the tribute of his supple knee,
With Thanks, my countrymen, my loving friends,
As were our England in reversion his,
And he our subjects' next degree in hope.
Richard II, I, iv, 23–36.

It is interesting, too, to contrast Hengist's attitude towards the common people with that of Vortiger.

34–39. There are frequent references in the old comedies to the emphasis laid by the vulgar on position and precedence. Perhaps the most amusing of all is in Gertrude's speech in *Eastward Ho,* I, ii, 3–5, where she is anticipating her projected marriage with Sir Petronel Flash:

> O sister Mil., though my father be a low-capped tradesman, yet I must be a lady; and, I praise God, my mother must call me madam.

42. *Of yᵉ same parish.* The two MSS merely read "of yᵉ same" here. Obviously a word has dropped out, and *Q* fills the gap by inserting "Town" after "same." Though "parish" is only a guess, it can at least be claimed that it makes better sense than "Town," since Simon and his fellows are obviously all intended to be fellow-townsmen of Queenborough.

57–90. "Neare vnto this Castle, the same King *Edward* did at the same time also, erect (as I saide) the towne of *Quinborow,* which he created a free Borough, and made the Townsmen *Burgesses,* giuing them power to choose yeerely a *Maior* and two *Bailifes,* that should make their oath of allegeance before the Constable of that Castle" [of Queenborough].

W. Lambarde, *Perambulation of Kent,* 252.

74. Through stitching is the simplest form of stitching. "To go through stitch" is to go through with something, "a tailor's expression for finishing anything once begun" (*N.E.D.*). Cf. "Wee might haue made round worke, and gone thorough stitch," Nashe, *Works,* ed. R. B. McKerrow, iii, 32, 11–12, and "Indeed sweet Lady you must pardon this young man, 'tis his fault, he has not yet the true handling of his worke, he cannot goe through stich yet," W. Rowley, *A Shoo-maker a Gentleman,* II, i, 64–66.

75. A pun on "collar" and "choler" also occurs in the opening lines of *Romeo and Juliet* (I, i, 3–4):

> *Samp.* . . . if we be in choller, wee'l draw.
> *Greg.* I, while you live, draw your neck
> out o'th Collar.

The primary meaning in this passage, however, is "choler"; nevertheless, the spelling is significant, and lends colour to Mr. F. Meynell's suggestion (in the Nonesuch Press edition of *The Temple,* 231) that George Herbert's *The Collar* should more properly be *The Choler.*

76. *linsey woolsey,* a material woven from a mixture of wool and flax. The word was also used to denote a strange medley in talk or action, and, as an adjective (cf. line 78) to mean neither one thing nor the other.

78. *Coyle,* a slang word of unknown origin, first appearing in the sixteenth century, meaning a tumult or disturbance.

108. *M^rs^*. It may perhaps be necessary to point out that this is here an abbreviation, not of "mistress," but of "master's."

117. *fustian,* a kind of coarse cloth made of cotton and flax. "Elizabethan statutes of apparel limiting the use of silk materials to rich nobility made fustian a fashionable substitute for middle-class persons. . . . From its substitution for silk materials, grew the figurative meaning of falseness, pretence, or bombast." Linthicum, *op. cit.,* 106–109.

133. *hampen.* This variant spelling of "hempen" is not recorded in the *N.E.D.*

138–141. "Lucian in his *Somnium* (14) has a story about a man named Simon, who, from squalid poverty was suddenly advanced to opulence. A quondam acquaintance, meeting him, addressed him Χαῖρε ὦ Σίμων: whereupon the upstart, turning in anger to his retainers, said—Εἴπατε τῳ πτωχῷ μὴ κατασμικρύνειν μου τοὔνομα· οὐ γὰρ Σίμων ἀλλὰ Σιμωνίδης ὀνομάζομαι. Doubtless Middleton had this passage in mind." *Bullen.*

167. *Callimoocher.* This is apparently a nonce word; at any rate, no other example of its use was known to the compilers of the *N.E.D.* There it is defined as "a raw cadger, a greenhorn," and a possible relationship with "moucher," a loafer, is suggested. Halliwell, in his *Dictionary of Archaic and Provincial Words,* is still more vague, and writes: "A term of reproach. It is probably connected with *micher.*"

168. *Alecunner.* An examiner or inspector of ale: "An officer appointed in every court-leet, and sworn to look to the assize and goodness of bread, ale, and beer, sold within the jurisdiction of the leet." Phillips, 1786. (*N.E.D.*)

170. *Baldrib,* "a joint of pork cut from nearer the rump than the spare-rib, so called 'because the bones thereof are made bald and bare of flesh' (Minsheu). Humorously used of a lean bony person." *N.E.D.*

175. An amusing piece of Puritan jargon aptly introduced.

177–178. The cithern for the entertainment of waiting customers was an invariable piece of furniture in the Elizabethan barber's shop.

192–193. Cf. the proverb "The devil is a gentleman."

218–235. Various phrases in Simon's speech on the Seven Deadly Sins suggest a conventional visual representation of them. For example, they were doubtless to be found portrayed in old wall paintings in churches. They were also used as a tapestry design, and, if Donne is to be trusted, such a tapestry hung in the great hall of the old Palace of Westminster:

> Tyr'd, now I leave this place, but pleas'd so
> As men which from gaoles to'execution goe,
> Go through the great chamber (why is it hung
> With the seaven deadly sinnes?).
>
> *Satire IV,* 229–232.

243. *bowlt,* to sift, and hence to find out or separate by sifting. The *N.E.D.* quotes from Sir Benjamin Rudyard in Rushworth's *Historical Collections,* iii (1692) I, 25: "Let the matters bolt out the Men; their Actions discover them."

257. *sackbuts.* A pun: (i) bass wind instruments, (ii) butts of sack.

260–262. "Hengist perceiuing that his people were highlie in Vortigernes fauour, began to handle him craftilie, deuising by what means he might bring him in loue with his daughter Ronix, or Ronen, or Ronowen (as some write) which he beleeued well would easilie be brought to passe."

Holinshed, *Historie of England,* 79.

263. It is clear that Roxena leaves the stage shortly after this speech, but there is no direction for her exit. Her father apparently nods over his book in a corner until he is aroused at line 320. Whether he was meant to overhear the conversation of Vortiger and Horsus, and whether there was any point in making him do so, it is difficult to say. Probably, however, he did so.

275. *an ember weeke.* "The English name of the four periods of fasting and prayer appointed by the Church to be observed respectively in the four seasons of the year. Each of these fasts occupies three days, viz. a Wednesday and the following Friday and Saturday; these are called *Ember days,* and the weeks in which they occur are called *Ember weeks.*" *N.E.D.*

ACT IV, SCENE I

Parodies of the crudity of rustic shows and symbolism such as this scene contains occur elsewhere in the drama of the period, as in Munday's *John a Kent and John a Cumber* (*M.S.R.,* 367–395):

Enter Pembrook, Moorton, Oswen, Amery, to them this crew <> marching, one drest lik a Moore, wth a Tun painted with <> yellow oker, another with a Porrenger full of water an<> a pen in it, Turnop speaketh the Oration.

Turnop. Lyke to the Cedar in the loftie Sea,
or milke white mast vppon the humble mount:
So hearing that your honors came this way,
Of our rare wittes we came to giue account.
ffor when as princes passe through pettie townes
they must be welcomd, least they tearme vs clownes.
Our presents precious, first the golden Tunne,
borne by that monstrous Murrian black a Moore,
Mortonus Earlus in thy praise is doone.
This shining brook hemd in with this fierce shoare
That hath <
Is peereless Penbrook, if I roue not <w>yd<e>
As for the two last rymes, right woorshipfull, <an>d m<
wise, by the error of the Authour ouerslipped, is th<

mothie Turnop the Oratour newly corrected, to wit <
This princely pen vp prauncing by the sydes,
And so we wishe ye both two blessed brydes.
Oswen. My Lordes, my fathers tennants after their homely guise,
welcome ye with their countrey merriment,
How bad so ere, yet must ye needes accept it.
Pemb. Else Oswen were we very much to blame,
thankes gentle freendes, heere drinke this for my sake
Morton. And this for me, cõmending your great paynes
which in more liberall sorte we will requite.

Such symbolism and riddling, however, was not disdained even by the loftiest in the land, as the following passage will show:

> On an October morning in 1582, as the Queen was mounted to "ride abroad in the great park to kill a doe," Heneage emerged from a thicket, to hand her three tokens, a book, a bucket, a jewelled bodkin. The bucket referred to Ralegh, whose nickname with Elizabeth was "water" (a play on the pronunciation of his name). The meaning of this touching little drama was that her bellwether would kill himself unless measures were taken to remove the water. Elizabeth was delighted and affirmed to Hatton that "there never was such another." She tried to fix the bodkin, but her horse was excited by her excitement, and she had to give back bodkin and book (containing letter) till she had managed him to a standstill. Then she and Heneage went through a little flirtation by proxy.
>
> E. Thompson, *Sir Walter Ralegh,* 26.

ACT IV, SCENE II

8. *Consumation,* not to be confused with "consummation" but a formation from "consume."

11. Horace's "Exegi monumentum aere perennius" (*Odes,* III, 30) had long been a commonplace with the sonneteers, so it is not surprising to find a reminiscence of the phrase in a different context.

124. *Mother,* hysteria. Cf. *Lear,* II, iv, 56.

128. *faithes Anchor.* It is usually the anchor of hope—*ancora spei.* The image of the anchor, however, is linked with faith in some lines of Herbert, the occasion of which is thus related by Walton:

> A little before his death, he [Donne] caused many Seals to be made, and in them to be ingraven the figure of *Christ crucified* on an Anchor, (the emblem of hope) and of which Dr *Donne* would often say, *Crux mihi Anchora.*—These Seals, he gave or sent to most of those friends on which he put a value; and, at Mr. *Herberts* death, these Verses were found wrapt up with that Seal which was by the Doctor given to him.

When my dear Friend could write no more,
He gave this Seal *and so gave ore.*
When winds and waves rise highest, I am sure,
This Anchor *keeps my faith, that me secure.*
The Compleat Walton, ed. G. Keynes, 416.

257. *habitt.* An allusion to the difference between the costumes of married and unmarried women in the sixteenth and early seventeenth centuries.

DUMB-SHOW III AND CHORUS IV

"For this, and for that, that the king had maried a woman of vncought beleefe: well neare all the Britons forsooke hym and hys workes."

Fabyan, *Chronicles,* 72.

"Shortlie after, Vortigerne forsaking his lawfull wife, maried the ladie Roxena or Rowen, Hengists daughter, to the high offense of God, and great displeasure of his subiects. . . . Herevpon the Britains for the stay of such mischiefe as they saw at hand, deposed Vortigerne from his kinglie seat, and placed his sonne Vortimer in his roome."

Holinshed, *Historie of Scotland,* 95–96.

"This mariage and liberalitie of the king towards the strangers much offended the minds of his subiects, and hastened the finall destruction of the land. . . .

"When the nobles of Britaine saw and perceiued in what danger the land stood, by the dailie repaire of the huge number of Saxons into the same, they first consulted togither, and after resorting to the king, mooued him that some order might be taken for the auoiding of them, or the more part of them, least they should with their power and great multitude vtterlie oppresse the British nation. But all was in vaine, for Vortigerne so esteemed and highlie fauoured the Saxons, and namelie by reason of the great loue which he bare to his wife, that he little regarded his owne nation, no nor yet anie thing esteemed his owne naturall kinsmen and chiefe friends, by reason whereof the Britains in fine depriued him of all kinglie honour, after that he had reigned 16 yeeres, and in his steed crowned his sonne Vortimer."

Holinshed, *Historie of England,* 79.

Vortimer "left not til he had byraft from thẽ the more parte of suche possessions as before time they had wonne, and kepte them onelie to the Isle Tenet, the which Vortimer often greeued by such nauye as he then had.

"When that Rowen doughter of Hengiste perceaued the great mischiefe, that her father & the Saxons were in, by ye marcial knighthode of Vortimer: she sought such meanes, that shortly after, as testifieth Gaufride and other, Vortimer was poysoned, when he had ruled the Britaynes after moste concorde of writers seuen yeres."

Fabyan, *Chronicles,* 76.

"When Ronowen the daughter of Hengist perceiued the great losse that the Saxons susteined by the martial prowesse of Vortimer, she found means that within a while the said Vortimer was poisoned, after he had ruled the Britains by the space of 6 or 7 yeares and od moneths. . . .

"After all these bloudie broiles and tempestuous tumults ended, Vortigerne was restored and set againe into the kingdome of Britaine, in the yeare of our Lord 471. All the time of his sonnes reigne, he had remained in the parties now called Wales, where (as some write) in that meane time he builded a strong castle called Generon, or Guaneren, in the west side of Wales nere to the riuer of Guana, vpon a mounteine called Cloaricus, which some referre to be builded in his second returne into Wales, as shall be shewed hereafter."

Holinshed, *Historie of England,* 80–81.

"At length the said Vortimer through treason of his stepmother Roxena was poisoned, and died. Then was Vortigerne againe restored to the rule of the kingdome, first forced by oth to promise neuer to aid the Saxons, nor to receiue by way of aid anie forreine people into the realme."

Holinshed, *Historie of Scotland,* 96–97.

ACT IV, SCENE III

1–131. "Shortlie after that Vortigerne was restored to the rule of the kingdom, Hengist aduertised therof, returned into the land with a mightie armie of Saxons,* whereof Vortigerne being admonished, assembled his Britains, and with all speed made towards him. When Hengist had knowledge of the huge host of the Britains that was comming against him, he required to come to a communication with Vortigerne, which request was granted, so that it was concluded, that on Maie day a certeine number of Britains, and as manie of the Saxons should meet togither vpon the plaine of Salisburie. Hengist hauing deuised a new kind of treason, when the day of their appointed meeting was come, caused euerie one of his allowed number secretlie to put into his hose a long knife (where it was ordeined that no man should bring anie weapon with him at all) and that at the verie instant when this watchword should be vttered by him, *Nempt your sexes,* then should euerie of them plucke out his knife, and slea the Britaine that chanced to be next to him, except the same should be Vortigerne, whom he willed to be apprehended, but not slaine.

"At the day assigned, the king with his appointed number or traine of the Britains, mistrusting nothing lesse than anie such maner of vnfaithfull dealing, came vnto the place in order before prescribed, without armor or weapon, where he found Hengist readie with his Saxons, the which receiued the king with amiable countenance and in most louing sort: but after they were a little entred into communication, Hengist meaning to accomplish his deuised purpose, gaue the watchword, immediatlie wherevpon the Saxons drew out their kniues, and suddenlie fell on the Britains, and slue them as sheepe being fallen within the danger of woolues. For the Britains had no weapons to defend themselues, except anie of them by his strength and manhood got the knife of his enimie. . . .

"Vortiger was taken and kept as prisoner by Hengist, till he was constreined to deliuer vnto Hengist three prouinces or countries of this realme, that is to say, Kent & Essex, or as some write, that part where the south Saxons after did inhabit, as

* [side-note] Matth. West. saith 4000. He might easilie returne, for except I be deceiued he was neuer driuen out after he had once set foot within this Ile.

Sussex and other: the third was the countrie where the Estangles planted themselues, which was in Norfolke and Suffolke. Then Hengist being in possession of those three prouinces, suffered Vortigerne to depart, & to be at his Libertie. . . .

"Thus by what meane soeuer it came to passe, truth it is (as all writers agree) that Hengist got possession of Kent, and of other countries in this realme, and began to reigne there as absolute lord & gouernor, in the yeere of our Lord (as some write) 476, about the fift yeere of Vortigerns last reigne: but after other, which take the beginning of this kingdome of Kent to be when Hengist had first gift therof, the same kingdome began in the yeere 455, and conteined the countrie that stretcheth from the east Ocean vnto the riuer of Thames, hauing on the southeast Southerie, and vpon the west London, vpon the northeast the riuer of Thames aforesaid, and the countrie of Essex."

Holinshed, *Historie of England,* 81–82.

"Hengistus then hauinge the kinge as prisoner, & a great parte of the rulers of Britain thus as before is sayde subdued: was some deale exalted in pride, and compelled the kinge to geue vnto him as witnesseth Policronica, thre prouinces in the East parte of Brytayne, which three prouinces should be Kente, Southsaxon or Sussex, and Eastenglys, which is to meane Norlff, and Sulff, as afirmeth the authoure of the floure of histories. But Guydo de colluma sayeth, that the foresayd thre prouinces was Kent, Eastesaxon or Essex, and Eastanglis, whiche is Norff. and Suff. Of the which said prouinces when Hēgist was possessed, he suffred the king to go at his libertie. . . .

¶ "The kingdome of Kent here beginneth. . . .

"This Lordshippe or Kyngdom of Kente, hadde hys begynnynge vnder Hengyste. . . . Hengist kept his lordshyppe in peace and warre by the space of foure and twenty yeres, as moste writers testifie."

Fabyan, *Chronicles,* 77–79.

24–25. Compare

Look like the time, bear welcome in your eye,
Your hand, your tongue: look like the innocent flower,
But be the serpent under it.

Macbeth, I, v, 64–66.

33. *nerues.* Used, of course, in the old, and original, sense of "sinews."

53. *Nemp your sexes.* From the Old English "Nimað ēowra seaxas," take your knives.

127. *Captiuate.* Used in the obsolete sense of "to take prisoner."

134–136. Compare

For murder, though it have no tongue, will speak
With most miraculous organ.

Hamlet, II, ii, 622–623.

18. *sencelesse.* This malaprop was originally Dogberry's: "You are thought here to be the most senseless and fit man for the constable of the watch." (*Much Ado about Nothing,* III, iii, 22–24.)

19. *pumps.* "A pump was a single-soled, low shoe, which fitted the foot closely without ties. . . . Pumps were the footwear of servants." In 1612 they cost from 12 to 22 pence a pair. See M. C. Linthicum, *Costume in the Drama of Shakespeare and his Contemporaries,* 253–254.

79–82. Cf. "The best actors in the world, either for tragedy, comedy, history, pastoral, pastoral-comical, historical-pastoral, tragical-historical, tragical-comical-historical-pastoral, scene individable, or poem unlimited. Seneca cannot be too heavy, nor Plautus too light. For the law of writ, and the liberty, these are the only men."

Hamlet, II, ii, 415–421.

83. *strong ith wrists.* A feeble pun, referring to all the words ending in "-ist" which the cheater has just used.

87–93. Compare *Histriomastix,* II, i, 144–147, where the travelling players have the choice of playing before the Mayor or before a lord, and choose the latter:

> *Steward.* My maisters, my Lord Mavortius is disposed to hear what you can do.
> *Belch.* What! fellows, shall we refuse the Town play?
> *Post.* Why, his reward is worth the Mayor and all the Town.

98. *a play wherein we vse a horse.* W. J. Lawrence ("Shakespeare's Use of Animals" in *Those Nut-Cracking Elizabethans*) maintains that, contrary to general belief, horses did actually appear sometimes on the Elizabethan stage, notably in *Thomas of Woodstock* and Heywood's *Late Lancashire Witches.*

105–117. There has been some discussion over this list of plays, especially as to whether or no Fletcher's *Wildgoose Chase* is referred to in line 111. Since nothing is known of the original date of Fletcher's play beyond the fact that it was acted at Court in 1621, it is impossible to decide. Dyce also mentions that "Taylor, the water-poet, in the preface to *Sir Gregory Nonsense*" (1622) alludes to a book called *Woodcock of our side,* but, he adds, "perhaps he merely invented the title, for the expression was proverbial." Certainly no one has ever found evidence pointing to the existence of plays bearing any of the other titles mentioned, although a play called *Cupid's Whirligig* has survived. The list seems, on the whole, to be a purely fanciful one, particularly appropriate for a band of cheaters, with perhaps a satirical glance at the fashion for giving plays catch titles which afforded no clue as to their plots.

In *Histriomastix,* II, i, 216–221, a similar list of plays occurs when the travelling players are questioned as to their repertoire:

> *Usher.* One of you answer the names of your playes.
> *Post.* *Mother Gurtons neadle* (a tragedy)
> *The Devel and Dives* (a comedie)

A russet coat and a knaves cap (an Infernall)
A proud heart and a beggars purse (a pastoral)
The widdowes apron stringes (a nocturnall).

Here the humour appears to consist in the assignment of the plays to their various categories. Whether any of the titles other than the first were those of real plays we have no means of determining. On the other hand, the repertoire ascribed to "my Lord Cardinalls players" in *Sir Thomas More,* IV, i, 41–43, consists largely of real plays, and seems to represent a genuine attempt on the part of the dramatist to achieve historical accuracy.

108. *whible,* a variant form of "quibble."

Carwidghin. The *N.E.D.* suggests that this word is a variant of "carwitchet," a hoaxing question or conundrum.

115–116. "Woodcock" was a common term for a simpleton, on account of the ease with which the bird was snared. The point of Simon's remark is that if the player consorts with a fool, as his title implies, he is no fit company for Simon.

128–130. Dyce quotes here by way of illustration the first part of the passage from Nashe cited in the note on lines 299–306 below, and adds two lines from the Praeludium to Goffe's *Careless Shepherdes* (1656), 5:

I never saw Rheade peeping through the Curtain,
But ravishing joy enter'd into my heart.

147–153. Cf. Hamlet's "No, no, they do but jest, poison in jest, No offence in the world." (*Hamlet,* III, ii, 244–245.)

175. *Ansterdam,* the home of the Puritan refugees.

179. In the public theatres the beginning of a play was announced by three trumpet blasts.

182. *golls,* a cant term for hands.

299–306. "Amongst other cholericke wise Iustices, he was one, that having a play presented before him and his Towneship by *Tarleton* and the rest of his fellowes, her Maiesties seruants, and they now entring into their first merriment (as they call it), the people began exceedingly to laugh, when Tarleton first peept out his head. Whereat the Iustice, not a little moued, and seeing that with his beckes and nods hee could not make them cease, he went with his staffe, and beat them round about unmercifully on the bare pates, in that they, being Farmers and poore countrey Hyndes, would presume to laugh at the Queenes men, and make no more account of her cloath in his presence."

Nashe, *Pierce Penniles,* in *Works,* ed. McKerrow, i, 88.

314. *in Kent or Kirsendom,* a proverbial expression. It is also alluded to by Simon in lines 42–46 above.

398. *a dog and a bell,* a blind beggar's companions.

1–202. "Now will we returne to Vortigerne, of whome we read in the British historie, that after the Saxons had constreined him to deliuer into their hands a great part of the south and east parts of the realme, so that they had in possession London, Yorke, Lincolne, & Winchester, with other cities & townes, he not onelie fearing their puissance, but also the returne of Aurelius Ambrosius, and his brother Vter pendragon, withdrew him into Wales, where he began to build a strong castell vpon a mounteine called Breigh, or after other Cloaric, neere to the riuer of Guana, which is in the west side of Wales in a place within the compasse of the same hill called Generon or Gueineren. . . .

"Whilest Vortigerne was busied in building of this castell, the two foresaid brethren Aurelius and Vter prepared a nauie of ships, and an armie of men, by helpe of such their kinsmen and freends as they found in Britaine Armorike, and so passed the sea, and landed at Totnesse: whereof when the Britains were aduertised, the which were scattered abroad and seuered in diuers parties and countries, they drew vnto the said two brethren with all speed that might be. When Aurelius and his brother Vter perceiued that they were sufficientlie furnished of people, they marched foorth towards Wales against Vortigerne, who hauing knowledge of their approch, had fortified his castell verie strongly with men, munition and vittels, but yet all auailed him nothing, for in the end after his enimies had giuen diuers assaults to the said castell, they found meanes with wild fire to burne it downe to the earth,* and so consumed it by fire togither with the king, and all other that were within it."

Holinshed, *Historie of England,* 83–84.

"Shortlie after Hengist returned, and what by force and subtill shifts, at length got possession of the more part of Britaine, so that the Britains were constreined to flie into Wales, whither also Vortigerne fled, and remained there a certeine time, till at length Aurelius Ambrosius, and Vter, the sonnes of king Constantine came ouer out of little Britaine, and besieging Vortigerne in a castell, burnt him with the house and all, when they could not otherwise come by him, according to that which Merline the British soothsaier had prophesied before."

Holinshed, *Historie of Scotland,* 97.

2–15. "Diffugerat enim eo uortigirnus. ut tutum refugium haberet. Erat autem opidum illud natione herging. super fluuium guaie. in monte qui cloartius nuncupatur. Ut igitur ad illud peruenit ambrosius. proditionis patri ac fratri illate reminiscens. eldol ducem claudiocestrie affatur. Respice dux nobilis huius loci urbes & menia. utrum poterint uortegirnum protegere. quin gladii mei ipse mucronem infra ipsius uiscera recondam. Promuerit enim necem. Nec tibi ignotum esse existimo ipsum eam promuerisse. O hominem omnium sceleratissimum. o ineffabilibus tormentis pendendum. Primum prodidit patrem meum constantinum. qui ipsum & patriam a pictorum irruptione liberauerat. deinde constantem fratrem meum. quem ut proderet in regem promouit. Denique eum ipsemet uersucia sua insignitus fuisset. intromisit cum conciuibus paganos. ut ipsos qui fidelitati mee adherebant exter-

* [side-note] Wild fire not yet invented as some think.

minaret. Set permittente deo. in laqueum quem fidelibus suis parauerat: incautus cecedit. Nam ut nequitiam ipsius saxones compererunt: eiecerunt illum ex regno. quod neminem pigere debebat. Illud uero dolendum censeo quod nefandus ille per paganos quos inuitauit. nobiles ciues exterminauit. fertilem patriam deuastauit. sacras ecclesias destruxit. & christianitatem fere a mari usque ad mare deleuit. Nunc igitur ciues uiriliter agite. & uindicate uos in istum prius: per quem hec omnia accesserunt. Deinde uertamus arma in hostes imminentes. & patriam ab eorum ingluuie liberemus. nec mora diuersis machinationibus incumbunt. menia diruere nituntur. Postremo cum cetera deficissent: ignem adhibuerunt. Quod cum alimentum reperisset: non adquieuit adiunctus. donec turrim & uortigirnum exarsit."

Geoffrey of Monmouth, *Historia Regum Britanniae,* VIII, ii (ed. A. Griscom, 1929, 399–401).

32. "They [the Saxons] had in possession London, Yorke, Lincolne, & Winchester, with other cities & townes."

Holinshed, *Historie of England,* 83.

147. *ye flame follows me.* It is clear, not only from this and other speeches of Roxena (e.g., lines 163, 166, 182) but also from the speech of Aurelius at the beginning of the scene and from Vortiger's dying speech (ll. 191–197) that one of the attractions of the play must have been the startling display of fireworks with which it concluded. Fletcher and Massinger's *Island Princess,* which was performed at Court during the winter season of 1621–22, has a long scene (II, ii) during which a town is on fire, but there are no directions in the text for any fireworks. The most elaborate stage-directions referring to fireworks in any play of the period occur in Heywood's *Silver Age* (1611); e.g., "As he toucheth the bed it fires, and all flyes vp, Iupiter from thence taks an abortiue infant," and, a few pages later, "Hercules sinkes himselfe; the Diuels appeare at euery corner of the stage with seuerall fireworkes. The Iudges of hell, and the three sisters run ouer the stage, Hercules after them: fire-workes all ouer the house." (Heywood's *Works,* ed. Pearson [1873], iii, 155 and 159). Cf. also "he appeares more terrible then wilde fire at a play," *The Hogge hath lost his Pearle* (1614), C3v.

One cannot be certain how these pyrotechnical displays were managed on the stage, but it is interesting to notice that Nicola Sabbatini in his *Praticà di Fabrica Scene e Machine ne' Teatri* (Ravenna, 1638) describes how it was done on the contemporary Italian stage. Miss L. B. Campbell (*Scenes and Machines on the English Stage during the Renaissance,* 156) thus summarises his directions:

> A scene on fire may be provided if due care is exercised. It would seem that the triangular scenes are here considered preferable. A cloth wet with aqua-vitae is spread over the side of the scene not exposed to the audience, a man stationed near each scene applies a torch, the triangles are quickly revolved, and the buildings appear to be burning.
>
> An inferno may be presented by the judicious use of smoke and flames emitted through trap-doors on the stage.

A burning scene such as Sabbatini describes is illustrated in a design by Parigi for

Le Nozze degli Dei (Florence, 1637) which is reproduced at p. 112 of Miss Enid Welsford's *The Court Masque.*

212–257. "When this Aurelius Ambrosius had dispatched Vortigerne, and was now established king of the Britains, he made towards Yorke, and passing the riuer of Humber, incountred with the Saxons at a place called Maeshell, and ouerthrew them in a strong battell, from the which as Hengist was fleeing to haue saued himselfe, he was taken by Edoll earle of Glocester, or (as some say) Chester, and by him led to Conningsborrow, where he was beheaded by the counsell of Eldad then bishop of Colchester."

Holinshed, *Historie of England,* 84.

241. *reason.* This word is in all three texts, but it should perhaps be emended to "ransom."

APPENDIX

The Early Development of the Hengist Legend

THE universal acceptance, from the twelfth to the seventeenth century, of the early legendary history of Britain from Brut to Careticus is merely one further symptom of the boundlessness of human credulity. But not even the lively imagination of Geoffrey of Monmouth, its fabricator, could have foreseen the progeny which this offspring of his brain was to bring forth. Between such extremes as the stiff moralisings of *Gorboduc* and tragic heights of *Lear* there are a whole host of Elizabethan and Jacobean plays which can trace their descent back to the *Historia Regum Britanniæ,* among which Middleton's *Hengist* occupies not the least honorable place. But there was one portion of Geoffrey's *History*—the story of Arthur—which had enjoyed an imaginative appeal far outweighing that of any other part of the book, and a host of poets and romancers had transformed it long before Shakespeare brooded over the sorrows of Lear or visualised the graceful beauty of Imogen. The spell cast by the Arthurian legend has not waned even yet, though today it is not so much an incentive to the visions of poets as a battleground of scholarship,[1] and scholarship, in spite of its ranks of opposing theories, has rendered notable services in investigating the twilit regions behind Geoffrey. Though agreement will probably never be reached through sheer dearth of facts, there has been no dearth of discussion.

Vortiger, according to Geoffrey, was the murderer of one of Arthur's uncles, and, in his turn, met his fate at the hands of the brother of the man he murdered. His end, too, was prophesied by Merlin, who furnishes a further link between him and the great hero of romance. Thus the searchlight which has been concentrated on Arthurian origins has perforce brought the story of the play within the radius of its beam. Furthermore, whatever doubts one may cherish as to whether Kay and Gawain, or even Arthur himself, ever existed except in the world of romance, some of the characters in Middleton's play were undoubtedly real people, and confirmation of their existence has come down to us from a variety of sources. The true story of Constans (the Constantius of

[1] Nevertheless we have *The Waste Land* to show that poetry can be wrung even from a scholar's theory.

the play) and his father Constantine is most accessible in the pages of Gibbon,[1] and found its way into the English chronicles from the late Roman historians by way of Bede,[2] though a later misunderstanding transferred their actions from Gaul to Britain. In spite of the destructive criticism of Lot,[3] modern scholarship[4] has not rejected the legend, first related by Bede,[5] that Hengist and Horsa were the leaders of the original band of Saxon invaders which made Britain its home. Some scholars, indeed, have gone further and identified the Jutish leader with the Hengest of Danish legend (of whom the gleeman sang in Hrothgar's hall) who had taken part in the defence of Finnsburh against Finn's treacherous attack, and had survived the ensuing slaughter.[6] Whether or not they were identical is, fortunately, of small moment to the present discussion, for the tale that passed into the Elizabethan chronicles reached them overlaid with British, and not with Saxon, accretions. As for Vortiger, we may reasonably suppose that he too once existed,[7] but, if we are to believe M. Lot,[8] his very name is but an example of that process of accretion which rapidly transformed the legend. It is no more than a Celtic gloss translating the words *superbus tyrannus,* which are the contemptuous words applied by Gildas to the unnamed sovereign who summoned the barbarians to his aid.

Gildas, who wrote his book *De Excidio et Conquestu Britanniæ* shortly before 550, is the first British writer to discuss the Saxon invasion. The modern reader yearns for facts instead of tropes in Gildas's jeremiad, but in vain, for the facts are few. A certain proud tyrant (unnamed) had invited three shiploads of barbarians to help him to repel the inroads of the Picts and Scots. Once settled in the kingdom, the rapacious pagans attracted hordes of their fellow-countrymen, and to these Saxons were due in no small measure the woes which, for their sins, the miserable Britons had since endured.

Of far greater importance are the statements of Bede in his *Ecclesiastical His-*

1 *Decline and Fall of the Roman Empire,* chapters xxx and xxxi; ed. J. B. Bury (1898–1901), iii, 272–275 and 340–342.

2 *Eccl. Hist.,* I, xi.

3 "Hengist, Horsa, Vortigern: La Conquête de la Grande-Bretagne par les Saxons" in *Mélanges d'histoire offerts à M. Charles Bémont* (Paris, 1916), 1–19.

4 See R. H. Hodgkin, *A History of the Anglo-Saxons* (1935), i, 78 and 95–101.

5 I, xv.

6 *Beowulf,* 1070–1145; *Finnsburh Fragment,* 14–17. The identity of the two Hengists has been maintained, for example, by H. M. Chadwick, *Origin of the English Nation,* 49–50; R. Imelmann, *Forschungen zur altenglischen Poesie* (Berlin, 1920), 342 ff.; and, most recently, by A. C. Bouman, "The Heroes of the Fight at Finnsburh," *Acta Philologica Scandinavica,* x (1935), 130–144. It should, however, be mentioned that the identification has been opposed by such authorities as R. W. Chambers, *Beowulf* (1932), 443 ff. and A. G. van Hamel, "Hengist and his Namesake," *Studies in English Philology, A Miscellany in honor of Frederick Klaeber* (1929), 159–171.

7 Hodgkin, *op. cit.,* i, 96.

8 *Op. cit.,* 17–18.

tory of the English Nation, completed in the year 731. The famous fifteenth chapter of the first book of that work is the foundation on which all later historical speculations have been based, and there is little doubt that it represents the best Saxon tradition of the invasion.[1] The first band of settlers from Germany arrived in or just after the year 449 at the invitation of Vortiger (now first named) and were allowed to settle in the east of Britain. After describing the three races from which they came, Bede continues:

> The first two commanders are said to have been Hengist and Horsa. Of whom Horsa, being afterward slain in battle by the Britons, was buried in the eastern parts of Kent, where a monument, bearing his name, is still in existence. They were the sons of Victgilaus, whose father was Vecta, son of Woden; from whose stock the royal race of many provinces deduce their original.[2]

Bede then goes on to tell how the Saxons, having secured a firm foothold, joined the Picts and turned against their benefactors, thus initiating that period of rapine and conquest which ended in the subjugation of England. Earlier Bede had referred briefly to the usurpation of Constantine at the end of the Roman period, and had also mentioned the death of Constans, who had been brought by his father from a monastery to be elevated to the purple, at the hands of Gerontius, his father's count. In the chapters which follow the account of the Saxon invasion he relates the life and miracles of St. Germanus, who had come to Britain from Gaul to combat the Pelagian heresy.[3]

For the purposes of the present enquiry one may safely ignore the *Anglo-Saxon Chronicle,* which was compiled in the reign of Alfred, and which, though more circumstantial in the matter of dates and places, and therefore more suspect, is largely based on Bede. One cannot, however, ignore the somewhat earlier *Historia Britonum,* generally linked with the name of Nennius. It is in this work that the legend really develops into a story, wild and improbable perhaps, but with some imaginative appeal. But the book as a whole is so obvious and unsatisfactory a piece of patchwork that its origins have been much discussed, and there have been as many theories about it as there have been commentators. Since the story of Vortiger and the coming of Hengist and Horsa is one of the crucial sections of this work, it will be necessary to say something of these theories, though we shall concentrate as much as possible on the story alone, and ignore those sections of the book which are concerned with such topics as the early history of the world or the principal cities of Britain.

[1] See Hodgkin, *op. cit.,* i, 78.
[2] Trans. L. C. Lane, Everyman's Library edn., 23.
[3] Chapters xi and xvii–xxi.

Nennius's tale can be fairly briefly summarised. He first describes, in a chapter obviously derived from Bede, the arrival of the Saxons at the invitation of Vortiger, who was king of Britain at that time, and their settlement on the Isle of Thanet (chapter 31). About the same time St. Germanus came to preach in Britain, and an account of his miracles follows (32–35). The story then returns to the Saxons, who, after various successes, brought over to Britain more men, and with them the daughter of Hengist. Vortiger, meeting the maiden at a banquet, fell in love with her, demanded her of her father, and was given her in return for the province of Kent (36–37). After this success Hengist sent for still more Saxons, including his two sons (38). We are then told of Vortiger's domestic sins, which included incest with one of his daughters, and of the reproofs he suffered from St. Germanus (39). His attempts, too, to build a citadel were thwarted by magic, but the nature of the supernatural agencies opposing him was revealed by a mysteriously begotten child named Ambrosius, who also prophesied the king's end[1] (40–42). Meanwhile, Vortimer, the son of Vortiger, had taken things into his own hands and waged war against the Saxons, winning a succession of victories, in one of which Horsa was slain. He succeeded in driving the Saxons beyond the seas, but after his premature death they returned and re-established themselves (43–45). They made their position sure and extracted further territories from Vortiger by a treacherous attack on the British nobles at a banquet held to establish peaceable relations, and Nennius shows his knowledge, however slight it may have been, of the Anglo-Saxon tongue by quoting the words in which Hengist gave the signal for the attack: Nimed eure Saxes (46). Then follows an account of Germanus's "Hallelujah" victory over the Saxons, which had also been related by Bede, and then the story of Vortiger's death. He had fled from the wrath of the saint to a castle in the kingdom of Dimetae, but the castle and all those within it were consumed by a firebolt which fell from heaven in answer to the prayers of St. Germanus (47).

This, then, is the outline of the story which has been so much discussed. Fortunately, however, the disagreement between the most recent authorities on Nennius[2] is less real than appears at first sight, and there is a residuum of admitted fact in the various theories that one can accept with confidence. It is gen-

[1] Ambrosius is, of course, the original of Merlin. All Nennius's details in this part of the story were taken over by Geoffrey of Monmouth, who expanded them, and gave Merlin's prophecies a twelfth century application.

[2] E. Faral, *La Légende Arthurienne, Études et Documents* (Paris, 1929); A. G. van Hamel, Introduction to *Lebor Bretnach* (Irish Manuscripts Commission, Dublin, 1932); F. Lot, *Nennius et L'Historia Britonum* (Paris, 1934). See also F. Liebermann, "Nennius, the author of the *Historia Britonum*" in *Essays in Mediaeval History presented to T. F. Tout*, 25–44.

erally admitted that the work dates from the early years of the ninth century, most probably from the year 826; that it was put together of various incongruous elements, the most important of which was an earlier British History, since lost, which was a century or so older; and that it has probably undergone revision. There exists, however, at Chartres a shorter version of the work, obviously incomplete, containing the tantalising inscription "Exberta[1] fii Urbaoen de libro sti Germani." To Faral this manuscript represents one stage in the agglomerative process by which the work was formed, and a stage earlier than the final one; but van Hamel and Lot seem to be more correct in insisting that it is no more than an abbreviated version of the later work.[2] The Chartres manuscript, unfortunately, breaks off at the end of chapter 35. However, both this inscription and an acknowledgement in the fuller version as to the source of the account of Vortiger's death draw attention to what must have been one of the most important elements in the compilation: the life of the saint. This life, nevertheless, was obviously unlike any life of St. Germanus that has survived or was available to Bede, and the extravagance of many of the miracles attributed to him by Nennius suggests a British origin for it.[3]

It is also fairly well agreed that the miracles of St. Germanus in chapters 32–35 have been interpolated, probably by Nennius himself, into the historical narrative, but the extent to which the *Liber* supplied additional facts concerning Vortiger and Hengist is by no means clear, although chapters 39 and 47 would appear to have come from this source. Faral is inclined to glimpse traces of further Welsh legends which were incorporated either *via* the *Liber* or independently. Van Hamel, however, on the strength of the earliest Irish versions, believes he can reconstruct from them the pre-Nennian *Historia,* and that it ended immediately before the recital of the saint's miracles. Lot will have none of this, and to him van Hamel "a été victime d'une mirage"; chapters 31, 36–38, and 43–46, he thinks, may have come from the older *Historia,* but the *Liber Sancti Germani,* and any incidents which look as if they might have been derived from it,

[1] Variously emended to *excerpta* and *experta.*

[2] Faral, 56 ff.; van Hamel, xxx; Lot, 20–34.

[3] "He [Nennius] quotes repeatedly the *Liber S. Germani.* To judge from his excerpts it had nothing in common with German's almost contemporary biographer, Constantius, Bede's source. But it was read also by Nennius's countryman and younger contemporary, Mark, who after being educated in Ireland had been a British bishop for a long time and was now living in old age as a hermit near Soissons. There he told, about 859–76, to Heiric of Auxerre, the author of *Miracula S. Germani,* one miracle perpetrated by German which materially and in part even verbally agrees with Nennius. Mark, however, seems to me not to follow him, but rather his lost source, the *Liber,* since Heiric would hardly have failed to propagate German's miracles connected with Vortigern, if Mark had read them in Nennius. The proper names and two particular incidents in that tale, which are wanting in Heiric, seem to me to be added by Nennius to the *Liber.*" Liebermann, *op. cit.,* 35.

existed only in the fertile brain of Nennius, whose place is therefore beside Geoffrey of Monmouth and James Macpherson as one of the world's outstanding literary fabricators.

Nennius, then, is the furthest point to which it is possible with any certainty to trace back a large number of important incidents in the legend, such as the coming of Roxena, the King's sudden infatuation with her, the heroic resistance of Vortimer, the treachery of the Saxons, and the death of Vortiger. Faral suggests, not unreasonably, that the Ambrosius incident is a topographical legend,[1] and agrees with Liebermann that the story of the massacre is etiological—"l'invention d'un érudit"; Lot adds that Vortiger's flight to the West before his death was motivated by Nennius's desire to link the king's name with the petty kingdom of Gwrtheyriawn, which existed at the time when he wrote. But exactly what proportion of the contributions made to the development of the story by the *Historia Britonum* came from earlier Welsh chronicles, from the distinctly surprising life of the saint, or from the equally surprising imagination of Nennius, it would probably be fruitless to decide.

Between the reign of Alfred and the beginning of the twelfth century there was little historical writing, but the twelfth century was notable for a group of genuinely accomplished historians. Of them, Henry of Huntingdon and William of Malmesbury both recount the story of Hengist and Vortiger. It is true that Nennius is their source for these events, but they were both sufficiently enlightened to treat him critically and ignore his more imaginative extravagances. St. Germanus, in fact, virtually disappears from their pages. Henry of Huntingdon adds nothing of significance in his telling of the story, but William of Malmesbury introduces two new details. He describes how, in overpopulated Germany, it was the custom among the tribes to cast lots to decide who should emigrate, and he makes Hengist's daughter the cup-bearer at the feast at which Vortiger first met her. The second item was probably a picturesque touch prompted by the historian's imagination, but the first, as Faral has pointed out,[2] was gleaned from a passage in Paul Diacre's *Gesta Langobardum,* which, in its turn, may owe something to the well-known chapter in Tacitus which describes how the Germans made all their decisions by casting lots.[3]

Geoffrey of Monmouth, the junior contemporary of Henry of Huntingdon and William of Malmesbury, managed to overcome the initial scepticism of his brother historians—no very difficult task, for the rest of the world was only too

[1] Lot, while not denying this, goes still further and calls the incident "une interpolation dans une interpolation."
[2] *Op. cit.,* 218.
[3] *Germania,* x.

eager to applaud—with the invincible authority of the ancient book in the British tongue which his friend Walter the archdeacon had lent him. When Geoffrey wrote of Hengist and Vortiger, however, he did not need to use his talent for imaginative elaboration so extensively as in many other parts of his work, for here, as we have seen, he was not first in the field. Nevertheless, he did his best. The story that afterwards became the theme of Middleton's play occupies chapters 5–19 of book vi, and the first seven chapters of book viii of the *Historia Regum Britanniæ* (the intervening book vii being entirely devoted to the prophecies of Merlin), and Nennius is clearly their source. Constantine the Roman usurper, has now become the brother of the King of Little Britain, sent across the Channel after the end of the Roman occupation to help the Britons against the Picts and Scots. He led them to victory, and in return they elected him their king. After his death, his eldest son Constans was taken from the monastery of St. Amphibalus and raised to the throne by the ambitious Vortiger, who took advantage of the new King's inexperience and feebleness of wit to seize all the power into his own hands. Eventually he suborned the puppet king's Pictish guard, who, in an outburst of drunken enthusiasm for Vortiger, broke into the bedchamber of Constans and murdered him. Vortiger promptly possessed himself of the crown, but his drastic punishment of the murderers soon involved him in difficulties with their fellow-countrymen beyond his borders, so that when Hengist and Horsa arrived in Britain shortly afterwards their welcome was assured.

From this point the story follows lines which are already familiar, but Geoffrey tells it much more circumstantially, with the addition of many new details and a number of dramatically appropriate speeches after the manner of the classical historians. Sometimes these speeches are used as a means of incorporating information from his sources, as when Hengist is made to explain to Vortiger the German system of banishment by lot, and then proceeds to describe his people's religion. Among the "new additions" to the tale are several important episodes. Geoffrey is the first writer to relate the story of Thong Castle (vi, 11), although here Hengist is given permission to take as much land as a thong will compass, and his trickery lies in the fact that he has a large hide cut so that it makes but a single thong. Again, at the banquet at which Vortiger meets Hengist's daughter—here named Ronowen—she greets him with a cup, saying "Laverd King, wassheil," and teaches him to reply to her salutation with "Drinc heil!" We are told too of the influence which the Saxons had among Vortiger's retinue after his marriage with Ronowen, an influence which was instrumental in causing the Britons to depose Vortiger in favour of Vortimer, his son by a former wife. Geoffrey also makes Ronowen a poisoner, responsible for Vortimer's death. Finally, in the account of the treachery of the Saxons, Geoffrey is far more specific than previous writers had been; he describes the valour of Eldol, Earl of Gloucester, who alone escaped from the massacre, and states that the Saxons, after releasing Vortiger, took London, York, and Lincoln, as well as Winchester.

All the incidents in Nennius in which St. Germanus was in any way concerned have disappeared, and the saint's name occurs only in two incidental references. On the other hand, Merlin "that is also called Ambrosius" becomes an elaborate figure, and a whole book is devoted to his prophecies. Geoffrey wrote most of these prophecies with an eye to the events of his own time, but the last and least cryptic of them foretold the imminent death of Vortiger at the hands of Aurelius Ambrosius and Uther Pendragon, brothers of the murdered Constans. This prophecy was speedily fulfilled. At the word of their coming from Britanny with an army Vortiger fled to the "castle of Genoren on the mountain that is called Cloar." Hither his enemies followed him, and being unable to force an entrance "they set the place on fire, and the fire finding fuel, spread blazing up till it had burned up the tower and Vortiger therein." Aurelius then turned his forces against the Saxons, and Hengist was shortly afterwards captured on the field of battle by Eldol. His execution followed inevitably, and the Saxons were rapidly subdued by Aurelius.

Such an addition as the story of the first wassail in England is clearly etiological invention, but two at least of the incidents added by Geoffrey can be traced back to their sources. The story of the thong is nothing more nor less than the old legend of the foundation of Carthage, to which Virgil makes Venus refer when she addresses her son:

> ingentia cernis
> Moenia surgentemque novae Karthaginis arcem,
> mercatique solum, facti de nomine Byrsam,
> taurino quantum possent circumdare tergo.[1]

The origin of the legend is thus explained by a modern commentator:[2] "the original name of Carthage was the Semitic Bosra 'a citadel'; this was corrupted by the Greeks to Byrsa (βύρσα, a bull's hide) whence arose the legend that the new settlers were allowed as much land as they could cover with a hide; so they cut the hide into narrow strips and got enough for an adequate citadel."

[1] *Aeneid,* i, 365–368.
[2] A. Sidgwick, in his note on this passage in his edition of Virgil's *Works.*

Livy also has an allusion to the story,[1] but it is most likely to have become familiar to Geoffrey of Monmouth from Virgil and the Virgilian commentators, or from one of the compendiums of ancient history which were so popular in the Middle Ages.

In describing the death of Vortiger Geoffrey, as we have seen, abandoned the account given by Nennius, or, perhaps, it might be more true to say that he altered it so as to bring it more into accordance with the accounts of the end of the historical murderer of Constans. Indeed, the account given by Gibbon of the death of Gerontius[2] who, deserted by all except his wife and a barbarian friend, and surrounded by the rebellious troops who had set fire to his stronghold, affords an even closer parallel to the play than to Geoffrey of Monmouth. But there can be little doubt that Geoffrey here modified Nennius's story under the influence of one of the later historians of the last days of the Roman Empire.[3]

With Geoffrey of Monmouth the legend of Vortiger and Hengist took shape and crystallised, and, since none of the writers of romance took it up, it maintained its form until Elizabethan times. It had passed into the domain of authentic history. There is therefore nothing to be gained by tracing it through all the *Bruts* of the Middle Ages and the later chroniclers who repeated it. The story appears in them all, with a little condensation here or a little elaboration there, but with no fundamental alteration of its outlines.[4] It is more pertinent to enquire whether Middleton took the trouble to refer to Geoffrey as the *fons et origo* of the theme he was dramatising. To this question no definite answer can be given, although there is nothing inherently improbable in the suggestion that he may have done so, since he became official Chronologer to the City of London not long after the play was written, and it is reasonable to suppose that he was interested in the old chronicles. However, the play agrees with Geoffrey rather than with any of the Elizabethan chronicles in three respects. Geoffrey speaks throughout as if the succession to the throne depended not so much on primogeniture as on the will of the people, while Middleton emphasises both their influence and, being an Elizabethan, their fickleness; both writers

1 34, lxii, 12.

2 Chapter xxxi; ed. J. B. Bury, iii, 340–341.

3 The original source of the incident is Sozomen, *Hist. Eccl.*, ix, 13 (Migne, *Patrologia*, ser. Graec., vol. lxvii, columns 1621–1624).

4 Miss N. S. Aurner, in her *Hengist: a Study in Early English Hero Legend* (University of Iowa Studies, 1921), devotes a chapter to the handling of the story of Hengist by the Frisian chroniclers in the late Middle Ages and early Renaissance. But, since there is nothing to suggest that these accounts were based on local tradition or were derived from any other source than Geoffrey of Monmouth, they cannot be said to have any connection with the origin of the legend or to have exerted any influence on its development in England.

give the religion of the Saxons as the reason why they ought not to be granted land on British soil;[1] and both put indignant speeches into the mouth of Aurelius before the walls of Vortiger's stronghold.[2] These resemblances are slight, and may be accidental, so that, unfortunately, no definite decision can be reached.

[1] This was originally pointed out by Christ, *Quellenstudien*, 11–12.
[2] The passage from Geoffrey is quoted in the note on V, ii, 2–15.